50 WALKS IN
Herefordshire & Worcestershire

50 Walks in Herefordshire & Worcestershire

Published by AA Publishing (a trading name of AA Media Limited, whose registered office is Grove House, Lutyens Close, Lychpit, Basingstoke, Hampshire RG24 8AG; registered number 06112600)

Mapping in this book is derived from the following products:
OS Landranger 138 (walks 12–14, 24–27)
OS Landranger 139 (walks 10–11)
OS Landranger 148 (walks 38–45)
OS Landranger 149 (walks 28–31, 35–37)
OS Landranger 150 (walks 1–9, 15–23)
OS Landranger 161 (walks 46–50)
OS Landranger 162 (walks 32–34)
OS Explorer 189 (walk 32)
OS Explorer 204 (walk 17)

Maps contain data available from openstreetmap.org © under the Open Database License found at opendatacommons.org

ISBN: 978-0-7495-8373-6

A CIP catalogue record for this book is available from the British Library.

AA Media would like to thank the following contributors in the preparation of this guide:
Clare Ashton, Tracey Freestone, Lauren Havelock, Nicky Hillenbrand, Lin Hutton, Graham Jones, Ian Little, Richard Marchi, Nigel Phillips and Victoria Samways.

Cover design by
berkshire design company

Printed and bound in the UK by Oriental Press, Dubai.

A05851

We would like to thank the following photographers, companies and picture libraries for their assistance in the preparation of this book. Abbreviations for the picture credits are as follows:
Alamy = Alamy Stock Photo
Trade Cover, Neil Bussey/Alamy
Back Cover Advert, SolStock/istockphoto; 9, Richard Whitcombe/Alamy; 12/13, Neil Bussey/Alamy; 27, Michael Kemp/Alamy; 48/49, Shari Black Velvet/Alamy; 83, John Sutton/Alamy; 117, Greg Balfour Evans/Alamy; 130/131, Angela Hampton Picture Library/Alamy; 147, Robert Macdonald/Alamy; 163, Christiaan May/Alamy; 176, SolStock/istockphoto

The contents of this book are believed correct at the time of printing. Nevertheless, the publishers cannot be held responsible for any errors or omissions or for changes in the details given in this book or for the consequences of any reliance on the information it provides. This does not affect your statutory rights. We have tried to ensure accuracy in this book, but things do change and we would be grateful if readers would advise us of any inaccuracies they may encounter by emailing walks@aamediagroup.co.uk

We have done our best to make sure that these walks are safe and achievable by walkers with a basic level of fitness. However, we can accept no responsibility for any loss or injury incurred while following the walks. Advice on walking safely can be found on pages 10–11.

Some of the walks may appear in other AA books and publications.

Discover and book AA-rated places to stay at www.RatedTrips.com.

AA

50 WALKS IN
Herefordshire & Worcestershire

CONTENTS

The walks

HOW TO USE THIS BOOK

Each walk starts with an information panel giving all the information you will need about the walk at a glance, including its relative difficulty, distance and total amount of ascent. Difficulty levels and gradients are as follows:

Difficulty of walk

🟢 Easy

🟠 Intermediate

🔴 Hard

Gradient

▲ Some slopes

▲▲ Some steep slopes

▲▲▲ Several very steep slopes

Maps

Every walk has its own route map. We also suggest a relevant Ordnance Survey map to take with you, allowing you to view the area in more detail. The time suggested is the minimum for reasonably fit walkers and doesn't allow for stops.

Route map legend

⇢	Walk route	▨	Built-up area
❶	Route waypoint	▨	Woodland area
– – – –	Adjoining path	🚻	Toilet
•	Place of interest	🅿	Car park
⌒	Steep section	⊞	Picnic area
☀	Viewpoint	)(	Bridge
⊪⊪⊪⊪⊪	Embankment		

Start points

The start of each walk is given as a six-figure grid reference prefixed by two letters referring to a 100km square of the National Grid. More information on grid references can be found on most OS Walker's Maps.

Dogs

We have tried to give dog owners useful advice about how dog friendly each walk is. Please respect other countryside users. Keep your dog under control, especially around livestock, and obey local by-laws and other dog control notices.

Car parking

Many of the car parks suggested are public, but occasionally you may have to park on the roadside or in a lay-by. Please be considerate about where you leave your car, ensuring that you are not on private property or access roads, and that gates are not blocked and other vehicles can pass safely.

Walks locator map

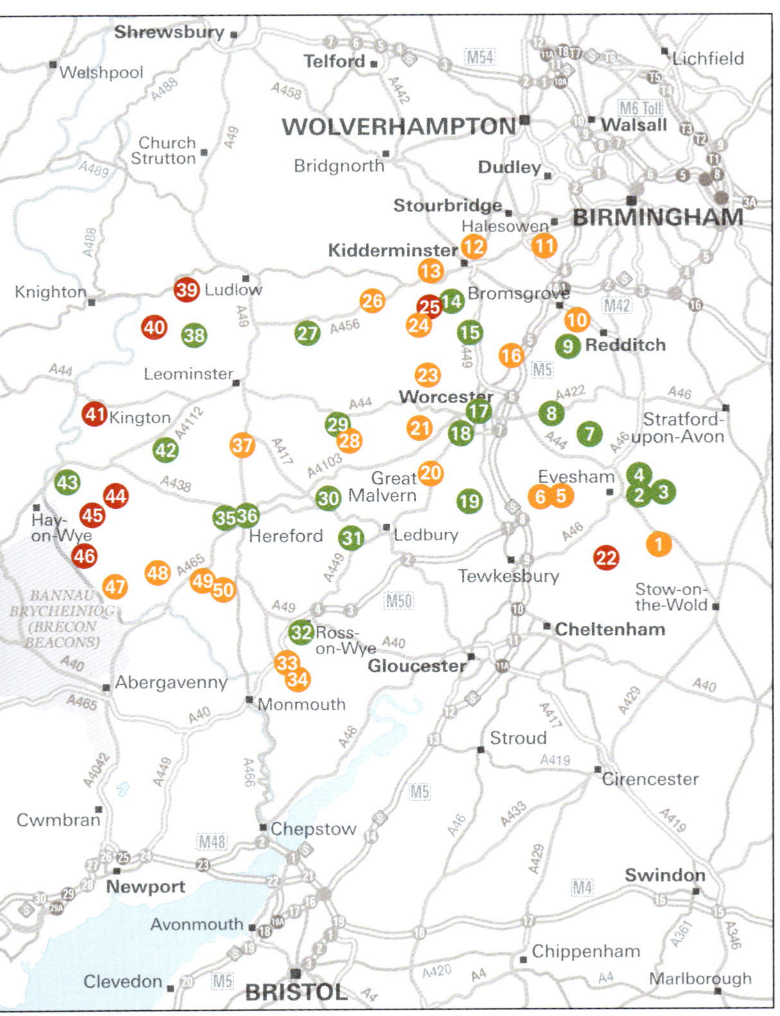

EXPLORING THE AREA

Worcestershire is a county of generally rolling hills, save for the flat and fruity Vale of Evesham in the east and the prominent spine of the Malverns in the west. Nearly all of the land is worked in some way; arable farming predominates – oilseed rape, cereals and potatoes – but there are concentrated areas of specific land uses, such as market gardening and plum growing. The county is not without surprises – in Stourport it has Britain's only town created because of a new canal; it has Droitwich Spa, a former site of inland salt production; and its long-distance footpath, the Worcestershire Way, has some fine 'ridge' sections, at Rodge Hill (see Walk 23) in particular.

In Herefordshire the land is hillier, abutting in the west with the Black Mountains ridge that defines the border with Wales. Crops are important here, but there are more green fields – for grazing, silage or hay – because this is livestock country. You may be surprised by the large number of sheep, since the 'Hereford' breed of cattle has acquired such fame. And you can't walk for long in this county without seeing an apple orchard.

There are short walks around each county's capital. In the city of Worcester (see Walk 17), which is by far the larger of the two, parts of the core have been reasonably well held on to – New Street, in particular – and Worcester's Commandery (museum) is a regular crowd-puller. The city of Hereford (see Walks 35 and 36) essentially escaped wartime bombing but suffered considerable damage from sorties made by trendy architects in the 1960s (and subsequently), but the cathedral area and the riverside – Castle Green and Bishop's Meadow – have retained, thus far, their charm.

The two counties offer plenty of other things to do. Highlights include spending some time on a river, enjoying the view from Hereford Cathedral's tower, seeing the Mappa Mundi and Chained Library Exhibition, drinking the cider and eating too many plums in the Vale of Evesham.

In these pages you will find much evidence of past activity: there are churches, castles and mansions (some in use, some in ruins), railways (disappearing and disappeared), canals (extant and extinct) and a pot-pourri of personalities. No conscious effort has been made to select routes beside rivers, yet there are several. Perhaps they hold a subliminal attraction, or is it just that their abundance makes them hard to avoid? They include the rivers Severn, Wye, Avon, Teme and Frome, to name just five, while in Herefordshire's Golden Valley (see Walks 44, 45 and 48), the river is called 'Dore', a name that possibly arises from a confusion of languages. The Welsh referred to the valley's river as *dwr*, meaning 'water', and some think that the Normans mistook this for d'or, the French for 'of gold' – if this is the case, it was an appropriate mistake to make! If it is coastal walking you want, then you've come to the wrong place, but otherwise you're sure to find something to delight you in Worcestershire and Herefordshire.

PUBLIC TRANSPORT

The three linear walks in this book are Walks 13, 20 and 35, using train, or bus. (It's always better to take your car to the end and use public transport back to the beginning.) Of the other 47 there are frankly few where you could reach the start by public transport if, say, staying here on holiday. The urban centres are the focus of bus service provision; for a village to have a bus service may mean no more than a bus into town on market day morning, returning in the afternoon.

WALKING IN SAFETY

All these walks are suitable for any reasonably fit person, but less experienced walkers should try the easier walks first. Route-finding is usually straightforward, but you will find that an Ordnance Survey walking map is a useful addition to the route maps and descriptions; recommendations can be found in the information panels.

Risks

Although each walk here has been researched with a view to minimising the risks to the walkers who follow its route, no walk in the countryside can be considered to be completely free from risk. Walking in the outdoors will always require a degree of common sense and judgement to ensure that it is as safe as possible.

- Be particularly careful on cliff paths and in upland terrain, where the consequences of a slip can be very serious.
- Remember to check tidal conditions before walking on the seashore.
- Some sections of route are by, or cross, busy roads. Take care, and remember that traffic is a danger even on minor country lanes.
- Be careful around farmyard machinery and livestock, especially if you have children with you.
- Be aware of the consequences of changes in the weather, and check the forecast before you set out. Carry spare clothing and a torch if you are walking in the winter months. Remember that the weather can change very quickly at any time of the year, and in moorland and heathland areas, mist and fog can make route-finding much harder. Don't set out in these conditions unless you are confident of your navigation skills in poor visibility.
- In summer remember to take account of the heat and sun; wear a hat and carry water.
- On walks away from centres of population you should carry a whistle and survival bag. If you do have an accident that means you require help from the emergency services, make a note of your position as accurately as possible and dial 999.

Countryside Code
Respect other people:

- Consider the local community and other people enjoying the outdoors.
- Co-operate with people at work in the countryside. For example, keep out of the way when farm animals are being gathered or moved, and follow directions from the farmer.

- Don't block gateways, driveways or other paths with your vehicle.

- Leave gates and property as you find them, and follow paths unless wider access is available, such as on open country or registered common land (known as 'open access land').

- Leave machinery and farm animals alone – don't interfere with animals, even if you think they're in distress. Try to alert the farmer instead.

- Use gates, stiles or gaps in field boundaries if you can – climbing over walls, hedges and fences can damage them and increase the risk of farm animals escaping.

- Our heritage matters to all of us – be careful not to disturb ruins and historic sites.

Protect the natural environment:

- Take your litter home. Litter and leftover food don't just spoil the beauty of the countryside; they can be dangerous to wildlife and farm animals. Dropping litter and dumping rubbish are criminal offences.

- Leave no trace of your visit, and take special care not to damage, destroy or remove features such as rocks, plants and trees.

- Keep dogs under effective control, making sure they are not a danger or nuisance to farm animals, horses, wildlife or other people.

- If cattle or horses chase you and your dog, it is safer to let your dog off the lead – don't risk getting hurt by trying to protect it. Your dog will be much safer if you let it run away from a farm animal in these circumstances, and so will you.

- Everyone knows how unpleasant dog mess is and it can cause infections, so always clean up after your dog and get rid of the mess responsibly – bag it and bin it.

- Fires can be as devastating to wildlife and habitats as they are to people and property – so be careful with naked flames and cigarettes at any time of the year.

Enjoy the outdoors:

- Plan ahead and be prepared for natural hazards, changes in weather and other events.

- Wild animals, farm animals and horses can behave unpredictably if you get too close, especially if they're with their young – so give them plenty of space.

- Follow advice and local signs.

For more information visit www.gov.uk/government/publications/the-countryside-code

WILLIAM MORRIS AND BROADWAY TOWER

DISTANCE/TIME	5.25 miles (8.4km) / 2hrs 45min
ASCENT/GRADIENT	787ft (240m) / ▲ ▲
PATHS	Pasture, rough, tree-root path, pavements, many stiles
LANDSCAPE	Flat vale rising to escarpment
SUGGESTED MAP	OS Explorer 205 Stratford-upon-Avon & Evesham
START/FINISH	Grid reference: SP095374
DOG FRIENDLINESS	Sheep- and horse-grazing country (some cattle too, and possibility of red deer by Broadway Tower) so only off lead in empty fields; some stiles may be tricky
PARKING	Church Close pay-and-display car park, just off Church Street, 4 hours maximum; other options are well signposted
PUBLIC TOILETS	Church Close car park and Fish Hill Picnic Place
NOTES	Cotswold Court shopping arcade gates shut overnight, roughly 7/8pm. If shut go round on road

If Caspar Wistar, the 18th-century American anatomist after whom the wisteria genus was named, were alive today, a springtime visit to Broadway would give him much pleasure. Visitors come in swarms to this Worcestershire village, which lies against the edge of the Cotswolds – understandably so, for it's one of the prettiest places in England. The honey-stone buildings stretch for the best part of a mile (1.6km). Horse chestnut trees flame with pinky-red candelabras and walls drip with the brilliant lilac flowers of wisteria.

There are many buildings of note in Broadway, not least the partly 14th-century Lygon (pronounced 'Liggon') Arms. Aside from being a fine building, this hotel is also notable for its historic neutrality in the Civil War, with both Charles I meeting his supporters there in 1645, and Oliver Cromwell reputed to have stayed there in 1651 on the night before the decisive clash in the Battle of Worcester.

Less historic but just as interesting is Broadway Tower. The 6th Earl of Coventry's four-storey folly built in 1798 has served as home to a printing press and a farmhouse, but is best known as a country retreat for William Morris (1834–96). Appropriately, in 1877 he founded the Society for the Protection of Ancient Buildings. Artistically, Morris empathised with the Pre-Raphaelite Brotherhood; a group, primarily of painters, founded in 1849 by William Holman Hunt. They believed that British art had taken a 'wrong turn' under the influence of Raphael, who, with Michelangelo and Leonardo da Vinci, had made up the trio of most famous Renaissance artists. The English Pre-Raphaelites challenged the teachings of the establishment, producing vividly coloured paintings, lit unconventionally, which had an almost flat appearance. Fascinated by pre-industrial techniques, Morris and some friends set up a company producing crafted textile and stained-glass products.

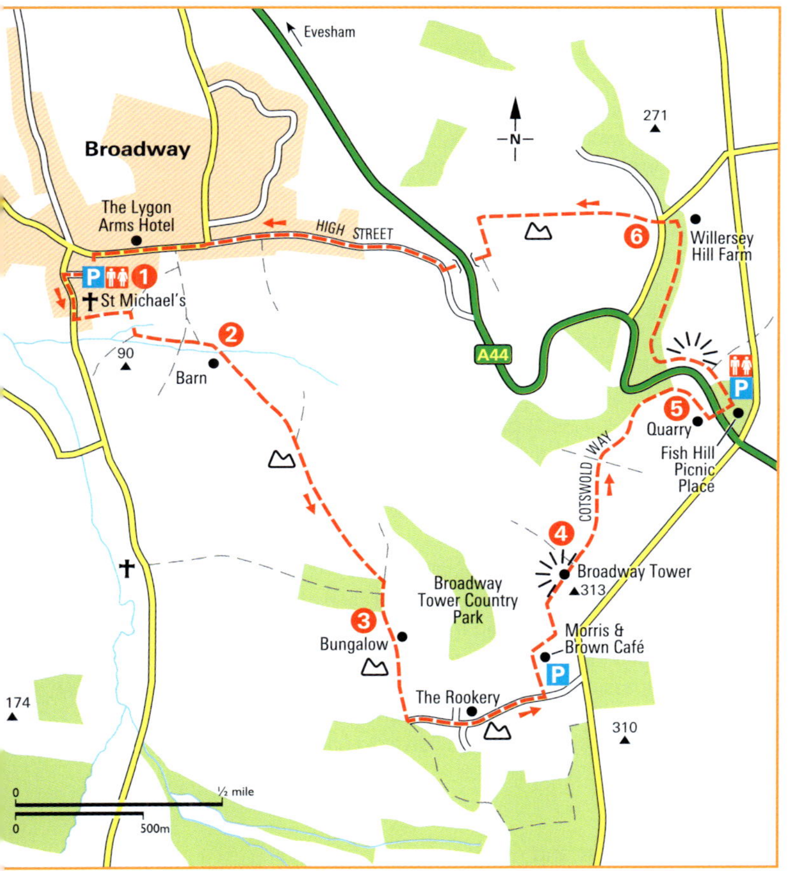

1. From the car park, walk back down Church Close then turn left. At the far end of the church wall turn left down a track, soon passing a tiny orchard. Continue straight ahead and through a gate by some horse jumps. Turn right along a grassy strip, through a gate and across a small bridge over a rivulet. Turn slightly left across uneven pasture. Go through a kissing gate and up to the far right-hand field corner and through a metal kissing gate. Go right, through a green kissing gate, and over a sleeper bridge beside a stone barn.

2. Go slightly left up a grassy field, passing a waymarker in a boggy patch to reach a stile. Continue over this and up a grassy field (horse jumps on right). Cross another stile, cutting slightly right across a small field corner to a large gap in the hedgerow. Continue along this line through a further long grassy field. Pass a prominent large sycamore tree and go through gates either side of Millennium Woodland. Maintain the line across a large field and down to go through a metal gate by a corner of woodland. Ignore a track leading immediately right, and go out of the woodland via a step-over gate.

3. Slant uphill, passing in front of a stone bungalow. Just before the woodland ahead, turn left through a gate. Join a tarmac road, heading left and steadily uphill. At the brow, turn left through a gate before the car park for Broadway Tower Country Park and pass the Morris & Brown café. Beyond this a tall kissing gate gives access to Broadway Tower with its spectacular views.

4. Beyond the tower go through a similar gate, then a little gate immediately on the right. Head slightly left above scrubby hawthorns to a gate in a dry-stone wall. Bear slightly left to meet a bend in a tractor track. Cross this, following Cotswold Way markers, to reach some metal gates among trees. Continue through these, bearing slightly downhill and left. Bend slightly right by each of the next waymarkers, contouring just above the road.

5. Ignore the first footpath sign leading to the road and follow the Cotswold Way signs towards Fish Hill Picnic Place as you join a tarmac track by a barn conversion. Continue to a main road, crossing this via a central refuge to reach Fish Hill car park. Follow Cotswold Way signs left, past picnic tables and up some steps to a toposcope with good views. Then follow the Limestone Trail signs ahead, to enter a wood. Bear right above a fence, then left down some steps shortly after. Bear right at the bottom of the steps, still following Limestone Trail signs. Head up some steps to exit the hollow, continuing straight ahead where the Limestone Trail forks left. Follow this narrow path (beware exposed tree roots) near the top of this dense wood. Eventually, just beyond a corrugated iron barn above, drop down on the left to cross a stile either side of a road junction.

6. Follow a footpath sign, descending an open slope just to the right of young woodland. Go through a kissing gate and continue downhill, then follow a vehicle track bending first left then right to a gate. Go through this, under the main road and through two more gates to reach the High Street. Turn right along this, passing a mini roundabout at the top of High Street in Broadway. Continue along High Street and then turn left by the war memorial in the centre of Broadway, and through Cotswold Court shopping arcade to emerge opposite Church Close car park.

Where to eat and drink

At the Broadway Tower, the smartly renovated Morris & Brown café welcomes walkers. A good range of drinks, savoury snacks, local ice cream and fantastic cakes are available. Dogs are welcome in the large outside patio area outside. Otherwise, options abound in busy Broadway.

While you're there

Information boards on walls above the four flights of stairs up the Broadway Tower add interesting details about the view. Inside there are displays about the tower's history, William Morris and the craftsmen who settled in the Cotswolds (open every day except in extreme weather).

A CIRCULAR WALK FROM BADSEY

DISTANCE/TIME	4.5 miles (7.2km) / 2hrs
ASCENT/GRADIENT	80ft (24m)
PATHS	Meadow and arable paths, tracks and minor lanes, many stiles
LANDSCAPE	Flat, market gardening and pasture
SUGGESTED MAP	OS Explorer 205 Stratford-upon-Avon & Evesham
START/FINISH	Grid reference: SP070431
DOG FRIENDLINESS	Can be off lead away from sheep pastures
PARKING	Roadside parking, Badsey village
PUBLIC TOILETS	None on route

This is market-gardening country. During World War I at least 20 locations in Worcestershire were used to house prisoners of war (POWs), as part of the Government's drive to plug the gap in the farming economy left by those who had been sent away to fight. Badsey's POWs were mostly employed by market gardeners – the most labour-intensive of agricultural activities – at a time of low mechanisation. The POWs received 1d of the 4d their employers had to pay the Government for their services. This became 5d after grumblings were made about these employers having access to preferential rates. Towards the end of World War I, the Manor House in Badsey, then a boys' home, was requisitioned to accommodate POWs. Originally built to house monks from Evesham Abbey who fell sick, the striking black-and-white building is now a private residence. Parts of it date from about 1350, but it is mostly 16th century.

Pockets of resentment existed in the local community towards the POWs. For example, the local paper gave a dressing-down to a farmer who gave cider to his workers, among whom were German POWs.

Yet, despite the prevailing air of uncertainty, a growing bond of friendship began to develop between many of the prisoners and the market gardeners. One story suggests that a local employee lent a prisoner a bicycle to ride to one of the fields on the other side of the village, one employer sent his small child to escort a prisoner to work, and there is even a tale of a German prisoner carving toys out of wood to make Christmas presents for the children of a local farmer.

In May 1918 three prisoners escaped while working at Langdon Hill. A search party was launched and a Badsey man stumbled on the three prisoners resting in a spinney near Wormington.

Although some prisoners attempted to escape, such stories are rare. What was their incentive? Despite the mental strain of being a prisoner abroad, and living in what must have been cramped conditions – according to an edition of the Evesham Journal, about 100 men were held in the Manor House – to be captured, uninjured, and taken away from the front to do essentially familiar, physical work was a dream ticket when set alongside the hell of trench life.

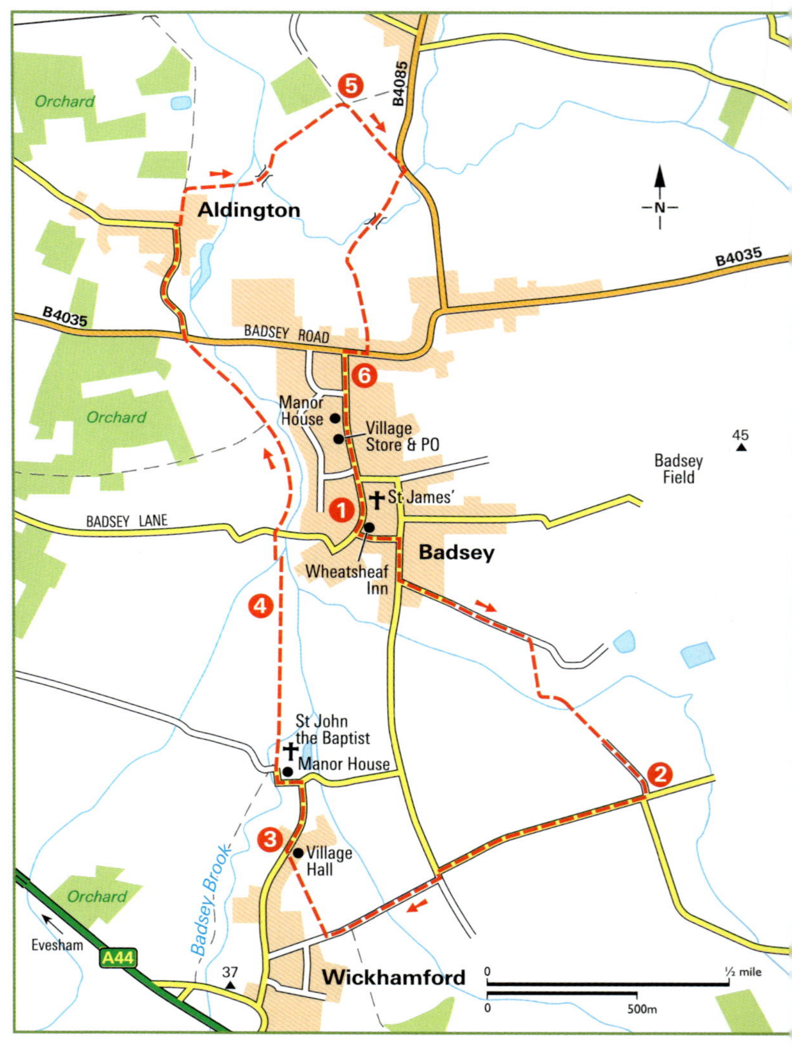

1. Walk south from St James' Church, turn left, past the Wheatsheaf Inn and along School Lane, then turn right into Willersey Road. After 125yds (114m), turn left into Sands Lane. Walk for 500yds (457m), to take a waymarked path right, opposite wire fence paddocks. Cross a field to a footbridge. Cross the next (small) field diagonally left to find, behind trees, a muddy right-hand field-edge. Follow this to a lane.

2. Turn right, signposted 'Badsey', and follow the lane for nearly 0.5 miles (800m). When this bends right, go straight ahead on a track. After 0.25 miles (400m), at the corner of the last field on the left before houses, find a stile in the hedgerow on the right then more meadow stiles lead to Wickhamford's memorial hall.

3. Turn right at the road, passing striking black-and-white houses, some thatched. After 275yds (251m), at a right-hand bend, go left, passing the spectacular Wickhamford Manor, to pass in front of St John the Baptist church, of weathered sandstone with a squat tower. A footbridge crosses Badsey Brook; follow the left-hand field-edge.

4. Close to a black wooden shed, keep right to join a green-centred track to Badsey Lane. Cross to take a similar track to Badsey Road. Cross this fast road carefully, taking the road through Aldington to a junction in front of The Old Stables. Turn right then almost immediately left. Just after the last house along Chapel Lane, go half-right, to a footbridge. Over this, cross one field, then in a plantation is the walk's only ascent, though hardly a taxing climb.

5. Continue to an intersection just before a large shed and nursery and turn right. At the B4085 go right for 40yds (37m). Turn right and down this tatty meadow, then swing right through a gap to a footbridge. Veer left a little to a metal kissing gate beside a shed with barbed wire gates. A track (green down the middle) leads to Bretforton Road. Turn right, then left at the sign for the village centre to view the Manor House on the right.

6. Continue along this street to the start at St James' Church, where the Manor House's POWs frequently attended services and had their own choir.

Where to eat and drink

In Badsey, the 17th-century Wheatsheaf Inn has bar meals and a broad restaurant menu. The local village store stocks supplies to get you round the walk.

What to see

Between Wickhamford and Aldington you'll see a long row of water outlets for the intensive market gardening here. Look out for all manner of produce in season – rhubarb, lettuce, spinach, broccoli, beetroot, courgettes, pumpkins and leeks.

BRETFORTON TO HONEYBOURNE

DISTANCE/TIME	6.75 miles (10.8km) / 3hrs
ASCENT/GRADIENT	65ft (20m) / ▲
PATHS	Quiet lanes, farm tracks and field footpaths
LANDSCAPE	Open vale with views
SUGGESTED MAP	OS Explorer 205 Stratford-upon-Avon & Evesham
START/FINISH	Grid reference: SP093438
DOG FRIENDLINESS	On lead near livestock though some off-lead opportunities crossing the old airfield
PARKING	Parking area between Bretforton Church and The Fleece Inn
PUBLIC TOILETS	None on route (pubs in Bretforton and Honeybourne for patrons only)

The village of Bretforton lies in the Vale of Evesham, a major fruit and vegetable growing area within Worcestershire. Indeed there is evidence of such produce being grown throughout this walk.

One of the most well known pubs in Britain, The Fleece Inn's name harks back to the biggest industry in the nearby Cotswolds in medieval times – sheep. The, now rare breed, Cotswold Sheep was renowned for its wool and provided the area with the wealth and prosperity from its shaggy coat. The tiny timber-framed pub, now owned by The National Trust, was once a long house, a farm dwelling that originally housed both a farmer and his stock. The building, with walls that defy gravity, is more than picturesque and has a large orchard for a beer garden.

With the area around Bretforton renowned for growing asparagus, The Fleece Inn is the leading venue for the annual British Asparagus Festival. Asparagus, thought of as an aphrodisiac and given to 19th-century bridegrooms because of its reputed powers, is celebrated all around the Vale of Evesham through many events during the Festival. The most famous is the annual Asparagus Auction, which takes place at The Fleece Inn followed by a Festival Day.

The Festival takes place each year from St George's Day (23 April) to Midsummer's Day (21 June), which are the official start and end dates of the Vale asparagus season. The auction and main festival day happen over the Spring Bank Holiday weekend.

Worth a small detour from the walk is a visit to All Things Wild, a zoo in the heart of a small Worcestershire village. Open all year round, with a wide range of small animals including monkeys, birds, insects and some not so small such as camels, rheas, zebras, snakes and caiman. Trails around various sections spotlight the farmyard, the outback and even the world of dinosaurs, on the Dino Land Train.

A section of the walk crosses the old RAF Honeybourne Airfield, including two of the defunct runways. The airfield was opened in December 1940 and was initially used for the training of Canadian pilots. The airfield was later home to No. 24 Operational Training Unit RAF, which used Vickers Wellingtons and Armstrong Whitworth Whitleys flying many operational bombing and leaflet dropping operations, including several prior to the D-Day landings in northern France. With a reduction in flying movements after the World War II, the airfield was closed permanently in 1948, with most of the ground returning to agriculture.

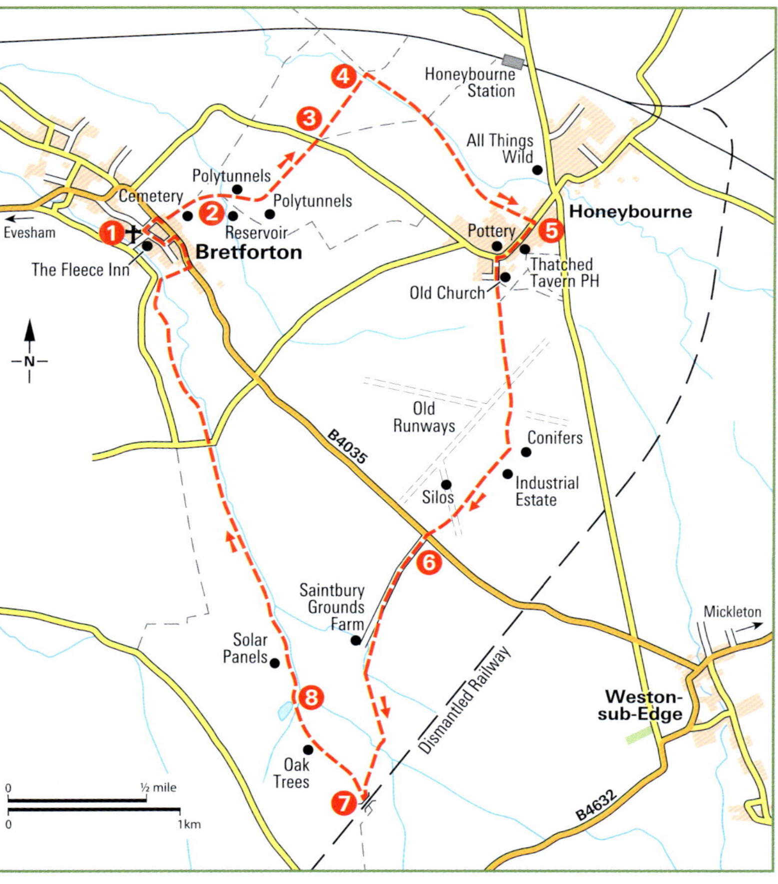

1. Walk past the front of the church, on Main Street, to School Lane and turn right. At end of the lane, cross the road taking a waymarked tarmac footpath, soon grass past the cemetery.

2. At a waymarked post 55yds (50m) from end of cemetery, cut across field at its narrowest point and bear right then left (at a 2nd waymarker) to a series of polytunnels. Turn right to run beside stream, then between the side of a

polytunnel and a small reservoir. At a large ash tree, turn left and follow the track for 0.6 miles (1km) passing between more polytunnels and a hedge gap to a road.

3. Turn right then, in 16yds (15m), left at a waymarker, past a shack. With a hawthorn in front of you, follow the right side of the hedge for 0.25 miles (400m). Pass through a hedge gap and cross a long meadow, then a brook to a metal gate.

4. Turn right and follow the right-hand field edge/brook, between further gates towards static caravans. In 0.25 miles (400m) turn right across a footbridge. Here are some of your first glimpses of Dover's Hill in the distance. Turn left keeping the brook and caravan site on your left, to an obvious stile. Continue on same line to pass beside stock fencing and a metal gate close to pale stone houses. Keeping houses on right, follow farm track crossing two further metal gates and exit paddock on far right, over a stile. Follow a narrow path for 21yds (20m) to gravel then keep same line to a road, arriving in Honeybourne.

5. Turn right. In 328yds (300m) turn left along Brick Walk towards the church. Follow the lane keeping the church on left and pass onto the playing field. Once again there are significant views of Dover's Hill and the main Cotswold ridge. In 219yds (200m) cross a footbridge. Continue line across field to a hedge gap. To your right is Bredon Hill and, beyond, The Malverns. Cross an old concrete runway and strike half-right across a further field following waymarked posts aiming towards a clump of conifers and an industrial estate. In 109yds (100m), crossing a track at a waymarked post, now fork right keeping conifers and buildings away to your left and farm silos to right to a further waymarker. Now, with conifer half-left behind and hangar on left, head across field towards two solitary pines and a double H-pole, keeping silos on right when crossing a second disused runway. Cross a stile then, carefully, the road to a track leading to Saintbury Grounds Farm.

6. Follow the track for 547yds (500m). At the stone-pillared entrance to farm, follow waymarkers left to continue along a parallel track. As the track bears right to farm buildings, keep straight through hedge gap. Follow ditch edge and cross footbridge where a second ditch converges. Immediately strike half-left keeping the double electricity poles on right, to a hidden stile in the far hedge, approximately 109yds (100m) from field corner. Cross a thin meadow to a stile and footbridge. Go half-left to a post and rise in ground level next to a disused railway.

7. Now track right to cross the same field widthways to a hedge corner by poplars. Cross a stile. Keep hedge on right admiring the two vast oak trees as you pass to a hidden footbridge in the field corner. Continue along hedge line and pass through it, over another footbridge approximately 33yds (30m) before field corner. Turn immediately left, skirting remaining edge of poplar wood and at a wide clearing left to a lake.

8. With lake in front of you, turn right and follow field edge, through a gap, passing solar panels on left. Pass through five fields, keeping to the right hand field edge at all times. Cross a minor road and, once again, maintain the right hand field edge for a further four fields, gaining a view ultimately of Bretforton church. Approaching a minor road on a bend, turn immediately right across a footbridge and take the well-trodden path to another road with pavement. Turn left and left again in 164yds (150m) into Main Street, to return to the church and parking.

Where to eat and drink
The Fleece Inn (owned by the National Trust) in Bretforton, serves real ales and excellent food. A large orchard at the rear serves as the pub garden. En route, Thatched Tavern in Honeybourne offers an extensive menu for lunches and dinner in either the bar or restaurant or in the pleasant garden.

What to see
Dover's Hill and much of the northern section of the Cotswold escarpment. You'll also see Bredon Hill and The Malverns.

While you're there
The walk passes the entrance to Honeybourne Pottery, which offers 1.5 hour 'crash' courses in making pottery and learning to use a potter's wheel on Friday, Saturday and Sunday (booking essential).

ALONG CLEEVE HILL

DISTANCE/TIME	4.5 miles (7.2km) / 2hrs 30min
ASCENT/GRADIENT	225ft (69m) / ▲
PATHS	Paths across fields, stony tracks and village roads, several stiles
LANDSCAPE	Level farmland with distant hills
SUGGESTED MAP	OS Explorer 205 Stratford-upon-Avon & Evesham
START/FINISH	Grid reference: SP077469
DOG FRIENDLINESS	On lead near sheep; some freedom in arable fields
PARKING	Outside village hall on School Lane, Middle Littleton, or on-street parking elsewhere in the village
PUBLIC TOILETS	None on route

The Vale of Evesham, renowned for its fruit, is virtually flat, but the growers who farm the land are constantly of the opinion that the economic field on which they play, slopes against them. The most frequently cited objection is that producers abroad get (more) governmental assistance, facilitating a large supply of cheaper imported fruit, which consumers are willing to accept.

Plums with such evocative names as Pershore Purple and Pershore Yellow Egg used to dominate the region, but nowadays the Victoria accounts for three-quarters of the commercially grown plums. The plum is the first tree to come into flower in spring, showing its delicate white petals even before the sloe (blackthorn). According to folklore, plums may, apparently, be used to make a love potion.

One of the ways in which cherry growers have made themselves more competitive is to grow the fruit on dwarfing rootstocks; as the name suggests, this means that the tree does not grow to any great height, making the labour-costly task of picking the fruit much easier. A further benefit is that the smaller trees can be covered by a plastic tunnel. Although there are now several types of plastic tunnel, in England the so-called 'French tunnel' has been around since the late 1980s, coincidentally roughly the time that the Channel Tunnel began to be drilled. Such a substantial investment is best thought of as an insurance policy, protecting the fruit from summer rainstorms.

There is considerable potential to be realised from combining these two simple technologies. Perhaps other trees, such as peaches, almonds, apricots and figs, will be grown in tunnels if suitable dwarf rootstocks can be cultivated.

Although growers are anxious to have soft fruits such as strawberries available early in the season, it is also an advantage to be able to prolong the season. This is achieved by taking plants out of the ground during the shortest days of December and January, then arresting their growth by keeping them in cold storage (which of course incurs a cost) until required, not planting out the last until August.

On our behalf, supermarket buyers make the assumption that we will only eat perfectly proportioned strawberries. Hives of honey bees are routinely used to maximise levels of pollination. Two separate studies have suggested that honey bees also reduce the percentage of misshapen fruit from about 30 per cent to below 5 per cent...presumably, as you read this, somebody is trying to work out why!

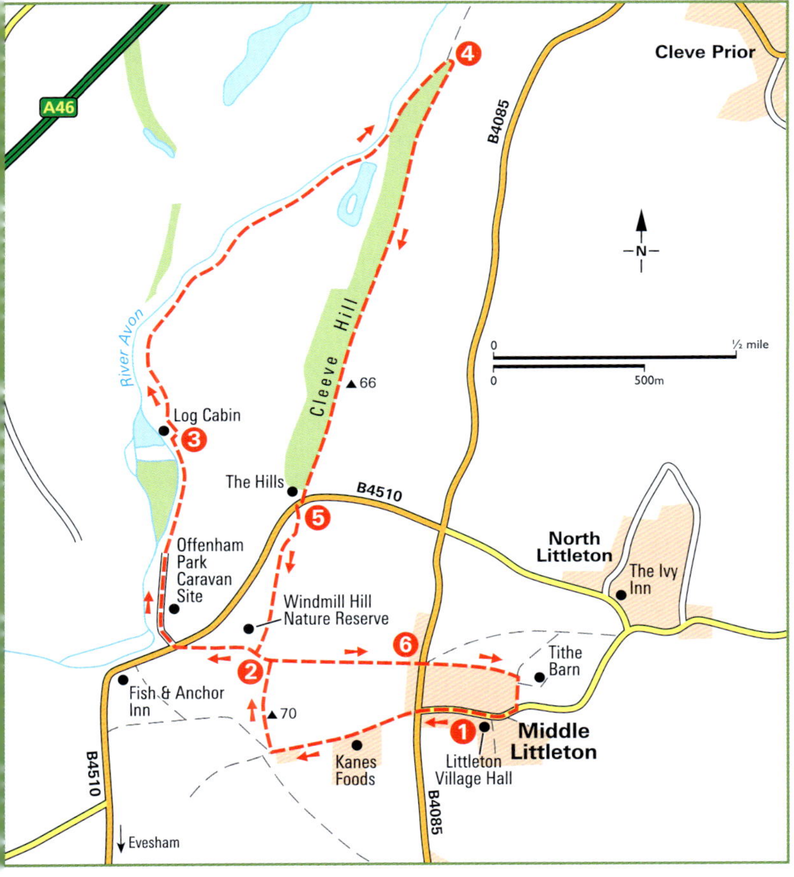

1. Walk westwards up School Lane to the B4085, here called Cleeve Road. Cross diagonally left to take a rutted, stony track, screened by a hedgerow from Kanes Foods. At a junction of tracks bear right by a nature reserve to join a bridle path, passing several gates. After 350yds (320m), you reach an opening on the right and a line of plum trees marking a field boundary; on the left is a metal gate.

2. Go through this gate, entering Worcestershire Wildlife Trust's Windmill Hill Nature Reserve. Descend steeply, ignoring crossing tracks, to another gate and across one field to the B4510. Follow the signposted 'Cleeve Prior' footpath through Offenham Park caravan site. (Turn left on the road for 220yds/201m for the Fish & Anchor Inn.) Go through a gate out of the caravan park to walk on a stone track beside the river.

3. At a log cabin move to the right to take a double-stiled footbridge and resume your riverside stroll. Continue through mostly ungated pastures for over 0.75 mile (1.2km). Ascend through trees to a clearing and a path junction.

4. Turn sharply right, back on yourself, soon walking into trees again, to follow a popular (and sometimes muddy) bridleway. In a shade under 1 mile (1.6km) the B4510 cuts through the hill, beside The Hills. Cross over and move right to a fingerpost, but follow the path for just 75yds (69m).

5. Go through the gate into the nature reserve here, and follow either of the parallel contouring paths, giving fine views over to the west. After 440yds (402m) you will recognise your outward route. Turn left here, up the bank, retracing your steps for just 30yds (27m), to Point 2. Once at the top go straight across, walking with the line of plum trees on your left-hand side. When this ends, maintain this direction until you reach the B4085.

6. Cross the road and go straight ahead. From the fields you will see the tithe barn. Before some young trees take a kissing gate to the right. In 15yds (14m) turn left to visit the tithe barn, or keep ahead to reach the village road. Turn right again, shortly to reach the start of the walk.

Where to eat and drink

Rather early on in the walk, and just a couple of minutes off the route, is the Fish & Anchor Inn, which welcomes both dogs and children. South Littleton has a post office stores and in North Littleton, The Ivy Inn serves hot food and a range of ales. The Ivy Inn also has an outdoor seating area to enjoy in fine weather.

What to see

As you walk through the caravan site you may notice that the caravans are raised, standing on breeze-block pillars about 3ft (1m) high. This flood-protection measure reduces the risk of damage by flooding, but by no means removes it.

While you're there

In the 1970s the Middle Littleton Tithe Barn (now NT), once used for tithe payments to the Abbey of Evesham, was lovingly restored. It's open from 10am to 5pm (April to October), so time your walk so as not to miss it. Documents show that the barn was in use in about 1370, but carbon dating puts its construction nearly 100 years earlier. Eleven magnificent bays span its 136ft (41m) length – that's about two cricket wickets – and the apex of its roof is over 40ft (12m) above its stone-slabbed floor.

ELMLEY CASTLE

DISTANCE/TIME	4.5 miles (7.3km) / 2hrs 30min
ASCENT/GRADIENT	705ft (215m) / ▲ ▲ ▲
PATHS	Meadows and woodland paths
LANDSCAPE	Farmland, woodland and panoramic views
SUGGESTED MAP	OS Explorer 190 Malvern Hills & Bredon Hill
START/FINISH	Grid reference: SO982411
DOG FRIENDLINESS	Lots of opportunities for off-lead walks; on lead around livestock
PARKING	On-road in Elmley Castle or Elmley Castle Picnic Place 219yds (200m) from start
PUBLIC TOILETS	None on route

Elmley Castle is a particularly attractive village that sits at the foot of the northern slopes of Bredon Hill. It has many black and white half-timbered buildings and old brick cottages, clustered around a cricket pitch. A tiny, channelled stream flows along the main street. The name of the village of Elmley Castle dates from the 11th century, when Robert le Despenser built a castle on an eastern outlier of Bredon Hill, half a mile south of the village, shortly after the Norman Conquest. It was later part of the estate of the powerful Beauchamp family, whose name can still be found in Worcestershire and neighbouring South Warwickshire. The castle remained the Beauchamp's chief seat until William de Beauchamp inherited the earldom and castle of Warwick from his maternal uncle. Thereafter it became a 'second home' until it was surrendered to the Crown in 1487. By the middle of the next century the castle was in ruins. Stones from the castle were used to build some of the houses in the village and the old Pershore Bridge, adjacent to the A44 road bridge. Today, while there is no building present, you can still see the fortified earthworks of the castle (on private land).

In 1234, with the increasing importance of the castle at Elmley, Walter Beauchamp received a gift of 10 does and 3 bucks from King Henry III for the Deer Park behind the church. Elmley still has its deer today, and you may see the herd while on the walk.

The Church of St Mary the Virgin stands at the head of the village, just below the Deer Park. The chancel of the church was probably built before 1100, a supposition based in part on the 'herringbone' style of stonework in the chancel wall. Its font has a 15th-century octagonal bowl on a 13th-century square base, decorated with carved serpents and dragons. Of particular note in the church is a set of three 17th-century effigies of the Savage family, lying down, with four children kneeling before them. The Savage family lived in an Elizabethan stone mansion in Elmley Castle, which Christopher Savage built having been granted the land around the ruined castle and the Deer Park. Christopher Savage, who died in 1545, had been an Esquire of the Body of

King Henry VIII. The mansion remained as the home of the Savage Family until 1822. In 1948, the mansion sadly made way for a housing estate.

The public house, The Queen Elizabeth, is named after Queen Elizabeth I who stayed in the village, with the Savages, for two days in 1575. The Queen was allegedly presented with a hat upon her arrival in the village on the road from the nearby town of Pershore. The place of the presentation, on the edge of the village, is still known as Bess Cap.

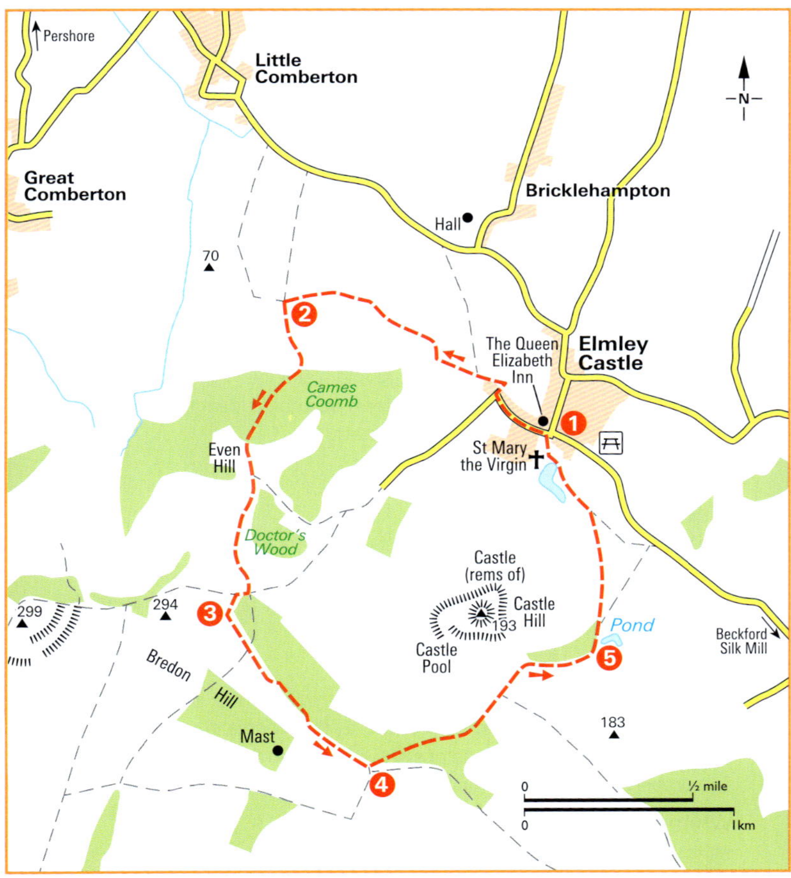

1. Facing the churchyard of St Mary the Virgin, with the Queen Elizabeth Inn on your right, go right, past the end of the pub. Pass several black-and-white houses, some of which are thatched. At a sharp left bend take a fingerpost to the right, passing beside a farm building. Turn sharp left at the end of this building, using gates to cross a concreted area; leave the farm through two more gates. Follow the right-hand field-edge. In the third field, after 40yds (37m), turn three-quarters right at a redundant stile, soon regaining your line. To the right is Bricklehampton Hall. Continue for three fields, crossing some quite rickety stiles and plank bridges over ditches. Reach a metal kissing gate to a track and turn left at Point 2 to walk uphill.

2. Once in woodland, briefly follow a level forestry road and fork left in 200yds (182m) to maintain line up through Cames Coomb. Cross the flat open meadow, Even Hill, to an obvious gate in stock fencing. Continue the climb along the well-trodden path, past Doctor's Wood, through a gate. Beyond, veer left then right through a green hollow to a wooden gate into woodland. Don't enter the wood but veer right then left to follow a stony track uphill beside woodland. In 110yds (100m), at a single post waymarker take the bridleway left to skirt the wood, not the route following the Wychavon Way.

3. Go through the gate and walk an easy 0.6 miles (1km) on a firm, fenced path, flanked by a steep wooded slope and open fields. Where the fence kinks there are gates on the right, and Wychavon Way indicators.

4. Go half left, into the woods, descending steadily on a wide bridle path. Leave this woodland for open meadow. Lower down, veer right, following single post waymarkers. Cross a wooden footbridge over a ditch. Continue descending through light woodland with bracken. At a possible fork keep left to another footbridge. Here go left, alongside a wire fence, passing a long and narrow pond on your right-hand side. Within 100yds (91m) of this pond, reach a new metal gate.

5. Through this, turn left over a leaning stile and across a two-plank footbridge. Go three-quarters right in parkland with a large, dead tree in the middle. In the next, large field, veer left to find a stile between a garden hedge and small paddock. A wooded path crosses a decorative dammed pond to reach the churchyard and a return to the start.

Where to eat and drink
The Queen Elizabeth Inn in Elmley Castle, at the start/finish of the walk is a community run venture that not only serves as pub but also as a restaurant, a take-away, a tea room and a library. Open all day (9.30am to 11pm) every day except Mondays (evenings only).

What to see
Bricklehampton Hall, close to the start of the walk, is an elegant Regency style house built in 1848 and surrounded by thirty acres of parkland. Though built in Cotswold limestone, the Hall has an Italianate exterior. The property is now a care home.

While you're there
Skirt the edge of Bredon Hill to visit Beckford Silk Mill, where silk fabric is designed, dyed and printed. Located in the village of Beckford on the southern side of Bredon Hill, there's a small shop on site and a café too.

BREDON HILL

DISTANCE/TIME	7.5 miles (12.1km) / 3hrs 55min
ASCENT/GRADIENT	1,115ft (340m) / ▲ ▲
PATHS	Tracks, woodland paths, bridleways, minor lanes, many stiles
LANDSCAPE	Farmland, woodland, panoramic views into Wales
SUGGESTED MAP	OS Explorer 190 Malvern Hills & Bredon Hill
START/FINISH	Grid reference: SO955423
DOG FRIENDLINESS	Close control needed – cows, horses and lots of sheep
PARKING	Roadside parking, Great Comberton village
PUBLIC TOILETS	None on route

Bredon Hill is a solitary outcrop of hard, yellowish limestone. The fort on its plateau summit enclosed 22 acres (8.9ha). Today the hill is one of English Nature's National Nature Reserves.

As the name Pershore – 'Pearshore' – suggests, the area around nearby Pershore has long been synonymous with pears, and plums too. Although perry remains a popular drink, with some manufacturers of perry apparently planting new orchards, many traditional pear orchards have, like apple orchards, been wiped off the map, either for more lucrative forms of agricultural activity, or for house building. An interesting legacy is the presence of pear trees in local hedgerows.

The pear's gene pool is being maintained by a national collection. As many as 120 varieties of perry pear have been recorded; about half of these have been traced in recent years. Specimens have been planted at the Three Counties Showground, near Malvern. In addition, the Worcestershire County Council's Countryside Greenspace Team runs a fruit-tree scheme, like its counterpart in Herefordshire. Pear, along with other fruit trees such as cherry, apple and plum, is a popular wood for turning; also, the fine grain of pear wood makes it suitable for engraving when the favoured box wood is not available. In Worcester, look out for the city's coat of arms – it bears three black pears. The story goes that when Queen Elizabeth I visited Worcester, the city's 16th-century events manager arranged for a Worcester Black Pear tree to be placed along her route; this pleased Her Majesty, who pronounced that the city's coat of arms ought to display these splendid fruits. Doubtless she didn't actually taste one for the fruit is too tough to eat uncooked; it needs to be served in a pudding such as a crumble, or preserved in syrup. (The name is also inaccurate – the fruits are no more black than white grapes are white.) Nevertheless, to encourage some sense of heritage among its children, Worcestershire City Council has provided every one of the city's schools with a Worcester Black Pear tree. On the top of Bredon Hill is Parson's Folly. Named after Mr Parson, a resident of nearby Kemerton, it stands on the perimeter earthwork of Kemerton Camp, an Iron Age hill fort. The name of the village of Elmley Castle dates from the 11th century, when Robert le Despenser built a castle on an eastern outlier of Bredon Hill. It was later part of the estate of the Beauchamp family. The castle was again fortified in the 14th century, after interim decay. It is said that stones from this castle were used to build the old Pershore Bridge, adjacent to the present-day A44 road bridge. Today there is precious little to see of the castle itself (on private land).

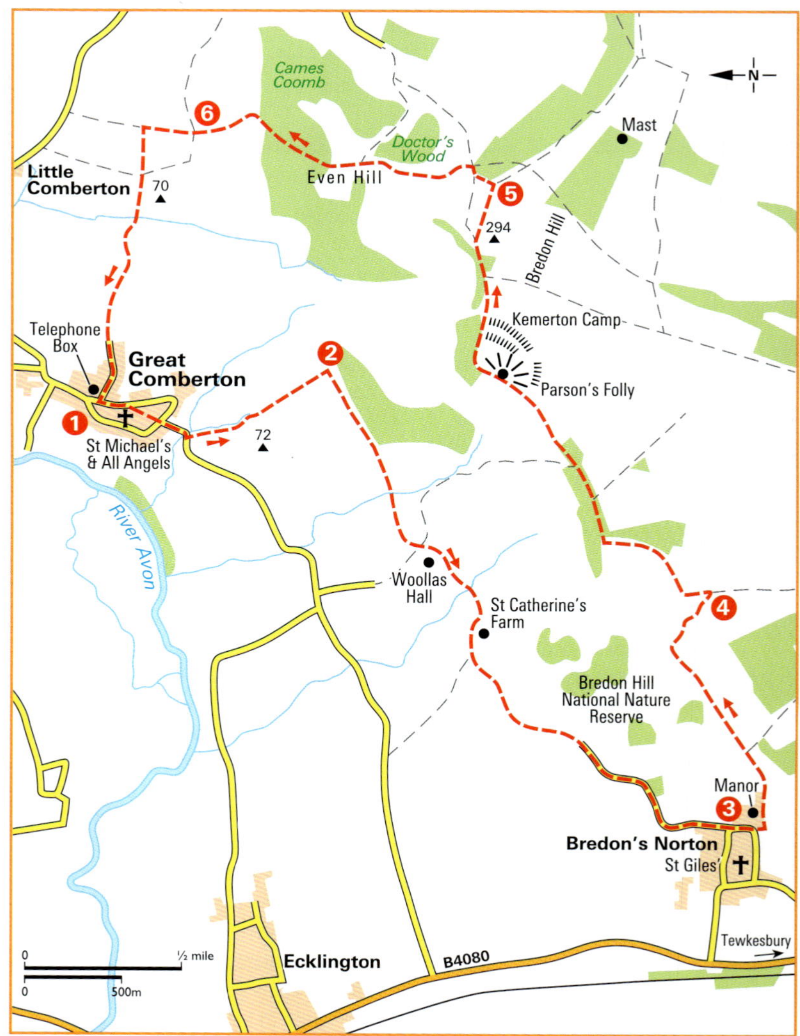

1. Begin beside the telephone box, now a community book exchange in Great Comberton. Follow Church Street. Go through the churchyard; leave by an old iron kissing gate. At the road, go down the '11%' gradient. In the dip find a metal gate. Ascend two fields (this bit is quite strenuous), with a stream on your left-hand side. In the third field, there is a (wobbly) signpost after 90yds (82m).

2. Turn right, initially beside trees. Soon a good farm track strikes across meadow. Ahead is a perfect Malvern Hills view. Follow waymarkers for the next 1.5 miles (2.4km), taking the gravel driveway beside Woollas Hall and skirting St Catherine's Farm. Take a hard track, later tarmac, down into Bredon's Norton. After the first few houses, you reach a junction.

3. Keep ahead for 100yds (91m) to another junction. Turn right if visiting St Giles' Church; otherwise go ahead again, then round a left bend. Go into a field, to the right of two buildings – there's a waymarker on a telegraph pole. Now follow an excellent track steadily upwards, through several gates, eventually swinging southeast, for at least 0.75 mile (1.2km). Less than 100yds (91m) beyond a single marker post reach a T-junction with 'no right of way' ahead.

4. Turn left, shortly veering right along a field-edge. Ascend for 600yds (549m), then turn right to walk all the way along the wooded escarpment ridge, before an open field leads to Parson's Folly on the edge of Kemerton Camp. Follow the escarpment eastwards, keeping the wall on your left until you reach a small conifer plantation. Just past this, ignore a downward fork, instead following a wire fence for over 0.25 mile (400m), to a wood.

5. Don't enter the wood; turn left, beside it. Within 150yds (137m), bend right to a junction. Turn left, facing away from the gate into wood, down a green hollow. At Doctor's Wood veer left to cross an oddly level field, Even Hill (no contours on the map). Find a gate hidden in a dip at the edge of woodland to the right. Descend steeply through Cames Coomb, along a wide, well-trodden path. Briefly follow a level forestry road, then leave the trees, descending on a track for 400yds (366m) to a metal kissing gate on the right.

6. Walk a further 275yds (251m) on the good track to find a path on the left (ignoring the first signposted path to the left), initially between two hedges. When it ends, go straight ahead. Keep this general line – later a hard track – back into Great Comberton. Turn right to the telephone box.

Where to eat and drink
This walk is 'dry' but you could try The Bell public house in Eckington on the B4080 or the Anchor Inn, just off the same road.

What to see
St Giles' church in Bredon Norton dates from the 13th century and has many fine and unusual tombs within the church, one of which is a pair of arms emerging from beneath a shield and clutching a heart, this a memorial to a Crusader who died in the Holy Wars in about 1290.

While you're there
A few miles to the north and clearly seen from Bredon Hill is Pershore Abbey in Pershore. Founded in the seventh century, the oldest surviving parts, hewn from local limestone, are Norman.

THE LENCHES

DISTANCE/TIME	7.2 miles (11.6km) / 3hrs
ASCENT/GRADIENT	607ft (185m) / ▲
PATHS	Quiet lanes, farm tracks and field footpaths
LANDSCAPE	Rolling countryside, pastures, orchards and woodland
SUGGESTED MAP	OS Explorer 205 Stratford-upon-Avon & Evesham
START/FINISH	Grid reference: SP014513
DOG FRIENDLINESS	On lead near livestock though lots of off-lead opportunities between Points 2 and 3
PARKING	Layby next to church in Rous Lench (avoid parking next to bus stop)
PUBLIC TOILETS	None on route

On a ridge at the northern boundary of the Vale of Evesham sits a collection of five villages. All five bear the same name – Lench – each one with a preceding clue as to who once owned the villages.

Collectively, the villages are known as The Lenches. All five villages once belonged to neighbouring abbeys – Rous Lench, Church Lench and Ab Lench owned by the abbey of Worcester, Sheriff's Lench and Atch Lench by the abbey of Evesham. Rous Lench was latterly occupied by the Rous (or Rouse) family. Church Lench and Ab Lench both fell into the hands of the Sheriff of Worcester, Urse d'Abitot, who in turn gave it to his heirs and hereditary sheriffs the Beauchamp family (who also owned Elmley Castle). With the Beauchamps then overlords at Church Lench during the 14th century, the manor was held by the Roculfs, hence Church Lench has an alternate name, Lench Roculf.

Odo, Bishop of Bayeux – William the Conqueror's half-brother, stole Sheriff's Lench from the church. Odo latterly gave it to Urse d'Abitot, the Sheriff who again gave it to his heirs, the Beauchamps. Hence, it's thought that this is how the village gained its name.

Ab Lench, which is sometimes incorrectly named Abbot's Lench because of its association with the abbey at Worcester, is thought to have derived from a personal name, Aebba from Saxon times.

At the beginning of the walk in Rous Lench you'll pass a medieval moat. Classified as an ancient monument, it used to surround the 14th-century manor, which no longer exists. The owners, the Rous family, were staunch Parliamentarians and it is reputed that Oliver Cromwell dined at Rous Lench Court in 1651 on the eve of the Battle of Worcester, the final conflict of the English Civil War in which he defeated King Charles II and the Royalists.

On your way around the villages, you will see several black and white half-timbered properties. Three in particular, all of differing size, to look out for are Rous Lench Court, The Cot and Toy Cottage.

Today's Rous Lench Court, across the parkland from the original manor house, actually dates from the second half of the 19th century, built in Elizabethan style to match its predecessor. The property, the landscape park and arboretum are all Grade II listed, including the yew avenue, considered one of the finest in England.

The Cot, in Sheriff's Lench, was built in 1871 in Tudor style by a landowner to house his workers. He incorporated a rather sobering inscription beneath the eaves reminding them – and visitors – to contemplate the next life rather than earthly pleasures.

Toy Cottage, in Malthouse Lane, Church Lench is a Grade II thatched dwelling from the late 17th century. Blink and you'll miss it! It is arguably one of the smallest houses in Worcestershire, quite literally a one-up, one-down but for the small 20th-century extension.

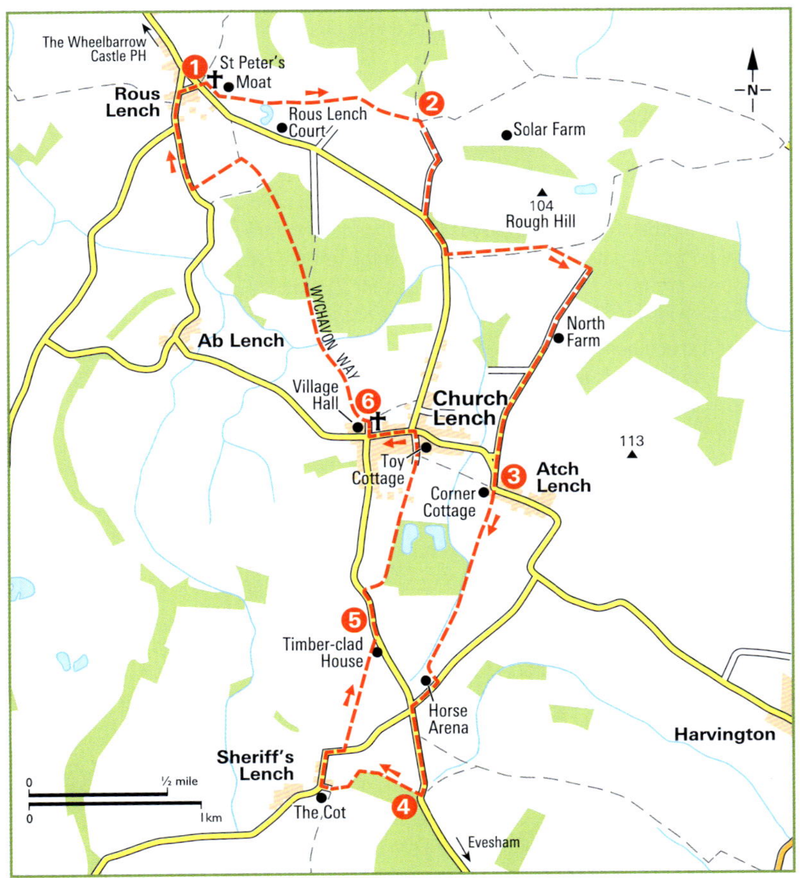

1. Head into churchyard and exit via a kissing gate into a field. Instantly, you'll see views of the impressive Rous Lench Court ahead. Pass up the side of an old moat on your left and follow the line up beyond a very tall Wellingtonia to a stile. Cross a track to a further stile and climb towards pines and a stile (turn around for your first glimpse of The Malverns). Cross a field using the same line to a copse beyond.

2. Beneath a lime tree, cross a stile, skirt the edge of a fenced plantation to a stile. Maintain the right hand field margin to a metal gate. Pass between trees to a further gate and farm building. Take the bridleway half-right for 546yds (500m) to a road. Turn left and in 328yds (300m) left again beside decorative double electric gates (and just before a bridge) to walk beside a driveway then sunken path for 0.5 miles (800m). Arriving at a gravel track in woodland, turn right. Follow the track, becoming a lane, for 0.75 miles (1.2km), before joining a road to 'Atch Lench'. Atch Lench has attractive half-timbered black and white houses that are worth a look on a short detour along the main street.

3. As the road turns a sharp corner, take a footpath between gardens, left of Corner Cottage. In 11yds (10m), take the right of two paths, by a gate, to keep the hedge on your left. At a metal gate, keep the hollow hedgerow ash on left and maintain left-hand field margin to a hedge gap and large oak, then swap sides. Over a stile, cross a field to a footbridge and keep a hedge on the right. Ignore footpath on right in 219yds (200m) and move straight on, around the field edge to a gate then fingerpost in the top left-hand corner of field, beside a horse arena. At a minor road, turn right for 219yds (200m) and at staggered crossroads, left. Take care on the road for 656yds (600m).

4. At a sharp bend, take a bridleway on right beside an orchard. At the top left field corner, cross a gap and follow left-hand field edge, arriving in Sheriff's Lench. At a road turn right, through the village and right again in 109yds (100m). In 328yds (300m), around a sharp bend in the road, take a footpath by a hidden fingerpost and gulley drain. Walk the right-hand field edge until fencing runs out, then across centre of field, maintain same line, towards a clump of small ash trees in the hedge. Pass through hedge into the next field and aim for the black, timber-clad house. Leave the field by a gate to the road.

5. Walk left along the road. 55yds (50m) past the sign for Lenches Lakes, turn right to a waymarked bridleway. In a further 295yds (270m), ignoring first public footpath sign, take fingerposted bridleway, becoming a lane, for 0.6 miles (1km). At a crossroads, turn left into Main Street to the church. Through the churchyard to a gate, you'll find a comfortable bench by the village hall car park with views of the Malverns and Shropshire Hills.

6. Leave the car park by a gate marked Wychavon Way. Through a further gate, take right-hand field edge to a gate and wooden steps. Descend straight down towards woodland. Cross a stile then footbridge and ascend along right-hand field margin. Into woodland, maintain the same line. At a fork, bear left for Wychavon Way, then a second, straight on, beside stock fencing crossing several tracks to clear the wood. Exiting the wood at a metal gate, walk the edge of the ridge and admire the views of the entire length of the Malvern Hills. Take the left-handed of two gates (in the corner). Walk the right-hand field edge and turn right at the lane to return to Rous Lench and the church.

Where to eat and drink

The Wheelbarrow Castle, Radford is 1.2 miles (2km) from Rous Lench. It is very handy owing to its proximity to the beginning and end of the walk. An alternative is the Apple Barn Restaurant at Evesham Garden Centre.

What to see

The Tower behind Rous Lench Court is Grade II listed and was built in the 1860s by Dr William Kyle Westwood Chafy, owner of the property. Italianate in style, it has a square plan with a circular stair turret and a crenellated parapet. The Tower can be seen from various viewpoints along the walk.

While you're there

The Valley Evesham, 6 miles (9.6km) from Rous Lench, has a garden centre, a selection of places to eat including a restaurant and café, over two-dozen shops and the Evesham Vale Light Railway. Many events take place throughout the year.

UPTON SNODSBURY AND HUDDINGTON

DISTANCE/TIME	5.25 miles (8.4km) / 2hrs 30min
ASCENT/GRADIENT	70ft (21m)
PATHS	Meadows and field paths, tracks and lanes, several stiles
LANDSCAPE	Gentle farmland, picturesque, historic house
SUGGESTED MAP	OS Explorer 204 Worcester & Droitwich Spa
START/FINISH	Grid reference: SO943543
DOG FRIENDLINESS	Mixed farmland throughout
PARKING	Roadside parking, Upton Snodsbury
PUBLIC TOILETS	None on route

A Grade I listed manor house, 16th-century Huddington Court is privately owned and not open to the public. The black-and-white timber-framed residence, considered 'the most picturesque house in Worcestershire' by prominent 20th-century architectural historian Sir Nikolaus Pevsner, is surrounded by a moat that was possibly dug for an earlier property on the site, the village of Huddington being of Saxon origin. From the 15th to 17th centuries the house belonged to the Wintour family. Brothers Thomas and Robert Wintour, who both resided at the property, were among the 13 men involved the Gunpowder Plot. During his reign, Henry VIII had broken from the Roman Catholic church and the authority of the Pope, and established the Church of England. His Dissolution of the Monasteries stripped them of their vast wealth. Later, Elizabeth I introduced (lucrative) fines for people not attending Church of England services. Catholic recusants established a form of 'closet Catholicism' – almost literally, since harbouring a Catholic priest was punishable by death and priests' holes were built to help priests avoid detection by the authorities.

In 1603, after Elizabeth's death, James I inherited the English throne, joining the crowns of Scotland and England. As the new king had a Catholic wife, it was hoped that he would provide greater security and tolerance for English Catholics, but this was not to be. Historians cannot agree precisely why the Gunpowder Plot took place. Was it a (misguided) attempt to spark the reinstatement of Catholicism in England or a means for the government to tarnish the Jesuit movement covertly by blaming them, thus strengthening the Protestant position?

Guy Fawkes, born a Protestant but converting to Catholicism in his early 20s, was not the principal conspirator within the Plot – just inept enough to get himself caught on the night of 4 November, 1605 following a tip-off received in the form of an anonymous letter to a prominent Catholic, Lord Monteagle.

The Wintour brothers and other plotters fled to Huddington Court to hide within its three priests' holes, following the arrest of Guy Fawkes. Eventually found, Robert and Thomas Wintour were executed for treason, along with Fawkes, in January 1606. They were hung, drawn and quartered.

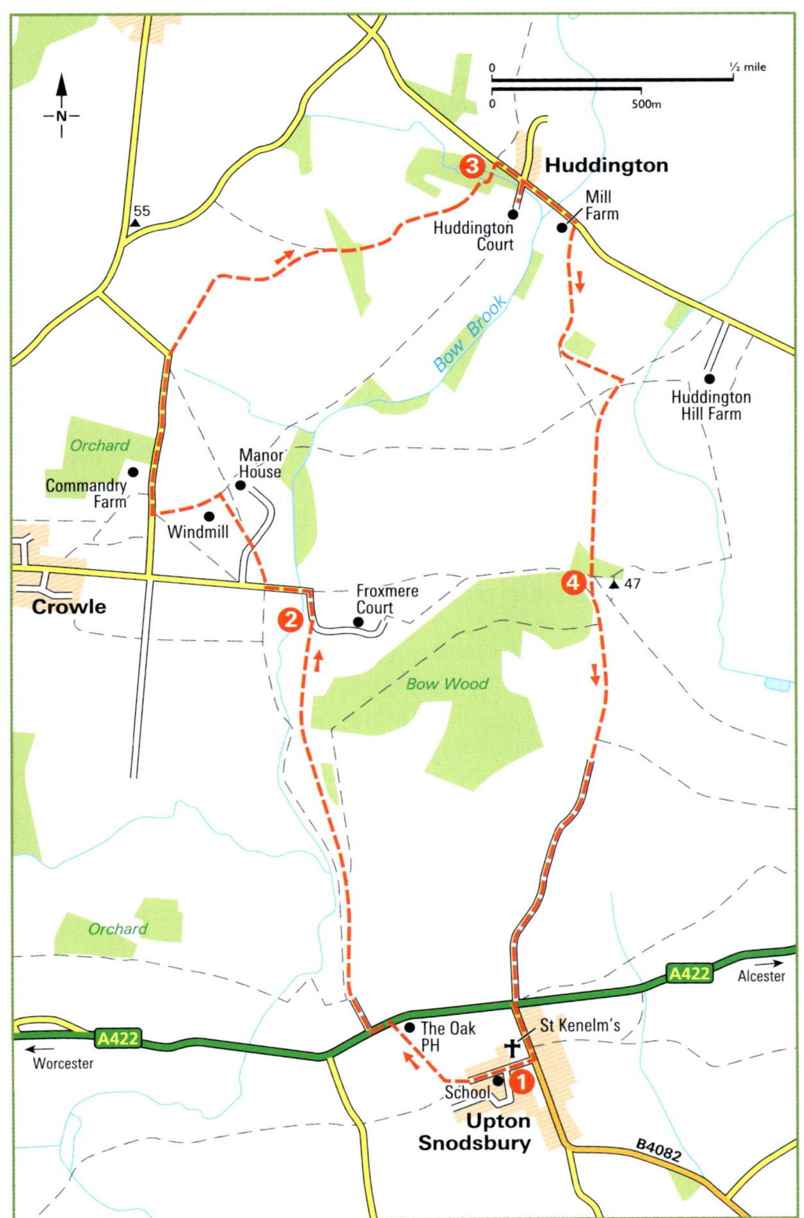

1. Begin on Church Lane, south of St Kenelm's Church (1874). Go west, past the school then between some bungalows and a private car park. Go diagonally right, through two kissing gates, then cross a field to the left of power lines, down to conifers fringing the car park of The Oak on the A422. Cross over. Turn left, then right after 50yds (46m) into Bow Wood Lane. In 100yds (91m) go ahead. Walk through a long field, scarcely gaining any height.

Eventually leave by a pair of narrow metal gates, crossing another field to a further metal gate beyond.

2. Join a driveway. When 90yds (82m) beyond Bow Brook's bridge go half right, reaching a metal kissing gate beside the drive to Manor House. Despite a waymarker pointing to a stile close to Manor House, aim one pylon right of a rusty windmill to another metal kissing gate. Turn half left to a gate in trees. Turn right on this minor road for 650yds (594m). Now follow a right-hand field-edge (fingerpost). Just before the field corner go through a gate on the right, continue with the hedge now on your left. At the next corner go through a gate and turn right. At an opening into a big field aim 10yds (9m) left of a two-poled power pylon ahead. In and out of woodland, take the right-hand field-edge. At the bend cross a double stile and three-planked bridge. Go diagonally, to a waymarked stile 40yds (37m) before a metal gate. Emerge beside a black-and-white house and a greenhouse through two garden gates, opposite Huddington Court.

3. Turn left, not towards Huddington Court, crossing a dam at steps, to a minor road. Turn right. In 120yds (110m), turn into Huddington Court's driveway. When it swings right, stop to admire the house. Back at the minor road, walk on to Mill Farm. Follow the fingerpost by the farm entrance. In a big field, aim for a prominent ash at a far woodland corner diagonally opposite. Walk with the plantation on your left. At its second corner, turn left. At the end of this field keep within it, turning right. In 120yds (110m), go for 500yds (457m) diagonally towards trees, passing 50yds (46m) left of the first pylon. Through an aperture in the trees, reach a stile within 50yds (46m).

4. Go half left, but on reaching a field boundary turn half right, staying within the field to walk parallel with Bow Wood. From the brow, continue with this field-edge on your left for 400yds (366m) to gates. A stone track leads to the A422 and thus Upton Snodsbury village.

Where to eat and drink

There is a store and post office in Upton Snodsbury. Near the start is The Oak Steakhouse and Grill, which has a characterful interior and beer garden. Within the pub is The Twisted Spoon tea house serving breakfast, lunch and afternoon teas.

While you're there

Adjacent to the lawn of Huddington Court is the largely Norman and 14th-century Church of St James. Between his arrest and execution, Robert Wintour admitted that he had told the chaplain, a Jesuit priest, about the Gunpowder Plot.

AROUND HANBURY

DISTANCE/TIME	4.75 miles (7.7km) / 2hrs 15min
ASCENT/GRADIENT	250ft (76m) / ▲
PATHS	Meadows, tracks and easy woodland paths, many stiles
LANDSCAPE	Parkland, woodland, country house
SUGGESTED MAP	OS Explorer 204 Worcester & Droitwich Spa
START/FINISH	Grid reference: SO957652
DOG FRIENDLINESS	Not good; not allowed in Hanbury Hall's garden (or house), lots of sheep
PARKING	Piper's Hill car park, on B4091 between Stoke Wharf and Hanbury (fast road and no sign – easily missed)
PUBLIC TOILETS	None on route

The motor car, the television and the contraceptive pill were arguably the three most socially influential inventions of modern times. Further down the list, but a candidate for a top-ten position, would come the domestic refrigerator. The commercial exploitation of the refrigeration principle was not realised until 1877, when the world's first refrigerated ship, equipped with a system designed by Frenchman Ferdinand Carré, brought frozen meat to France from Argentina. The now ubiquitous fridge-freezer did not begin mass production until much later, at a General Electric factory in 1939.

Prior to this refrigeration, the only way of keeping things cold was to use ice. It was stored in ice wells or ice houses. When ice was not available, salting was the primary method of preserving meat. Records show that Britain imported ice by ship from Scandinavia right up until 1921, a trade that had begun about 100 years earlier. Before that time it was collected in the winter from any practicable place – ponds, rivers and canals, and even by crushing snow. The ice house at Hanbury Hall (NT) is a wonderful specimen and Grade II listed. It's a shame that there aren't enough volunteers around to bring it back into use once more.

Built in the mid-18th century, it was sunk 11ft (3.4m) into the ground and topped with a mound of earth. Internally it is 20ft (6m) high and over 15ft (4.6m) across, making it roughly egg-shaped. The dome has a hatch in it (now covered with perspex, providing a useful skylight) and the entrance is a corridor nearly 28ft (8.5m) long. Melted ice drained through a grid in the brick floor. To some extent it was possible to manufacture ice. Close to the ice house, two deep pools with sluice gates served as reservoirs and, on frosty nights, water would be released into a third, shallow pool, yielding an ice 'crop' to be cut the next morning. Additionally, after heavy snowfalls, all available hands were put to shovels. The snow was compressed using feet, and then flung down the hatch.

The Orangery at Hanbury Hall is a wide, nine-bay building, with a lot of glass at the front – sufficient to protect oranges and other frost-sensitive plants from all but the harshest of winters. Architecturally, its highlights are the intricate carvings of fruit and foliage. Built in the 1740s, it was on its own until the 1770s extension to the gardens embraced it. In recent years the formal gardens at Hanbury Hall have been largely recreated in their original design, using detailed documentation and, when necessary, best guesses.

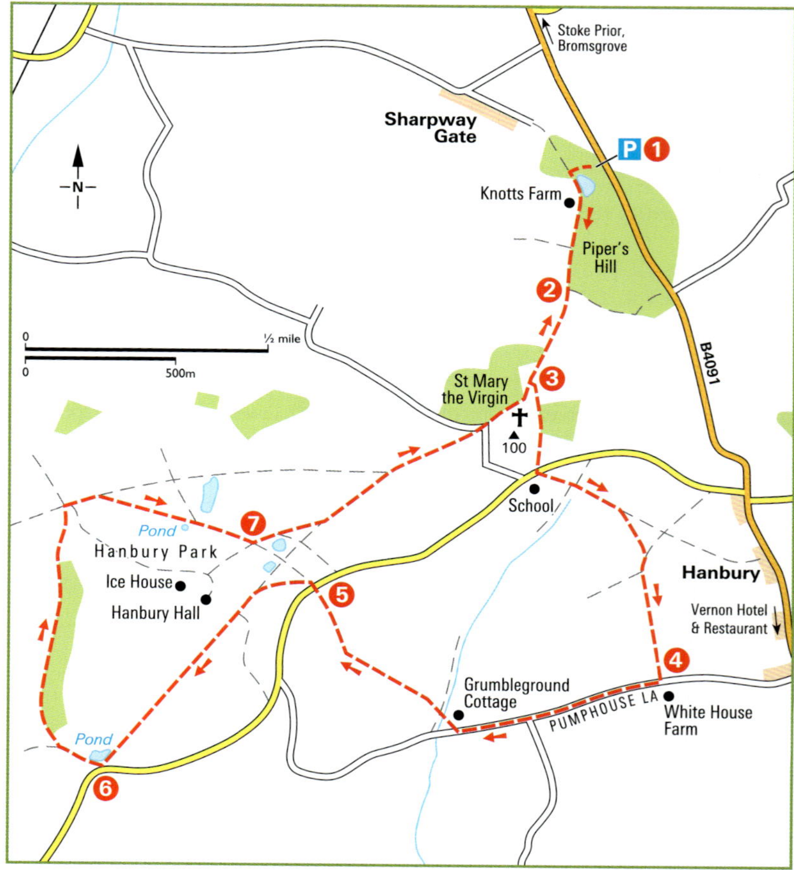

1. From the bottom of the car park, follow the driveway to Knotts Farm. Keep ahead at a post then, about 350yds (320m) after the farm, reach a gravel track.

2. Go straight ahead, with a field boundary on your left. Climb towards the church, until you reach a stake with two waymarkers.

3. Fork left, soon passing a spinney, then losing height across a meadow. Take care as the stile and steps here spill you straight on to a minor but fast road. Across this, go beside the school. Cross one field directly then a fraction right, walking diagonally in the third field, 30yds (27m) right of a young fenced oak, to a metal gate. In 70yds (64m) cross a footbridge on the left. Two more stiles lead to Pumphouse Lane.

4. Turn right. Take a stile and gate on the right just beyond black-and-white Grumbleground Cottage. In 40yds (37m), cross a three-plank footbridge. Follow electricity poles for two fields. Turn right, alongside a wire fence. Cross a stile to reach a road.

5. Cross the road to the footpath opposite. At a stile go half left, guided by a wire fence. Keep left to a kissing gate. Pass close to Hanbury Hall's entrance, soon easing away from the perimeter wall to walk 700yds (640m) across parkland, striking a minor road just beyond a picturesque pond on your right. (A line of young trees will be to your left.)

6. Ignore the minor road, turning immediately right. Hug the boundary fence of the coppice. Continue down the right-hand field-edge. In the corner cross a bridge and stile. At a junction turn right at a National Trust sign and stile, into this former deer park. After just 60yds (55m), at a small drainage ditch, edge right. Go straight, to a stile to the left of a clump of fenced trees, which hides a round pond. Maintain this line going up the incline – look out for Hanbury church tower on the left – to reach a tarmac driveway.

7. Turn left. When it curves right, go straight ahead to walk in an oak avenue. Keep this line for 700yds (640m), to a minor road. Turn right, then left up to the church. Through the churchyard, find a gate. Shortly rejoin the outward route at Point 3. Retrace your steps to return to the car park.

Where to eat and drink

The Vernon Hotel and Restaurant is located at the junction of the B4091 and the B4090 at Hanbury, a short drive to the south of Piper's Hill car park. It offers an extensive menu, sourced with fresh local produce. For visitors to Hanbury Hall (NT) and/or gardens, the tea room serves soup of the day, jacket potatoes and afternoon cream teas.

What to see

Some interesting agricultural artefacts adorn the front of Knotts Farm, including a buggy, a butter churn and a cider press. At the White House (adjacent to White House Farm) notice how, despite only being rebuilt in 2000, the boundary walls appears 'old', thanks to the use of mostly reclaimed bricks.

While you're there

The National Trust's Hanbury Hall is open daily.

TARDEBIGGE FLIGHT AND TUNNEL

DISTANCE/TIME	7.75 miles (12.5km) / 3hrs 15min
ASCENT/GRADIENT	380ft (115m) / ▲
PATHS	Tow path, pastures, field paths and minor lanes, many stiles
LANDSCAPE	Generally rolling rural scenery, and a whole lot of locks
SUGGESTED MAP	OS Explorer 204 Worcester & Droitwich Spa
START/FINISH	Grid reference: SO974682
DOG FRIENDLINESS	Off-lead on tow path, under control in fields
PARKING	Limited space, so park tightly and considerately, on north side of road bridge
PUBLIC TOILETS	None on route

In some respects the British are a nation of slow learners: how often do we hear of a large construction project for which the final bill was vastly in excess of the original projected cost? The canal builders of the 19th century were often not much better. In 1791 an Act of Parliament gave the go-ahead to build the Worcester and Birmingham Canal, setting aside £180,000. It was only in 1815 – 24 years later – that the route to Worcester was available to commercial traffic, and the sum that had been spent was a whopping £610,000. It seems that cost projections were invariably optimistic, rather than realistic. Even at that price, the project had been scaled down, literally, for the plan to take the larger barges that plied the Severn was abandoned.

The Tardebigge Flight was just one of the challenges of constructing the Worcester and Birmingham Canal. The tally of locks along the 16-mile (25.7km) stretch between Tardebigge and Worcester is 56. Add to that five tunnels and several reservoirs, some of which the canal builders were obliged to provide for mill owners along rivers affected by the canal, and it is not only the locks that escalate!

The Worcester and Birmingham Canal benefited from the discovery of salt at Stoke Prior in 1825 – the salt works were built around the canal shortly after. The works are now gone, replaced by housing, but the former brine reservoir remains at grid ref SO 947664. This was the works that John Corbett purchased in 1845. While Corbett must take the credit for the subsequent pre-eminence of his factory there, he must have been assisted by the competition between canal and railway. The Birmingham and Gloucester Railway had opened in 1841, and in 1851 another line followed: the Oxford, Worcester and Wolverhampton Railway.

Back in 1771, long before the Worcester and Birmingham Canal was conceived, James Brindley had engineered the broad-beamed Droitwich Barge Canal, right into the town's salt production centre. It ran for 5.75 miles (9.2km) to the River Severn, taking salt down and bringing coal up. Perhaps as a response to the railway threat, this 'cul-de-sac' was opened up in 1853 by cutting a mere 1.5-mile long (2.4km), narrow-beamed channel from the centre of Droitwich to Hanbury Wharf, joining the Droitwich Barge Canal with the Worcester and Birmingham Canal – the so-called Droitwich Junction Canal. Transportation of salt by canal ceased in 1914.

Even if you are not a canal-boat lover, the Tardebigge Flight is a memorable spectacle – it just goes on and on. It has a total of 30 locks within 2 miles (3.2km).

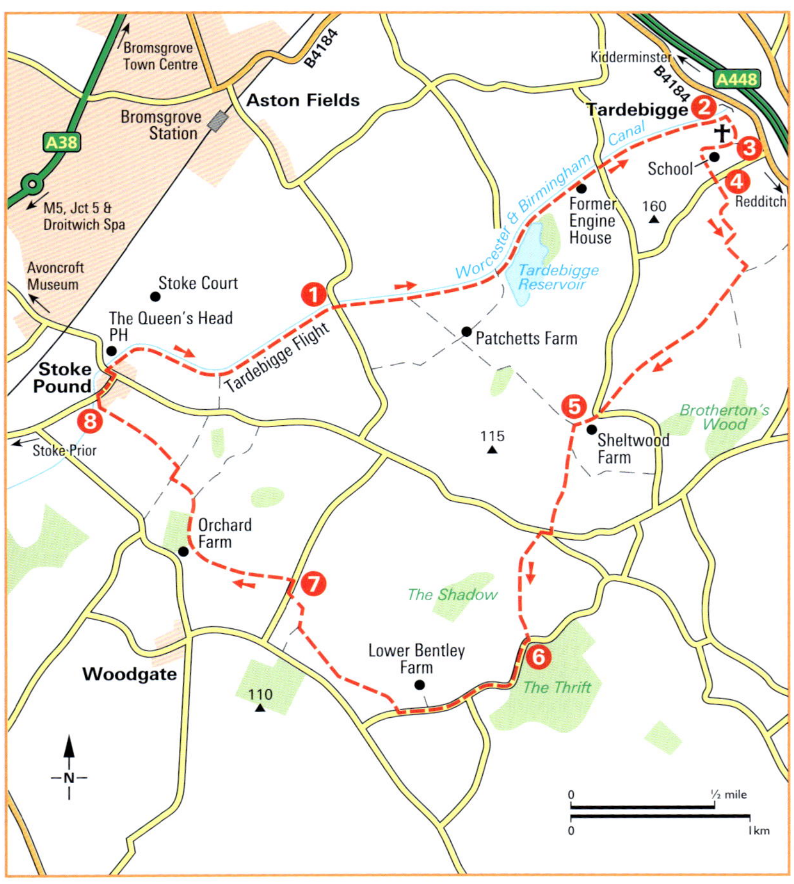

1. Cross bridge No. 51 and turn left, taking the towpath on the south side of the canal. Keep on the towpath for a little over 1.25 miles (2km). On your way, at a bend, the embankment of the Tardebigge Reservoir looms. Whenever a boat passes through a lock, heading either up or down, a lockful of water is shunted downstream by gravity. Although the locks are not built any wider or longer than is necessary, maintaining an adequate flow of water can be a problem at any time, not just when there is a dry summer. Hence the need for the reservoir, approached from its dammed end.

2. Beyond the topmost lock of the 30 is another striking feat of engineering – Tardebigge Tunnel. Turn right through a kissing gate just before the tunnel, but first descend steps to the tow path to see the light at the tunnel's far portal, 580yds (530m) away. Doubtless some of the extra money went into the making of this tunnel, which was bored through solid rock.

3. Bear right, up the bank, with the distinctive, baroque needle spire of St Bartholomew's ahead. The tower was completed in 1777. Cross the gravel car park then walk past the church it serves. Walk, with the primary school on your left, for just 30yds (27m). Turn left, beside the school and later its playing field, to reach a minor road.

4. Cross the road by a kissing gate and then a stile. Importantly, in the first field strike right of the fingerpost's direction to reach a stile at the offset corner in 150yds (137m). Follow waymarks through two field gates. Turn right beyond the second, towards the wind turbine. At the corner gate bear right within your field on a hedge-side path to cross two stiles, the second followed by a flat bridge. Keep ahead to the stile visible 140yds (128m) beyond a remnant hedge. Cross this double stile and shadow the field boundary to a stile at the far end of the copse. There's a field gate into a lane at the diagonally opposite corner. Bear left a few paces to the 'No Through Road'; here take the gate, right, and walk to the decrepit oak at the far end of the barns here at Sheltwood Farm.

5. Bear left. Within 110yds (100m) use the gate-side stile ahead. Drift right to use a stile through a wire fence, maintaining the same direction to cross a three-plank foot-bridge. Head half-right to use a corner stile near a pylon; turn left to a minor road junction. Turn right along the road to a waymarked stile, left, in 60yds (55m). Walk the left edge of two pastures, then climb the high stile and use the nearby handgate, swapping sides of the hedge. Continue hedge-side to a lane at a bend.

6. Turn right. Follow this for 0.5 miles (800m), taking 'Woodgate' at a junction, to Lower Bentley Farm's driveway. Go 140yds (128m) further, to a fingerpost on the right 5yds (4m) up a farm track. Head a quarter-left to the field gate; then another to the right of the cottage at the field head. Continue to the far-right corner of the long field, where two handgates bracket a plank bridge. Continue another 70yds (65m) to use a double stile, left. From here head a quarter right to a stile onto a lane.

7. Turn right, and in 75yds (69m) take a hand-railed, three-planked footbridge on the left. Pass through the kissing gate and walk ahead, to the right of the nearby offset field corner to find the first of a series of three in-line handgates across fields. At Orchard Farm's garden, turn right to reach the top-left corner of the field and a handgate. Continue ahead to cross the double stile across a ditch. Look ahead-right to locate a fingerpost at twin metal kissing gates beneath trees. Once through, continue beside the hedge, use an awkward corner gate and then aim a quarter-left to a corner gate and handgate 50yds (46m) left of the field-head oak. A grassy track leads to a road.

8. Turn right. At the T-junction turn left. Join the canal towpath this side of the bridge (The Queen's Head pub is opposite). Turn right beside the canal to return to Bridge 51, nearly 1 mile (1.6km) distant.

Where to eat and drink

Strategically located beside the bridge at Stoke Pound is The Queen's Head, where you can enjoy a canalside beer garden. It has a restaurant as well as a bar menu. Children are welcome.

What to see

You'll pass the former engine house (whose life as a pub ended in 2006). In conjunction with the Tardebigge Reservoir, it controlled the lock system's water levels. Repeated wetting and drying takes its toll on the lock gates – they are being constantly replaced. Each has a metal plate showing when and where it was crafted. Which is the newest gate you can see?

While you're there

Conceptually the Avoncroft Museum of Historic Buildings is unique – a collection of historic structures dismantled and reassembled in one place. Perhaps a 'dry' topic, but lots of effort has been put in to making it a family-friendly trip. At Stoke Prior is St Michael's Church. It was here that, in 1901, John Corbett (salt works owner) was buried.

A CIRCULAR ROUTE IN THE CLENT HILLS

DISTANCE/TIME	3.5 miles (5.7km) / 2hrs
ASCENT/GRADIENT	660ft (201m) / ▲
PATHS	Woodland paths (sometimes muddy), tracks, several stiles
LANDSCAPE	Rolling rural scenery, woodland, huge views
SUGGESTED MAP	OS Explorer 219 Wolverhampton & Dudley
START/FINISH	Grid reference: SO938807
DOG FRIENDLINESS	Plenty of running on tops, under control near livestock
PARKING	National Trust pay-and-display car park, Nimmings Wood (free for NT members)
PUBLIC TOILETS	At start

If you are a visitor to Worcestershire then the Clent Hills provide an excellent starting point. More people visit the Clent Hills than Worcester Cathedral. Four car parks provide easy access and make the hills the county's number one non-paying attraction. Of course, proximity to the West Midlands conurbation has much to do with it, but there is something satisfying in standing on the top as dusk falls, watching the city lights begin to sparkle in the distance.

Come up to the ridge along the Clent Hills in late April or early May and you may see not only vertical grey blocks of suburban Birmingham, but horizontal yellow blocks of modern rural Worcestershire, created by the flowers of oilseed rape. In 1971 the amount of oilseed rape grown in Britain was a mere 12,500 acres (5,059ha), but it is currently about 1.6 million acres (0.65 million ha). Most is sown in winter. Since it is prone to disease, it is advisable to plant it not more frequently than one year in six. Daffodils aside, it is now the main source of early spring colour in the countryside – Worcestershire and Herefordshire are no exceptions.

Oilseed rape, a brassica, derives its unfortunate name from the Latin word for turnip, rapum (whereas the verb comes from rapere, to snatch). Rapeseed oil is just one of many vegetable oils grown for human consumption. If your food has to be fried then rapeseed oil is a good choice – not only is it without cholesterol (as are all vegetable oils), but of the known vegetable oils, it is the one with the lowest level of saturated fatty acids. In spite of all this nutritional worthiness, however, only about 65 per cent of the rapeseed oil is made into cooking oil, with 22 per cent going to biofuel production; it is used in a number of industrial applications, too, such as lubricants.

Oilseed rape typically begins to flower in mid-April – earlier than traditional crops – for a five to six week period, so beekeepers have to mobilise their bees earlier, to exploit the available nectar. The nectar sets very quickly, so the beekeeper must extract it from the honeycomb just as the yellow hue is turning to green. Honey derived primarily from oilseed rape is almost white, has a soft texture, and a comparatively bland favour. So much oilseed rape is now grown that it has taken over from white clover as the country's largest source of honey, although some say that white clover produced the best honey (which is not white but pale straw in colour), especially when it grew in long-established, permanent pasture.

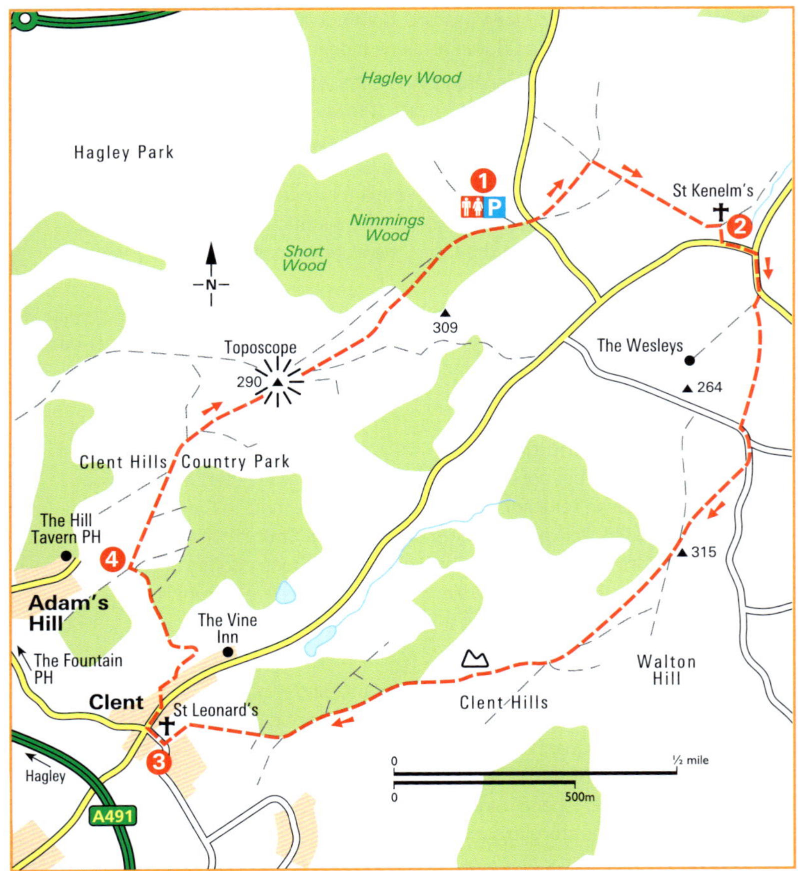

1. From the car park entrance, turn right and walk 10 paces to a stile on the left. Cross the stile and walk downhill, left of the horses' exercise yard, to a corner field gate. Head half-right to the offset hedged corner and waymark post; turn right beside the hedge, then jig left beneath trees in 50yds (45m) to a stile into horse pasture. In 50yds (45m) climb another stile and aim half-right, pass through the old hedge-line then look diligently ahead for a kissing gate near yews into the churchyard of St Kenelm's Church.

2. Leave by the lychgate. Turn left along the road for a short distance, then right at the T-junction. At the bend use the stile, on the right, off the driveway corner to The Wesleys. Climb gently uphill, aiming for the left edge of the hill-top woods, where steps lead to a lane. Turn left. Ignore a left turn but, just 30yds (27m) beyond it, take a muddy, gated narrow path into woodland up on

the right, angled away from the road and not signposted. Emerge from the trees to the trig point on Walton Hill. Turn left, taking the right-hand of two options. This wide way descends, in 800yds (730m) becoming a wood-edge path beside pastures on your left. Pass by a waymarked bridleway joining sharply from the right, shortly thereafter passing a National Trust sign for Clent Hills (right). At the waymarked fork here, bear right, over a cross-path to reach a kissing gate into steep pasture. Continue ahead, downhill through two fields to find St Leonard's Church at Clent, hidden by trees.

3. Turn right then right again, along Vine Lane. At Church View Cottage, opposite the church's driveway, turn left. (Please follow these woodland directions especially carefully!) In 180yds (165m), take the upper, left fork. In 80yds (73m), at a crossing, go left. After a further 100yds (91m) ignore options to turn right or half right. Continue downhill for another 160yds (146m). Ignore the gate and stile on the left, instead starting a stiff climb ahead, up widely spaced old wooden steps. At the top of the woods cross the path to a wider track and turn right.

4. Keep on this broad, open path, ignoring a right fork, to reach a semi-circular, five-panel toposcope. From this take the initially level path ahead, directly back to the car park.

Where to eat and drink

There is a small but popular National Trust café at the start, serving hot chocolate, bacon rolls and so on, with outdoor seating. In Clent, there is The Vine Inn, 250yds (229m) up the lane from Church View Cottage (passed during the walk). Hill Tavern, the Four Stones Coffee and Brunch and the nearby Fountain at Adam's Hill lie downhill-right from route marker 4. All serve food and are family friendly.

What to see

At St Kenelm's Church – a Grade I listed building – in Romsley parish, there is supposedly a crypt containing a holy spring; indeed, a 'Well' is shown on the suggested map. Reputedly the water sprung up when, in the year AD 819, Kenelm, the boy King of Mercia, was killed here. The truth behind this legend may be questionable, but something must have happened for the story to survive over 1,200 years.

While you're there

If you think you have done well to reach the dizzy heights of the Clent Hills, then go along to the Falconry Centre at Hagley, near Stourbridge, to put your achievement into perspective. Here you can see all manner of birds of prey soaring overhead. Lord Lyttleton's Hagley Hall (1760) is a striking Grade I listed house in formal gardens and parkland.

KINGSFORD FOREST PARK AND VILLAGES

DISTANCE/TIME	7.25 miles (11.7km) / 3hrs 30min
ASCENT/GRADIENT	560ft (171m) / ▲
PATHS	Forest rides, meadows, minor roads, village streets, canal tow path, many stiles
LANDSCAPE	Mostly pastures and woodland in rolling countryside
SUGGESTED MAP	OS Explorer 218 Wyre Forest & Kidderminster or OS Explorer 219 Wolverhampton & Dudley
START/FINISH	Grid reference: SO835820
DOG FRIENDLINESS	Much fun in woods but horses and sheep elsewhere
PARKING	Blakeshall Lane car park, Kingsford Forest Park
PUBLIC TOILETS	None on route

On this and other walks you may come across dense spindley woodland that somehow 'doesn't look right'. Such areas of trees may be to the oak what a pile of stones is to an old church: a ruin. The occurrence of the word 'coppice' on a map – Solcum Coppice, Gloucester Coppice – often indicates a woodland of historical importance to the local economy. With its proximity to the industries of the West Midlands, local charcoal production (especially in the Wyre Forest) was considerable.

Is charcoal an invention or a discovery? Probably it was 'discovered' by accident, and its subsequent uses were invented. It is wood that has been incompletely burned (in a controlled way) by being deprived of much of the oxygen that would otherwise render it a pile of ashes. Woods used for charcoal-making include hazel (a favourite because of its prolific regrowth), ash, oak and alder buckthorn, among others.

The raw material was cut and left to dry or 'season' for several months before use. This, together with how well and for how long the 'kiln' was burning, were key factors in determining the yield – 15–25 per cent was good, and 30 per cent exceptional. The kiln was a temporary structure, essentially a mound or dome of logs carefully constructed around a central airway, the whole being covered with turf, ideal since the roots of the grass bound the soil together tightly, and the turfs were easier to handle than soil on its own. Turf would also be used to cover the airway once a fire had been established at the core. It could take several days to complete the charcoal-making process. Of course, much of the weight lost is evaporated moisture. When re-ignited, the charcoal burns with an intensity capable of smelting metal, forging iron, and making glass, as well as blackening your burger. Gunpowder is concocted from three ingredients – charcoal, sulphur and saltpetre (potassium nitrate). Only when the coal derivative, coke, was introduced was charcoal superseded as an intensive heat source. (Coke later gave way to oil and gas, which also have the advantage of being easier to control.)

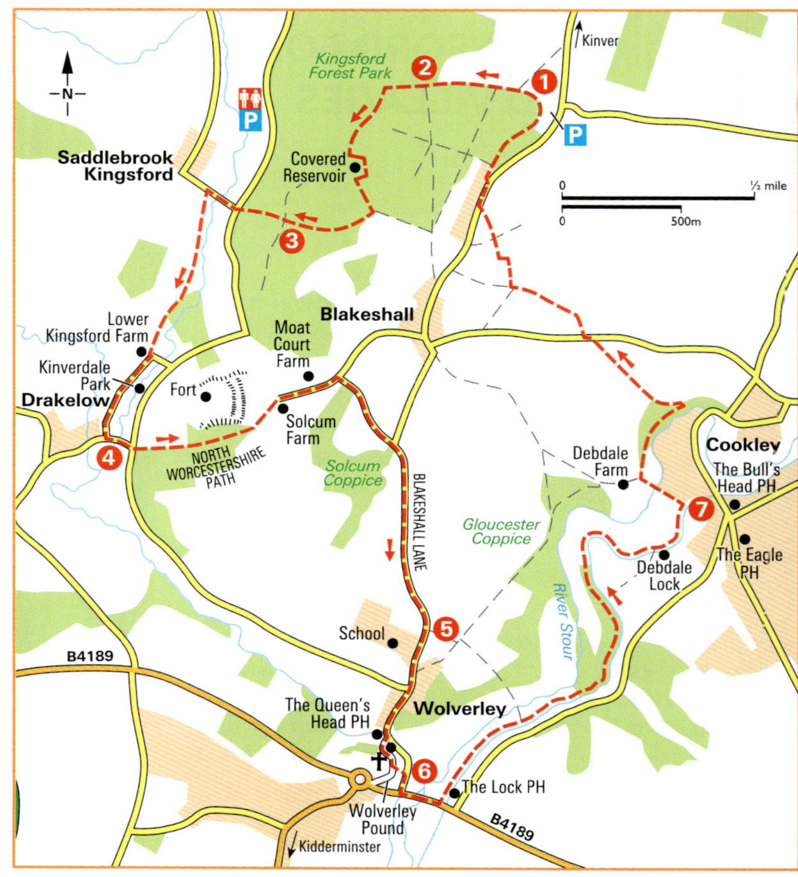

1. Take the sandy track inside the northern edge of the forest park (closest to the fence, not the path waymarked 'Woodpecker/Nuthatch Trail') for 550yds (503m), to the end of Kinver Edge Farm's extensive garden, flanked by panelled fencing. To the left is a wide glade, falling gently; ahead rises the woodland track.

2. With a National Trust 'Kinver Edge' sign on your right, and a track to your left, continue for 160yds (146m) to a fingerpost that includes 'Staffordshire Way', indicating the county border. Turn left down this good track. Soon fork left of a fenced-off, covered reservoir. At a junction turn right, but in 40yds (37m) – see Severn Trent Water's 'Blakeshall' sign through the fence – turn left. After 160yds (146m) at the forest edge, turn right on the inner path, that is, through gate posts, passing a bench 30yds (27m) beyond it. Go along here for 425yds (389m) to reach a T-junction.

3. Here, do not turn left along the Worcestershire Way, but turn right for just 10yds (9m), then immediately left on a path running through pines and silver birch. Reach a road junction within 200yds (183m) and go down Castle Hill Lane. Within 160yds (146m) take the waymarked path left, opposite the house, 'Saddlebrook Kingsford'. This green band improves to become a track, then a metalled road, passing houses on the right (not down Castle Hill). Turn right, passing Lower Kingsford Farm entrance and mobile homes, to reach a T-junction.

4. Here turn left, crossing over to the pavement set back from the road. At the next T-junction cross the road and go straight on, along a works access road, to reach a path into woods beside a timber-framed house. Ascend gently. Beside a house with decorative walling (Solcum Farm), join a lane that goes straight ahead. At the next junction, beside conifers, turn right, away from the North Worcestershire Path, following this minor road (which becomes Blakeshall Lane) towards Wolverley.

5. Descend into Wolverley past the school. See the footbridge alongside The Queen's Head, but take the route between two 'No Entry' road signs. Reach the Church of St John the Baptist by iron gates, zig-zagging up the concreted footpath through a deep cutting (if the gates are locked use the road). Leave the churchyard by modern steps. Go down the meadow opposite (with a fingerpost) to a minor road.

6. Turn right. At the B4189, turn left. In front of The Lock public house turn left, along the tow path. After about 1.25 miles (2km) is Debdale Lock, partly hewn into the rock. Some 220yds (201m) further, just before the steel wheel factory, is a kissing gate.

7. Turn left here along a track. (Alternatively continue for 150yds (137m) for refreshments in Cookley.) At a T-junction after a coniferous avenue, turn right on a broad gravel track. After about 350yds (320m) turn left (waymarker), up some wooden steps, into trees. Go up the left-hand edge of one field, past double electricity poles, and up the centre of another to a road. Turn left for just 15yds (14m), then right. Some 400yds (366m) along this hedged lane turn right, contrary to the blue arrow pointing ahead. At the next stile wiggle left, then right. Proceed straight ahead at a junction to the road. Turn right. In 150yds (137m), move left into the trees to re-enter the country park. Two paths run parallel to the road – both lead back to the car park.

Where to eat and drink

Wolverley has The Queen's Head (tables outside). Just outside Wolverley and on the canal is The Lock Inn and Old Smithy Tearoom. It has a road-noisy beer garden. Just off the route, in Cookley, there is The Bull's Head and The Eagle both of which have outdoor seating. Cookley also has a shop and several takeaways.

What to see

At St John the Baptist Church is a monument to five siblings, all of whom died between the ages of nine months and six years in the late 18th century. If the church is unlocked, you'll find inside some stained-glass windows made by William Morris's company and an effigy of a knight, well-preserved given its 14th-century vintage.

THE WYRE FOREST

DISTANCE/TIME	8.5 miles (13.7km) / 4hrs
ASCENT/GRADIENT	655ft (200m) / ▲ ▲
PATHS	Forest tracks, field paths, minor lanes, riverside, several stiles
LANDSCAPE	Undulating woodland, riverside, small town
SUGGESTED MAP	OS Explorer 218 Wyre Forest & Kidderminster
START	Grid reference: SO764799
FINISH	Grid reference: SO791753
DOG FRIENDLINESS	A train ride: yippee! Fun in forest too
PARKING	Between Arley station and River Severn or at Bewdley station
PUBLIC TOILETS	At Bewdley station; and also at Load Street (short-stay) car park in Bewdley

Flooding a market for manufactured goods with imports is not a modern phenomenon – back in the late 19th century, owners of woodland in the Wyre Forest were complaining about cheaper, Continental oak bark eroding their trade. Close to the Industrial Revolution's heartland and a large population, the Wyre Forest had been an important area for the tanning of leather (and for charcoal production).

Tanning, the transformation of animal hides or skins into stable, nonporous and durable leather, is a long, multi-staged and labour-intensive process. The animal hides have to be cured by salting or drying (or both). When oak bark (with a high tannin content) was used, skins were left in the tanning vat for anything from two to 90 days. The final stages may involve dyeing, rolling and polishing.

By the early 20th century, demand for timber oak had already fallen because of widespread availability of coal for heating and industrial uses, and iron had displaced it as the favoured shipbuilding material, but demand was propped up by the need for oak bark for tanning. Oak bark had to compete with synthetic tanning agents and the use of other, naturally occurring substances such as fish oil, and mineral-based agents such as chromium sulphate. The Bewdley tannery closed in 1928.

The Severn Valley Railway has regular steam-hauled passenger trains running throughout the year. The scenery, following and crossing the River Severn, is beautiful and unspoiled, while the tiny railway stations, lovingly tended by a band of volunteers, hark back to a bygone age. Passengers can simply turn up to purchase a ticket although it's worth checking the SVR website (www.svr.org.uk) for timetables and fares before setting out.

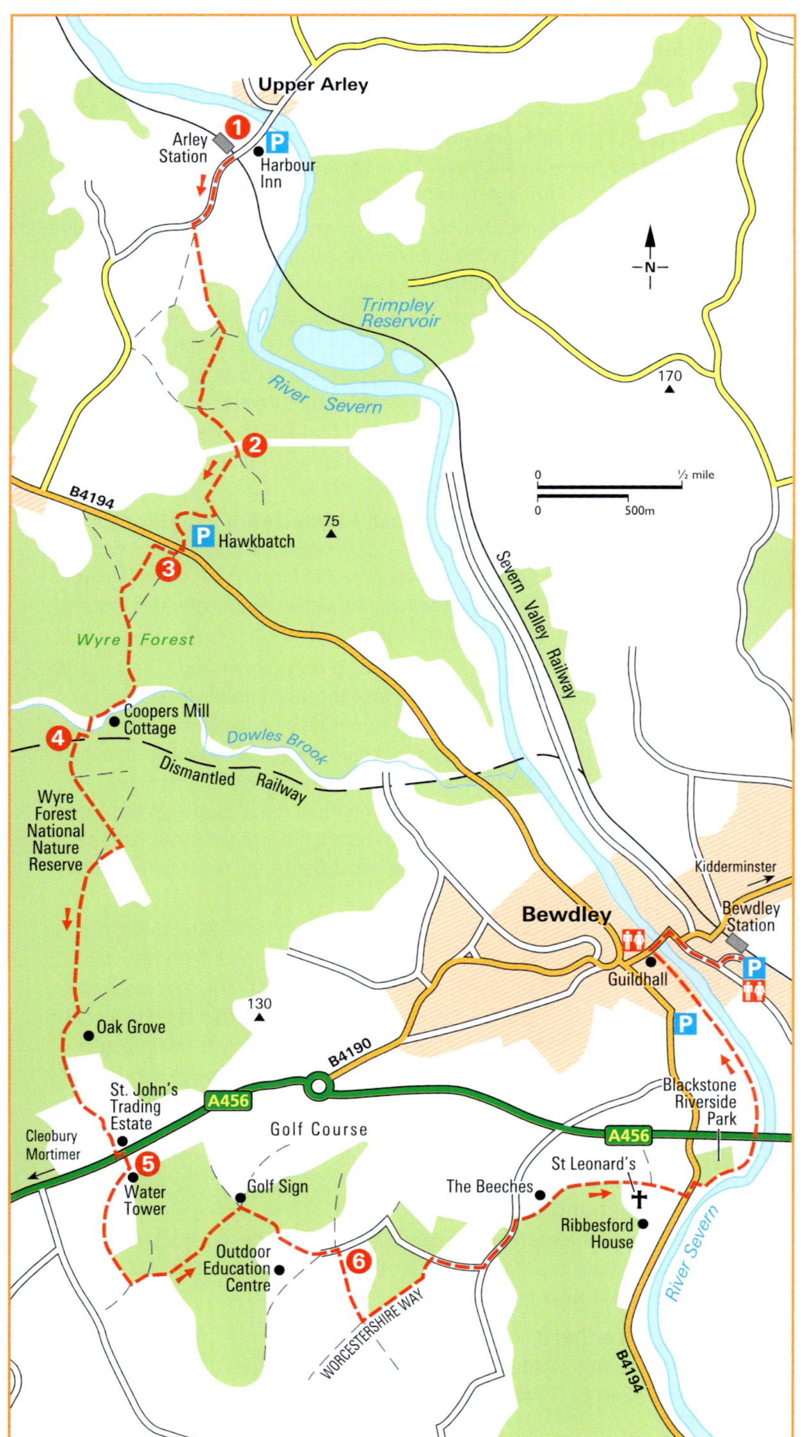

Upper Arley
Arley Station
1
P
Harbour Inn
Trimpley Reservoir
River Severn
170
N
2
B4194
75
P Hawkbatch
3
Wyre Forest
½ mile
0
0 500m
Severn Valley Railway
Coopers Mill Cottage
Dowles Brook
4
Dismantled Railway
Wyre Forest National Nature Reserve
Kidderminster
Bewdley
Bewdley Station
Guildhall
P
P
130
Oak Grove
B4190
Blackstone Riverside Park
St. John's Trading Estate
A456
Golf Course
A456
Cleobury Mortimer
5
Water Tower
Golf Sign
St Leonard's
The Beeches
Ribbesford House
River Severn
Outdoor Education Centre
6
WORCESTERSHIRE WAY
B4194

1. Turn right out of Arley Station to go uphill for 700yds (640m). Turn left. After a cottage follow a track into woodland, but soon fork right, ascending by a set of gates (not the driveway of Seckley Cottage). Roughly 30yds (27m) after the pasture on the right ceases, take the left-hand fork, leaving broken trees to your right. Soon bear right. After 500yds (457m), turn left at a track. Just 35yds (32m) on, reach a five-way junction. Go ahead, between blue-marked posts. In 310yds (283m) reach a fire break with low brick structures.

2. About 40yds (37m) beyond this, turn right down a conifer avenue. After some 440yds (402m), at a red-and-white orienteering post, turn right along a gravel path. At the car park bear right to the B4194.

3. Take a few paces right then cross over. Go only 15yds (14m) into the forest and turn right, walking parallel with the road. Before a house turn left (fingerpost), soon joining a better track. Keep on this for over 0.5 miles (800m), descending on concrete to Dowles Brook's miniature flood plain. Continue for under 0.25 miles (400m), passing Coopers Mill Cottage, then left to a timber-fenced footbridge. Turn immediately right. In 90yds (82m), ascend steeply (marked footpath) to an old railway.

4. Go through the gate opposite. After about 600yds (549m) just before you come to a cleared area, your path is half-right opposite a grass ride, into oaks (look for a public footpath waymarker). Follow this for over 0.5 miles (800m). Skirt a meadow, reaching a gravel track at Oak Grove. Eventually this reaches the A456 beside the St John's Trading Estate.

5. Turn left for 75yds (69m) then turn right by a water tower (sign, 'Tarn'). Just 30yds (27m) past a 'private garden' sign, take the stile into pasture then another into an abandoned orchard. Run alongside a hedge on the right, past a third stile, to a fourth 30yds (27m) further on, in the corner. Another stile leads into woodland. At a junction, turn left and in just 25yds (23m), fork right, descending slightly. Go ahead for 700yds (640m). At a golf club sign turn right. In 240yds (219m), turn two-thirds right. Go past a modern yet small cottage ignoring the stile opposite. Turn left at the road, by the entrance to the outdoor education centre, to a concrete lay-by.

6. Waymarked, go right across a huge field to a stile 25yds (23m) to the right of a gateway. Turn left. Follow this for 500yds (457m) to a road. Turn right for 300yds (274m). Turn left. In 350yds (320m) take the right fork, 'Worcestershire Way'. Avoid The Beeches using stiles. Descend to Ribbesford's church. A horse chestnut avenue leads to the (fast) B4194. Turn left for 110yds (100m), then cross road to Blackstone Riverside Park. Follow the River Severn into Bewdley. Cross Telford's stylish bridge, following signs to the Severn Valley Railway. Return to Arley Station and the start of the walk on the train.

Where to eat and drink

Arley Station or the Harbour Inn. In Bewdley, there's the Cock & Magpie, the Riverside Café, the Mug House Inn, the Merchant's Fish Bar and Tearooms and Ripleys tearooms.

While you're there

Arley Arboretum & Gardens (open in summer, Wed–Sun, 10am–5pm), exhibiting 30 acres (12ha) of specimen trees and plants dating back to the 1800s.

STOURPORT-ON-SEVERN

DISTANCE/TIME	3.25 miles (5.3km) / 1hr 30min
ASCENT/GRADIENT	328ft (100m) / ▲
PATHS	Tow path, tracks, good paths, some streets
LANDSCAPE	Urban, watery, and common with views
SUGGESTED MAP	OS Explorer 218 Wyre Forest & Kidderminster or OS Explorer 219 Wolverhampton & Dudley
START/FINISH	Grid reference: SO820704
DOG FRIENDLINESS	Good on common and tow path, not much fun in town
PARKING	Hartlebury Common Bog Car Park on A4025 opposite Cooks Garden Centre or layby 164ft (150m) further south
PUBLIC TOILETS	None on route

You will understand the rise and fall of Stourport-on-Severn if you look at a map of England. The infrastructural advantage realised by the opening of the Staffordshire and Worcestershire Canal was to link the River Severn with the rivers Trent and Mersey. Canals were conceived when road transport was not only uncomfortable for passengers but also extremely slow for goods, and railways had yet to be invented. Roads were in a poor condition, invariably worsened by poor weather in the winter months. River transport was, at least, an option along the Severn. (In comparison, Herefordshire's River Wye was usually too low in the summer months to give sufficient draught to even a small sailing barge.) A horse and cart could carry perhaps 300lb (136kg). Along a canal tow path, a horse could haul a barge carrying a vastly greater burden – up to 50 tons (50,679kg), a more than 300-fold weight advantage. Although the horse moved slowly, it is easy to see why those with money to invest fashionably threw it at all manner of canal projects. For Joe Public the main outcome was cheaper coal.

In 1771, when the Staffordshire and Worcestershire Canal opened, Stourport grew up, becoming what we might now call a 'new town'. As well as barge- and boat-building enterprises, other businesses, such as foundries and carpet factories, were opened. After just four decades, trade was hit by the new Worcester and Birmingham Canal, which had itself been 24 years in the making. Railway proliferation sent Stourport into further decline.

When the canals were nationalised in 1948, the days of commercial canal activity were already numbered. In the case of the Worcester and Birmingham Canal, the last two companies to use the canal regularly ceased doing so in the early 1960s; they were Worcester's Royal Porcelain (for coal) and Cadbury's of Bournville (for chocolate crumb). Commercial activity on the canal today centres on canal-boat cruising and in a sense we have the railways to thank for this. The initial response by the canal-boat operators to the commercial threat posed by the railways was to cut prices, and this meant cutting costs. Labour was not in short supply, so wages for boatmen were cut; their response, since so much of their time was spent on the water anyway, was to shed the burden of rent-paying by bringing their families on board their barges.

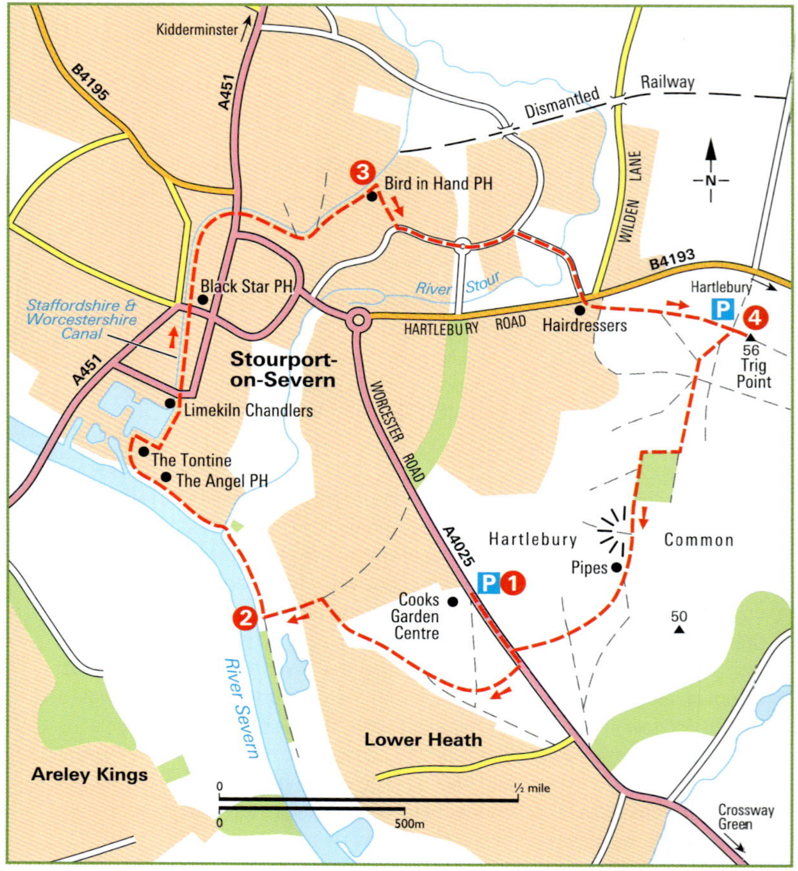

1. From the car park opposite the garden centre turn left for 370yds (340m) to take a footpath on the western side of the A4025. Strike across this bottom part of Hartlebury Common: you'll see some buildings in the far distance. Veer right, roughly following power lines, through silver birches, to find a sandy track at the back of some houses. At a modern housing estate join the tarmac briefly, aiming for a dirt track beyond the 'Britannia Gardens' sign and after Globe House. Turn left down a tarmac footpath, initially with wooden paling on the left, to the river.

2. Turn right. In 650yds (594m) you'll reach a lock and Stourport's canal basins. You'll probably want to spend some time exploring here but the route is neither across the two-plank walkway at the upper lock gate, nor the upper brick bridge with timber and metal railings; instead take the neat brick-paved path to circumnavigate The Tontine (see What to see). Now skirt the Upper

Basin, passing Limekiln Chandlers. Across York Street join the tow path. Follow this for a little under 0.75 miles (1.2km), leaving it at the Bird in Hand, before a defunct brick railway bridge.

3. Go down Holly Road, then half left into Mill Road, following it for 0.25 miles (400m), over a mini-roundabout and, bearing right at The Osiers, across the River Stour to the B4193. Cross and go to the left of the hairdressers to take a narrow, sandy, uphill path back on to the common. Soon, at a fork, go left, keeping in this direction as the ground levels and a parking area lies to the left. Go ahead to find, adjacent to a wire fence, the unpainted trig point.

4. Now retrace your steps for about 90yds (82m), passing a wooden waymarker, to a junction. Here turn left, away from the car park. Again in about 90yds (82m), at a T-junction with a marker post, turn left (signposted 'Heather Trail'). At the corner of a conifer plantation, 275yds (251m) further, turn right. After 100yds (91m) turn left, then in 220yds (201m), just after the far end of the plantation, enjoy views to the west. Now 65yds (60m) beyond this viewpoint, take the right option at a subtle fork. Go forward on this for another 250yds (229m), until an opening on the right. Here step very carefully over a pair of exposed and disused (but not actually hazardous) pipes. Follow the sandy track slanting downhill for 110yds (100m), then swing right, heading towards the road. Turn right and return to the car park.

Where to eat and drink

The Angel serves hot food and has outdoor seating overlooking the river and beside the canal, the Black Star offers home-cooked food and welcomes children and dogs. Additionally there are other pubs and several eateries within the town.

What to see

The otherwise delightfully restored canal basin in Stourport is overlooked by, The Tontine. It occupied a prime site when it opened for business in 1788; the middle of five terraced houses was a pub, while the remaining four provided accommodation for hop merchants. The building was saved from demolition in 1977 and today is a row of private homes. Nip up to Mitton Street from the canal beside The Black Star to view the petite but well-kept Villeneuve le Roi Garden, honouring Stourport's twin town.

While you're there

Just east of the common, off the B4193, is the vibrant Worcestershire County Museum, housed in the former servants' quarters at Hartlebury Castle. Open everyday except Mondays, and with great emphasis is on hands-on, interactive visiting, aimed at families (and schools). A little further afield, up the A450, is Harvington Hall, a 16th-century moated manor house that has had a turbulent history. It has a dazzling collection of priests' holes – in the 17th century any Catholic priest was guilty of treason just by being in England.

OMBERSLEY AND HOLT FLEET

DISTANCE/TIME	5.75 miles (9.2km) / 2hrs 30min
ASCENT/GRADIENT	200ft (61m) / Negligible
PATHS	Riverside paths, field paths and tracks, village street, several stiles
LANDSCAPE	Estate parkland, riverside meadows and general farmland
SUGGESTED MAP	OS Explorer 204 Worcester & Droitwich Spa
START/FINISH	Grid reference: SO844630
DOG FRIENDLINESS	Few off-lead opportunities unless very obedient
PARKING	On road parking towards southern end of A4133 (no southbound exit from village)
PUBLIC TOILETS	None on route

Ombersley must have been awful before the bypass, but now it verges on the tranquil. Ombersley Court was built in the 1720s. Apparently it has a superb interior, but the nearest you'll get to even a reasonable view of it is at the far end of the churchyard (beside a grim memorial tree). Sited on the Ombersley Park Estate, St Andrew's Church was built 100 years after Ombersley Court, but in the decorated style of the early 14th century, presumably to reflect the fragment of the original church (now a mausoleum) behind it.

Along the river towards Holt Fleet Bridge, to your right (and left also) is a classic stretch of woodland, adorning the steep slopes of the great River Severn's flood plain. If you were to walk along here at dusk you may be fortunate enough to see an owl, possibly even a barn owl. A survey conducted in Worcestershire in 1932 found 184 breeding pairs of barn owls, but a similar survey in 1985 found just 32. There were numerous reasons for its decline. Part of the blame is apportioned to the grubbing out of the hedgerows, thereby removing a good habitat for small mammals, a staple of the barn owls' diet. However, much of the decline is attributed to intensive agriculture's use of pesticides. These move along the food chain so that by the time a barn owl has eaten 100 or so slightly contaminated mammals (mice, shrews, voles), the cumulative dosage of pesticide is fatal.

The goal of the Worcestershire Barn Owl Society (WBOS) is to reverse the trend, partly by breeding barn owls and releasing them in carefully chosen locations. The WBOS builds and erects nest boxes in strategic places – you can even buy or sponsor one.

Like other owls, the barn owl flies silently, a useful hunting trick, achieved by having soft tips to its wing feathers – these tips effectively deaden any airflow noise.

The bridge at Holt Fleet replaced a ferry. It was the last in Worcestershire to cease taking tolls. (In Herefordshire tolls are still taken at the 1802 Whitney Bridge, near Clifford.) Such was the belief in a German invasion that mines were laid under the Holt Fleet Bridge during World War II. The Holt Fleet pub was built well before the bridge, and benefited greatly from the day-tripper business, being the northern terminus for paddle-steamer trips from Worcester, about 7 miles (11.3km) to the south. These trips ran until the 1930s. In contrast, The Wharf Inn, on the east bank, marks the site of a coal wharf. Holt Lock, a little way upstream, was completed in 1844.

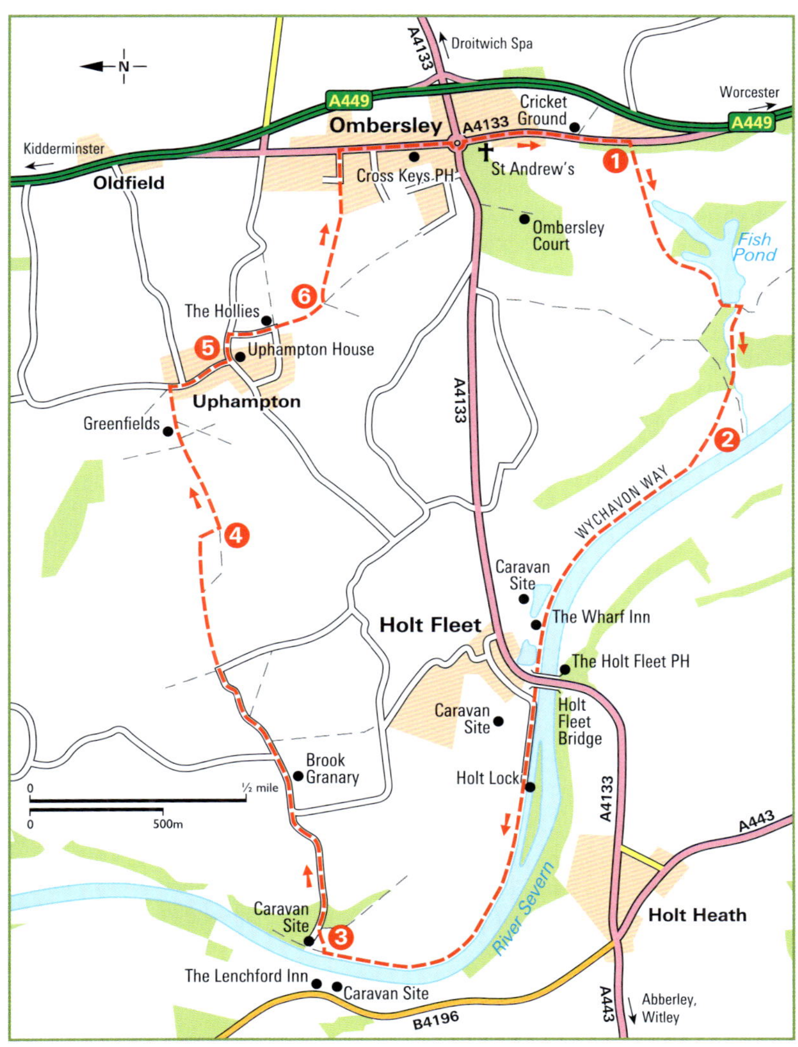

1. To the south of the village, and beyond the cricket ground, take a path on the right, signposted 'Turn Mill'. This is the Wychavon Way. Briefly in trees, walk across a meadow to a stile beside a willow. Go along the left-hand field-edges, and briefly by the water's edge. At the corner of the fish pond, fork right at a waymarker to a track. Turn left past the edge of the pond, following this track right in 80yds (73m), just beyond a gushing stream. After a slight incline in the open, take the left fork where it becomes a sunken path through woodland. Cross a meadow to the river.

2. Turn right. In 0.75 miles (1.2km) you'll pass by a caravan site to reach Holt Fleet Bridge. Go under this, continuing for 1 mile (1.6km), passing the staffed Holt Lock. When opposite The Lenchford Inn you'll come to a riverside gate.

3. Don't go through this gate; instead, turn right. In the field corner join the access road. At a junction go straight ahead on the public road by some static caravans. In 650yds (594m), at a right-hand bend, keep this line by moving left, on to a farm track. It's over 0.25 miles (400m) to the top of this field. Keep on the track, seeing a rusty shack ahead, tucked well into the hedge. When you are 30yds (27m) before it, turn right. Now, in 90yds (82m) go left, over a stile.

4. What could be mistaken for the fairway of a golf course turns out to be an enormous garden. Aim to pass to the right of the house called Greenfields, and a children's wooden watchtower, walking beside a walled vegetable garden. Keep ahead to go down its private, brick-paved driveway. Turn right, passing several black-and-white houses, to a T-junction – Uphampton House is in front of you.

5. Turn left for 110yds (100m), then turn right, uphill. In 150yds (137m), at The Hollies, don't bend right but go straight ahead, on a shingly track. About 220yds (201m) further, the main track bends right, a rough track goes ahead and a public footpath goes half left.

6. Take the public footpath option, along a field-edge. Continue through a small area of market garden, reaching a cul-de-sac. Shortly turn right, along the village street. There are many houses to look at, the churches of St Andrew (current and former), and several points of refreshment to delay your return to your car.

Where to eat and drink

On the route, The Wharf Inn has a riverside terrace and beer garden, and some children's play equipment. Close by, across the bridge, is The Holt Fleet. In Ombersley, at its northern end, is Cross Keys. Further down in a cluster are the quirkily named Venture In (restaurant), the Kings Arms and the Crown & Sandys.

What to see

The very ordinary and workmanlike single arch bridge at Holt was built by Thomas Telford in 1828 – he was responsible for six others over the Severn. It is the only Severn crossing between Stourport and Worcester.

DROITWICH SPA AND AROUND

DISTANCE/TIME	5.75 miles (9.2km) / 2hrs 30min
ASCENT/GRADIENT	230ft (70m) / ▲
PATHS	Pavements, field paths, stony tracks
LANDSCAPE	Agricultural lowlands, coppices, historical town
SUGGESTED MAP	OS Explorer 204 Worcester & Droitwich Spa
START/FINISH	Grid reference: SO898631
DOG FRIENDLINESS	Some country stretches but too urban to be much fun
PARKING	Long-stay pay-and-display. Alternatively, the Lido long-stay pay-and-display on Worcester Road
PUBLIC TOILETS	St Andrews Square shopping centre

Given that seawater is salty, it is not surprising to find salt pans by the Atlantic or on the Mediterranean coast. But how has salt been produced in Droitwich since prehistoric times? The answer is simply that the ground is rich in rock salt. The brine from the town's salt springs is far denser than sea water – 2.5lb of salt could be extracted by boiling a gallon of Droitwich's brine (about 250g from each litre).

Droitwich was an important Roman crossroads – the suggested map shows that the A38, the B4090 and the minor road to the north, Crutch Lane, all have Roman origins. They had a fort at Dodderhill (just north of Vines Park) and, when the railway was constructed in 1847, two mosaic pavements were stumbled upon. Later archaeological work found a Roman corridor house about 130ft (40m) long. Salt tax was a good earner for the monarch, up until its abolition in 1825. Ownership of 25 salt-evaporating pans contributed to the wealth of the Wintour family, who gained notoriety as participants in the 1605 Gunpowder Plot.

In 1845, when aged 28, John Corbett used capital from the profits of his father's canal business to buy and update a derelict salt works about 4.5 miles (7.2km) northeast, at Stoke Prior. He did the right thing at the right time. His works, Europe's largest, made him a fortune, much of which he pumped back into the company, improving working conditions and raising wages (to the extent that wives no longer needed to work), and also into the area, Droitwich Spa in particular. In France, in 1855, he met Anna (or Hannah) O'Meara, who lived in Paris with her French mother and Irish father. Corbett married her the following year. They had six children. Such was her apparent craving for France that he commissioned an architect to build him a French château, Château Impney, completed in 1875 for a staggering £247,000. Despite this, they separated after 28 years of marriage. In 1879 Corbett bought, and vastly improved, St Andrew's House. He renamed it the Raven Hotel, after the raven on the Corbett family's coat of arms (from the French le corbeau, meaning raven...which sounds a bit like 'Corbett').

To some extent, the use of ice and, later, refrigeration, as a means of preserving meats and other foods contributed to the decline of Droitwich's salt production, which ceased in 1922. Most recently, in a triumph of shopping over heritage, the Salters' Shopping Centre has been 'rebranded' as St Andrews Square.

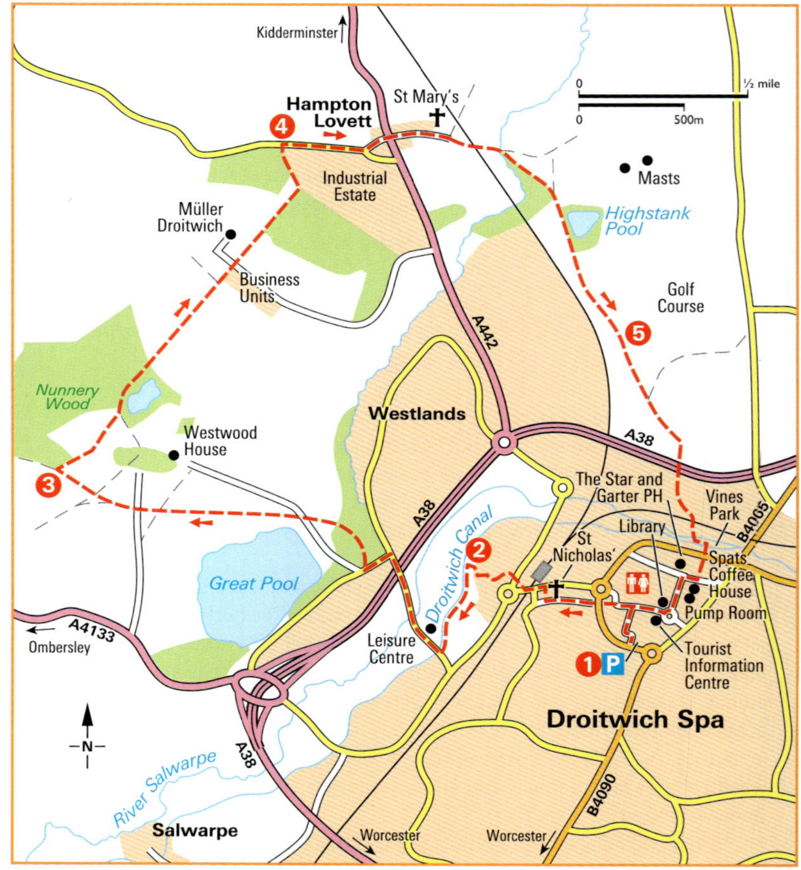

1. Begin outside the library walk west, along Victoria Square and then into Ombersley Street East. When it bends go straight on, passing a medical centre. After an underpass proceed to St Nicholas' Church. Go beyond the churchyard then right, to take another underpass. Turn left. Take the road over the railway to a roundabout, filtering right to go through a third underpass. Walk for 50yds (46m) to a fence corner, near a lamppost. Turn left, marked 'Cycleway 45'. In 30yds (27m) turn right. At the bottom of this cul-de-sac, Westmead Close, turn left. Soon take Ledwych Close, on the right. At the canal you are effectively out of Droitwich Spa.

2. Turn left. At the bridge turn right, passing sports facilities and schools. Turn left just beyond the A38 bridge, into Westwood Way. In 110yds (100m) reach the Westwood House slip road. Facing some allotments, take a gate to the left and walk parallel to the allotments. Beyond this woodland, through a kissing gate, reach a driveway. Cross a truly enormous arable field. Over a track and another driveway, finally reach a corner of Nunnery Wood.

3. Turn sharply right. Electric fencing shepherds you between paddocks before you veer left to walk briefly through Nunnery Wood. (Ignore tracks left.) Aim for two gates beside trees on the skyline. Keep straight on for 0.5 miles (800m), near the Müller Droitwich plant on the left, then curving left past an industrial estate to reach Doverdale Lane.

4. Turn right. Just before a '30' speed-limit sign, fork left. Cross the A442. Walk through the hamlet of Hampton Lovett to St Mary's Church. (It is asymmetrical, having a curved Norman column on its left side.) Take the meadow path under the railway. In 140yds (128m), at a footbridge, bear right, along a field-edge. Keep following this general, waymarked line for over 0.5 miles (800m), walking outside the right edge of the trees beside Highstank Pool. Go forward with hedgerow on your left; when it stops abruptly aim across a large field to clip corner greenery – young evergreens shielding a golf tee.

5. Keeping the same line, cross a vast field (in fact, just more of the same field!), through a kissing gate, a small new metal gate. Now aim slightly left to another metal gate. Follow the road under the A38 into a housing estate. Go forward, then down for about 150yds (137m), to find a tarmac path running between Nos 49 and 53 (51 is hidden). Go through two kissing gates flanking the level crossing. Turn left to The Gardeners Arms. Here turn right over the River Salwarpe, into Vines Park. Veer left to cross the Droitwich Canal. Cross this busy road and walk down the right side of a supermarket to High Street – in front of you is Spats Coffee House. Turn right, passing Tower Hill, then left into St Andrew's Street and then back to the start of the walk.

Where to eat and drink

Just about every need is catered for here. Along High Street, The Star and Garter serves cheap-and-cheerful food and a children's menu. The 15th-century Spats Coffee House at 22 High Street has home-made cakes, and you can get fish and chips down to the left.

What to see

Walk an extra 60yds (55m) at the allotments to view the arched gateway to Westwood House, with its distinctive stars and wheatsheaves on the Pakingtons' coat of arms. The drably coloured Westwood House (now upmarket flats) had four diagonal wings added to the 1600 building in the 1660s – presumably this shape was to reflect the stars on the Pakingtons' coat of arms.

While you're there

Go along Tower Hill to peep in at the Pump Room. The brine wells here were constructed in the 1890s but stood idle until 1921.

EXPLORING WORCESTER

DISTANCE/TIME	2.5 miles (4km) / 1hr 30min
ASCENT/GRADIENT	Negligible
PATHS	City streets and tarmac riverside path
LANDSCAPE	Urban with riverside
SUGGESTED MAP	OS Explorer 204 Worcester & Droitwich Spa
START/FINISH	Grid reference: SO846548
DOG FRIENDLINESS	Not dog friendly (except short stretch by river)
PARKING	Long-stay pay-and-display car parks at New Road, Tybridge Street and Croft Road (and elsewhere)
PUBLIC TOILETS	Near start at Croft Road and bus station; several elsewhere

The development of Lea & Perrins' Worcester Sauce was largely accidental. The story goes that the two chemists, who ran a store between Broad Street and Bank Street (just off High Street), were asked to make up a recipe brought back from abroad in the 1820s. This they did, making an extra jar for themselves. Finding it excessively hot, they put the jar aside. Some years later they stumbled upon it and, quite bravely, sipped it – eureka! It had mellowed to a pleasant piquancy. The secrecy surrounding the recipe is (apparently) retained, eccentrically but effectively, firstly by employing any given worker only on part of the process, and secondly by giving the ingredients meaningless code names. HP Foods, which is now owned by Kraft Heinz, bought the business in 1930. It has since gone on to achieve worldwide brand status.

Keep your eyes directed at least 10ft (3m) off the ground and New Street – actually rather old – is a visual feast. In the late 18th century, many merchants migrated from here, making their houses tenements and workshops. The merchants left partly because of the stench. Nowadays the most likely smell wafting down New Street is of fast food. An 1832 report said of The Shambles that 'filth of all description remains until it is perfectly alive', and in 1846 another said that in parts of Worcester 'pools of liquid filth perpetually stagnate the surface.'

Charles Hastings was a brilliant youth. He attended anatomy school in London when 16, became house surgeon to Worcester Infirmary aged 18, went to Edinburgh University aged 21, and returned to Worcester Infirmary. (He declined a professorship at Edinburgh.) Ahead of his time, Hastings believed that the state should be responsible for the health of its public. He conducted much research into what nowadays would be called 'occupational health' – of local porcelain workers, glovers, and salt workers, for example – and founded the Provincial Medical and Surgical Association. Twenty-four years later, with Hastings still at the helm, legislation formally established this body as the British Medical Association, which still oversees the work of medical practitioners today. It is said that he attended every case during the three cholera outbreaks in 1832, 1849 and 1853.

In 1854 Dr Hastings put much of his own money into innovative 'modern dwellings' (long-demolished, off Copenhagen Street) for artisans. He at least had the satisfaction of seeing the local death rate fall by 45 per cent in a decade. However, he still had a fight on his hands to persuade the city council to provide clean water. Amazingly, legislation compelling local councils to do this did not reach the statute books until 1872. He benefited the people of Worcester in several other ways too, such as by founding a natural history museum in the city. His grave lies in Worcester's Astwood Cemetery. When he died in 1866, aged 72, Sir Charles Hastings was Worcester's most lauded citizen; at that time Edward Elgar was only nine years old. One could argue as to which brought about the greater benefit to Worcester city.

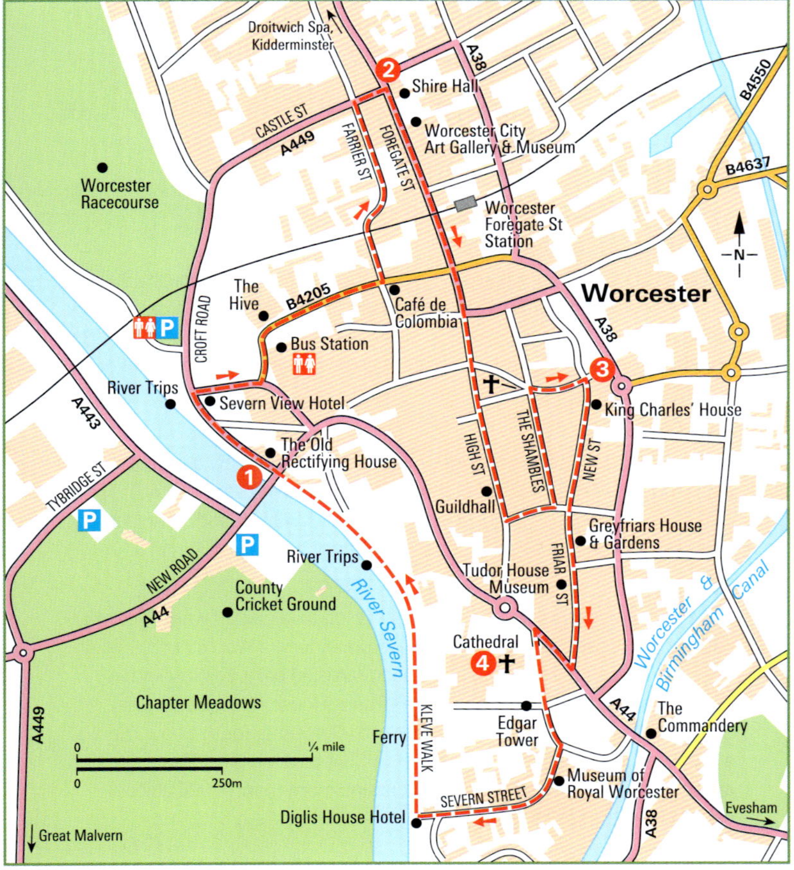

1. The route begins at the city side of the road bridge, but you can pick it up anywhere depending on where you have parked. Turn left, passing The Old Rectifying House. Turn right after the Severn View Hotel, then left, in front of the bus station, following the road round to traffic lights at Café de Colombia.

Turn left along Farrier Street, right into Castle Street, reaching the northern extremity of the route at its junction with Foregate Street.

2. Go right along Foregate Street, passing the Shire Hall and the Worcester City Art Gallery & Museum. Continue along The Cross and into the pedestrianised area called High Street. Virtually opposite the Guildhall, turn left into Pump Street. (Elgar's statue stands close to his father's piano shop, at the southern end of High Street.) Turn left again, into The Shambles. Opposite St Swithun's Church turn right into Mealcheapen Street. Another right turn and you're in New Street (which later becomes Friar Street).

3. Head down this partial time warp as slowly as you can, admiring Greyfriars House and Garden (a National Trust property) in particular, for a dual carriageway awaits you at the end. Turn right, then cross over carefully, to visit the cathedral.

4. Leave the cathedral along College Precincts to the fortified gateway known as Edgar Tower. (It is named after the 10th-century King Edgar, but was actually built in the 14th century. Go through this gateway to see College Green.) Walk along Severn Street, past the Museum of Royal Worcester and the King's School to reach the River Severn. Turn right, to complete your circuit, by following Kleve Walk, a leafy waterside avenue; this section floods frequently, as does the county cricket ground opposite at great cost to the club's revenue.

Where to eat and drink

Options abound. Try the Balcony Café at the partly baroque, partly Tudor Worcester City Art Gallery & Museum in Foregate Street: it's a delightfully airy place to sit for lunch, a snack, or tea and scones. In the cathedral, The Cloister's Café serves simple snacks in the tranquil surroundings of an ancient cloister.

What to see

In New Street, the half-timbered King Charles House (now a pub) is where the future Charles II sheltered after the Battle of Worcester in 1651. The magnificent Worcester Cathedral contains the tombs of both King John and Prince Arthur, elder brother of King Henry VIII.

While you're there

For a studied insight into the city's history, go on a guided walk (weekdays only) with a Green Badge Guide. The Commandery is Worcester's English Civil War museum – the Royalists headquartered here. History within living memory is easily recalled at the Tudor House Museum (in Friar Street). River trips depart from both North Quay and South Quay. There's a ferry too, from behind the cathedral to Chapter Meadows. The collection at the Museum of Royal Worcester contains more than 10,000 objects dating between 1751 and 2008.

AROUND POWICK BRIDGE

DISTANCE/TIME	6.5 miles (10.4km) / 3hrs 15min
ASCENT/GRADIENT	195ft (59m) / ▲
PATHS	Pastures, field paths, minor lanes, many stiles
LANDSCAPE	Mostly riverside and gentle slopes
SUGGESTED MAP	OS Explorer 204 Worcester & Droitwich Spa and OS Explorer 190 Malvern Hills & Bredon Hill
START/FINISH	Grid reference: SO834522
DOG FRIENDLINESS	Mostly sheep pastures, but off lead in middle of walk
PARKING	Car park, unsigned, on the A449/A4440 roundabout
PUBLIC TOILETS	None on route

The bridge across the River Teme, close to both the beginning and end of this walk, was the scene of one of the very first skirmishes of the English Civil War in 1642. It was a brief but aggressive engagement, from which the Royalists emerged victorious against the inferior cavalry of the Parliamentarians.

Barely a mile (1.6km) east of the starting point, the River Teme meets the Severn. This was the site of the decisive Battle of Worcester in 1651. The more famous of the two local battles, it brought an end to the Civil War. The exiled king, Charles II, had returned from France to drum up support, primarily among the Scottish army and die-hard Royalists, to overthrow Cromwell's Parliamentary forces. Die hard they did. During the Battle of Worcester, the church at Powick was used by Royalists as a lookout, due to its elevated position, enabling views of the surrounding area and the bridge. The church's tower still shows the marks of small-bore cannonballs, fired by Parliamentary gunners, extending up the south face of the tower from as low as head height to the very top. The original brick and stone Powick Bridge, dating from 15th century bears plaques commemorating the battles of 1642 and 1651.

Powick Bridge is a historic place. Mills have stood here since the 11th century or earlier. The big mill leat was cut in 1291. The buildings that still stand today, now sought-after private residences, were once part of a magnificent hydroelectric power station. This started out as a water mill and was converted in 1894 to become the world's first combined steam/hydroelectric power station, providing about half of the power needed by the city of Worcester. The station continued generating until the 1950s.

Powick Hospital was formerly known as the Worcester County Pauper and Lunatic Asylum (1847–1989). The asylum had workshops for a variety of trades, a gas works, a brewhouse, farm, bakehouse and chapel. In 1879, local musician and composer Edward Elgar was appointed bandmaster to the hospital band, made up from employees, after it was decided that music was therapeutic to the patients.

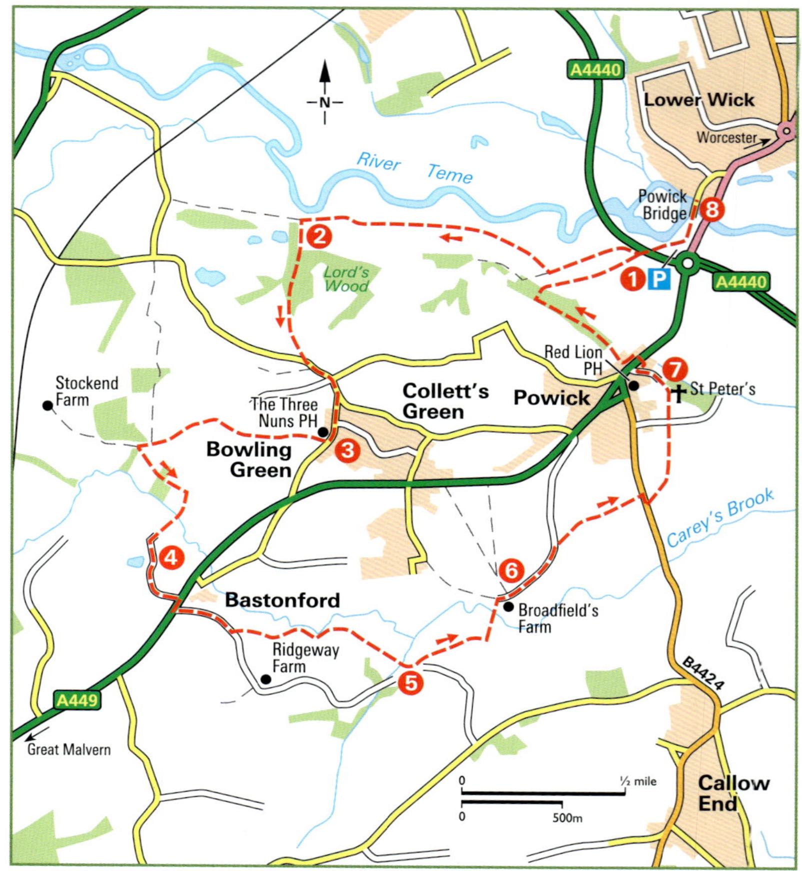

1. Walk 30yds (27m) towards the chimney. From the car park walk upstream, beside the River Teme. After just 200yds (183m), leave the river to go under the bypass. Aim towards a large white house (Ham Hill) but in the far corner of this meadow move right, beside huge trees perhaps standing in water. Roughly follow the river, keeping to the left of it, for over 0.5 miles (800m) passing over a steep wooden footbridge. Pass a solitary oak, mid-field, to locate a stile (with dog hatch) and hand-painted marker beyond.

2. Follow the right-hand field-edge, then turn left along the same field, in front of a large metal gate with waymarkers. At the top corner, a stile gives into Lord's Wood, to follow a discernible woodlander's lane. After 300yds (274m), stiles zigzag out of Lord's Wood. Pass a solitary house, then turn left onto the public road. Fork right 30yds (27m) beyond the signs 'Powick' and '30'. A few paces past The Three Nuns pub take the track on the right.

3. At the first bend take a stile, half right. Walk along two left-hand field-edges to a partially hidden stile in the top left, into a paddock. Follow the complicated but clear way-markers around a house and its grounds, before crossing stiles to emerge in a field. At the clear field opening on the left, turn left, to effectively double back along an obvious wooded track. Leaving the trees, aim for the far right field corner. Along this right-hand field-edge, walk 400yds (366m) to a broad entrance on the right, but cross left instead, aiming for a footbridge halfway down the block of woodland. Out of the trees, go forward 60yds (55m), striking half-right to a solitary oak smothering a telegraph pole. Carry on 40yds (37m) to find (perhaps with difficulty) a footbridge.

4. Skirt right of Elms (farm), picking up its driveway to the A449. At the main road, turn right briefly before crossing very carefully, to go 350yds (320m) along Ridgeway Farm's driveway to a fingerpost (walk around the hedge end). Walk 220yds (201m) up the left-hand field-edge, then pass into meadow. Edge along this narrow pasture, briefly going close to Carey's Brook, later moving to the right-hand field-edge. Go through a kissing gate beside a large oak, skirting the left-hand field-edge. In a corner take another kissing gate.

5. Just beyond a junction of tracks, a stile beside a rusted gate gives on to a wide, green lane. Through another gate in 100yds (91m) – not the pylon field – walk along the right-hand field-edge. At a pond turn left.

6. After Broadfield's Farm, follow its driveway for 400yds (366m) to a cattle grid. Over this, move immediately down to the right. Walk through, then beside young deciduous plantations, then one field to the B4424. Turn right on the pavement for 60yds (55m). Cross to a gate and gap where the remains of a stile can be seen. Cross a stile and go three-quarters left across former strawberry fields, for about 0.25 miles (400m), aiming to enter St Peter's churchyard by a metal kissing gate. From the outside, the stonework of different building phases is very noticeable, a mixture of 12th-, 15th- and 18th-century building.

7. Pass the church door to another kissing gate. Go ahead on a level path (not down to the right), which soon becomes a road to the A449. Cross at the pedestrian crossing to the right, before turning left, to take the route signposted 'Public Footpath, Bransford' on the left. Pass Severn Trent Water's Powick Hams installation, then take a waymarked path through young woodland for about 0.25 miles (400m). Steep wooden steps lead sharply down to the flood plain. Strike diagonally right, back to the underpass and car park, but you're not quite finished yet!

8. Make the short walk from the car park to Powick Bridge to see the plaques commemorating the important battles fought here during the Civil War. A little further on is the former hydroelectric power station, now desirable private homes. Return to the car park.

Where to eat and drink

Try The Three Nuns at Collett's Green, The Red Lion in Powick village or Powick's petrol station convenience store. Alternatively Worcester is just a few miles north and offers a whole range of places to eat.

What to see

The tower at Powick's church has small craters at about head height and higher up from small cannon, thought to have been fired by Parliamentarians at the Scottish Royalists soldiers using the tower as a lookout.

19

AROUND UPTON UPON SEVERN

DISTANCE/TIME	5.75 miles (9.2km) / 2hrs 15min
ASCENT/GRADIENT	80ft (24m)
PATHS	Meadows, lanes, tracks, village streets, riverside, several stiles
LANDSCAPE	Low-lying meadows, fruit farms, villages, small town
SUGGESTED MAP	OS Explorer 190 Malvern Hills & Bredon Hill
START/FINISH	Grid reference: SO850402
DOG FRIENDLINESS	Some opportunities for trustworthy dogs to be off lead
PARKING	Free car park opposite Church of St Peter and St Paul
PUBLIC TOILETS	At car park off B4211

The pretty town of Upton upon Severn sits at one of only a small number of crossings over the River Severn and as a result has long been of great cultural and strategic importance. During the English Civil War, Upton's craftsmen are believed to have aided the Parliamentarians in their preparations for the Battle of Worcester in 1651. They built two pontoons, which were hauled by the Parliamentary army from Upton to the confluence of the Teme and Severn rivers. They used these two 'bridges of boats' to cross each river, giving them a great strategic advantage. Today Upton stands as a cultural magnet too, with festivals and music events aplenty throughout the summer months.

At Upton upon Severn, the River Severn is only 36ft (11m) above sea level. Following storms and heavy rain, on 22 July 2007 a gauge at Saxon's Lode, just 1.5 miles (2.4km) downriver, measured a whopping 19.5ft (5.94m), exceeding the 18.9ft (5.76m) high-water mark recorded in 1947. Upton gained notoriety, and was dubbed 'Upton under Severn', when its flood defences could not be delivered in time due to surface flooding on the M5. According to the Environment Agency, even had those barriers been deployed, they would have been overrun.

This walk passes close to Tiltridge Vineyard and to the orchards and fields of Clive's Fruit Farm. At the end of January, it's possible to join in here with the ancient tradition of Wassailing – singing to the apple trees to encourage a good crop in the coming year. It's a good excuse to enjoy a cup of mulled cider, too.

Marked today only by a stand of large conifers, Hanley Castle stood in the 13th century as part of the Earl of Gloucester's estate. It was already a ruin at the time of Henry VIII and was mostly demolished, but some residual stone was later used to repair Upton's bridge.

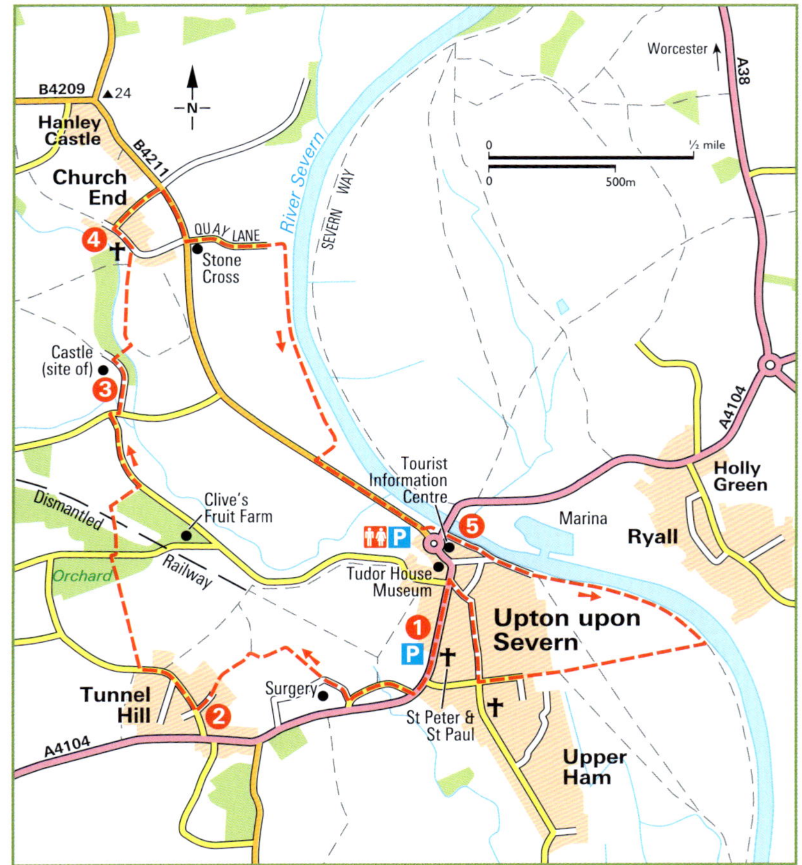

1. Begin opposite the Church of St Peter and St Paul, built in 1878–9 in a neo-Gothic style. Head away from Upton, along the A4104, and in 100yds (91m) turn right onto the old road, following the edge of the sports fields. Ignore the first signposted footpath and just before rejoining the A4104, turn right up a private road. At the bend near the Upton Surgery take stiles on the right. Near the field end go left, over a stile, ascending through a plantation. At a sunken lane turn left, to reach houses and a street.

2. Walk beside a playing field, then turn right, passing a children's play area. Take the second public footpath on the right, signposted 'Hanley Castle', along a field and straight through an orchard. Cross a road, going down another orchard row, admiring the Conference pears and Czar plums of Clive's Fruit Farm. At the end move left to cross the old railway by wooden steps, noting the original iron and concrete stiles. Cross through the gateway on the left to contour upwards to the steps on the other side of the cutting. From the far side, follow a sunken lane to a road and turn left. At a junction, turn right, soon taking a gravel driveway left between two bridges. Go right of the house to a stile beyond its sheds. Pass a hazel coppice on the right. A stand of huge conifers marks the site where Hanley Castle once stood.

3. Past the conifers, turn right to cross a stream. Go through a gateway (no gate) and a stile beyond it. In a few paces turn left through a rusty kissing gate just to the left of the large gate. Take the left-hand field edge and then enter the churchyard, ignoring way-markers. The church's tower, north chapel and chancel were added in 1674, whereas the stonework is largely 14th century.

4. Walk down the village street to the B4211. Turn right along the pavement for 220yds (201m). Cross over the road to the stone cross. Quay Lane leads down to the river. At the river, turn right, over a stile, to go along the edge of a large arable field. After 0.5 miles (800m) rejoin the B4211's pavement, before going under Upton Bridge then passing three pubs.

5. Keep beside the river on a road, to eventually go through a gate marked for Upton Ham. After 750yds (686m), at a fishery sign, turn right to cross the field. A kissing gate gives on to a vehicle track, then road. Go straight ahead, then right at the first proper crossroads, to join School Lane to the town centre. (Turn right for the tourist information centre in High Street.) Turn left along Old Street to return to the car park.

Where to eat and drink

In Upton there are many choices. The route passes three riverside pubs – The Plough Inn, the King's Head and The Swan Hotel – all within the town centre. Tearooms and cafés abound.

While you're there

The Tudor House Museum at 16 Church Street focuses on local history. At the end of June, Upton hosts a three-day Jazz Festival, attracting performers from around the world. There are also folk and blues festivals during the summer.

THE MALVERN HILLS

DISTANCE/TIME	4.5 miles (7.2km) / 2hrs 30min
ASCENT/GRADIENT	950ft (290m) / ▲ ▲
PATHS	Streets, railway bed, woodland paths, one short, steep grassy descent, several steady climbs, several stiles
LANDSCAPE	Suburban, recreational, wooded and pastoral
SUGGESTED MAP	OS Explorer 190 Malvern Hills & Bredon Hill
START	Grid reference: SO782457
FINISH	Grid reference: SO756424
DOG FRIENDLINESS	Few off-lead opportunities, must be controlled on ridge
PARKING	Car parks at both railway stations
PUBLIC TOILETS	None on route

The presence of spa waters in Malvern has been known for centuries. In 1756, a Dr Wall wrote of the waters' benefits and the 1820s saw the opening of the Baths and Pump Room – an early visitor was Princess Victoria in 1830. As a health spa, the town developed rapidly in Victorian times. A bracing combination of taking the waters and bathing was accompanied by brisk walks in the hills. Many of the well-engineered paths that criss-cross the slopes and link the peaks were built specifically to enable spa visitors to benefit fully from their medically managed visits. The railway in the 1850s brought the resort's attractions to a much wider market. Local architect Edward Wallace Elmslie designed Great Malvern's railway station (1861), considered elegant by the Victorians. Even today the wrought-ironwork of the station's mock pillars (actually drainpipes) is maintained in gaudy colours.

It isn't without reason that the Malvern Hills stand above the Worcestershire Plain. At their heart is a hard rock called gneiss, a metamorphic rock formed by intense pressure and heat some 700 million years ago. When work on the Colwall Tunnel started in 1856, labourers advanced 5ft (1.5m) per day through the softer, outer rocks, but progress slowed to just one-tenth of this through this ancient rock. The tunnel was not completed until 1860. Over its total 1,567yds (1,432m) length, it climbed 58ft (18m). The chief engineer was Stephen Ballard, who, in the previous two decades, had overseen work on the Hereford and Gloucester Canal. He was buried in his garden in Colwall, above the western entrance to the tunnel.

The Colwall Tunnel was so heavily used by steam locomotives that carriages would emerge with fallen lining bricks on their roofs. Modern trains use a broader, parallel tunnel, built close enough to the original to use its ventilation shafts by boring linking shafts. During World War II the old tunnel was used to store ammunition. The new tunnel's spoil was redeployed in 1959 to provide hard core for the M50 motorway from Strensham to Ross-on-Wye.

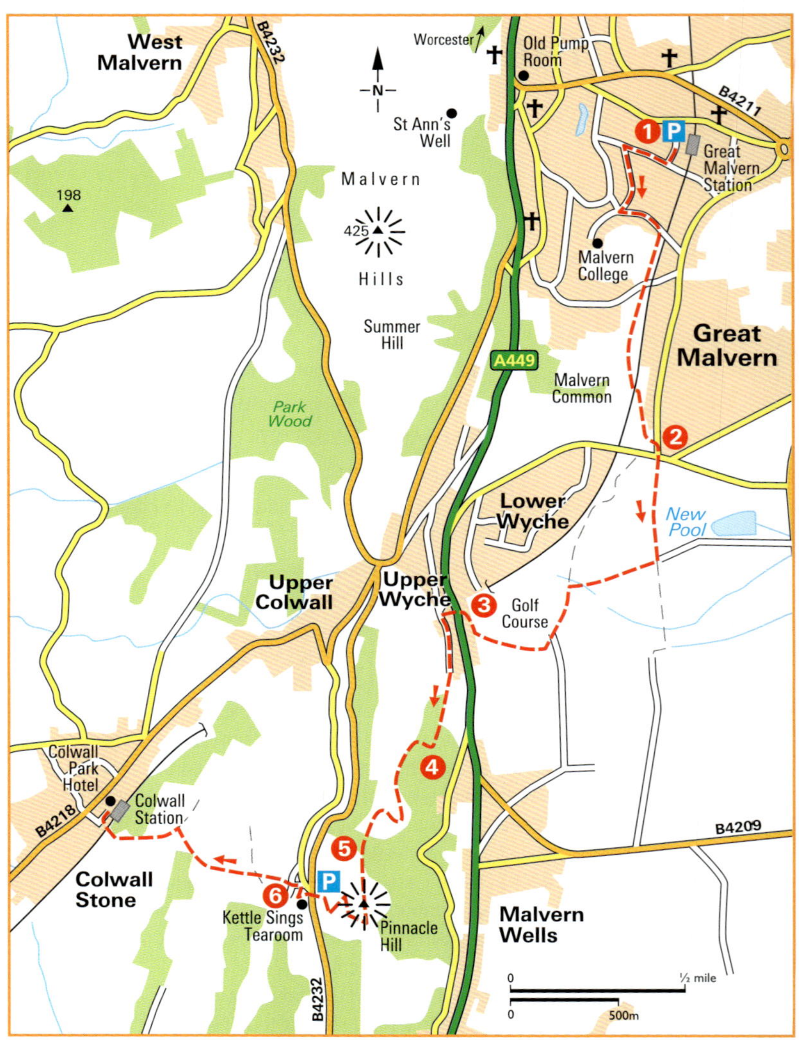

1. From Great Malvern Station go ahead; then left in 30yds (27m) into Imperial Road. Cross Tibberton Road, turning right up Clarence Road. At the skew junction turn back-left into Albert Road South. At the end turn left. Beside the railway bridge take a leafy pathway right, passing the extensive modern buildings of Malvern College. Cross the next road, then skirt the lower edge of Malvern Common. In 600yds (549m), at a dip and just by '60' on the track, pass under the railway. In 200yds (182m) drift left to a post box and road junction.

2. Cross the larger road to a fingerpost and fork right, through trees to a wide gate beside a garden, joining a dismantled railway. Descend wooden steps in 375yds (342m) and turn right to follow blue waymark discs (on white posts) across several fairways of the Worcestershire Golf Club. In dense woodland turn left – this track leads to the clubhouse and car park. Go diagonally, to the far side of a white building. Cross carefully beside a green, then another fairway, to reach a wide fenced path up between fields, soon reaching the A449 by houses.

3. Cross the A449, and the parallel higher road, to a steep path with a centre rail. At the top turn left along Eaton Road. The road becomes a green-centred tarmac track. In 40yds (36m) fork right up a woodland path before the house ahead. Follow the path for 275yds (251m) gently uphill, to a 'stretched-X' crossing. Keep ahead on the level path for a further 520yds (475m).

4. At another 'stretched-X', take the zig-zagging upward right fork beside an enormous yew and green seat; there is a cream-coloured house 130yds (118m) ahead. Very soon, at a second green seat, continue straight ahead, climbing gently up. After 275yds (251m) turn back-right by a third green seat, continuing gently up to yet another seat. Keep ahead. In approximately 200yds (182m) the dense woodland gives way to bracken and scattered silver birch. After 180yds (165m) ignore a downward right fork. Back into (less dense) woodland, after 140yds (128m) take an acute left turn, finally to meet the ridge path beside some pines.

5. Turn left to reach the grassy top of Pinnacle Hill. Less than 200yds (183m) beyond it, when a path forks right in the dip, turn fully right, down a steep grassy trod, over a crosspath and down to Gardiners Quarry Car Park. Cross to The Kettle Sings tea room.

6. Turn right in front of it; at the bend veer left to two field gates. Turn left beside a fence, then down the fenced path. At the corner, slip left down a sunken lane, soon reaching woods. Bear right to find waymarked steps, then half-left to a handgate and field-edge path to Colwall Station.

Where to eat and drink

On the route, strategically sited near the popular Gardiners Quarry Car Park, is The Kettle Sings tea room, and in Colwall, very close to the station, is the Colwall Park Hotel.

What to see

In keeping with the elegant period architecture, some Malvern streets are still lit by gas lamps. These are said to have inspired the opening section of C S Lewis's novel *The Lion, The Witch and The Wardrobe*. Lewis was a regular visitor to Malvern, as the Blue Plaque on The Unicorn pub testifies. Here, he would chat with friends including J R R Tolkien.

While you're there

Malvern Water is widely sold in shops throughout Britain. Few people realise that it's freely available from a series of wells and springs dotted along the fringes of the bald hills, from Earl Beauchamp's Spout in the north to Evendine Spring in the south. Those in the know take along bottles to fill from handy, ever-flowing roadside taps.

MALVERN HILLS AND SUCKLEY HILLS

DISTANCE/TIME	5.25 miles (8.5km) / 2hrs 30min
ASCENT/GRADIENT	344ft (105m) / ▲
PATHS	Firm or muddy tracks, meadows, some very short but steep, slippery sections, very little road
LANDSCAPE	Woodlands and rolling green fields
SUGGESTED MAP	OS Explorer 204 Worcester & Droitwich Spa
START/FINISH	Grid reference: SO752521
DOG FRIENDLINESS	On lead near livestock and in Nature Reserve, off lead in wooded areas elsewhere
PARKING	Opposite main entrance to The Knapp and Papermill Nature Reserve
PUBLIC TOILETS	At start

It's an unusual name for a nature reserve, but past land use explains the reason why. Making full use of the Leigh Brook, which runs through the reserve owned and managed by the Worcestershire Wildlife Trust, previous landowners once used mills here to make paper.

There were two mills within the 84 acres (34ha) now owned by the Trust. The remnants of Gunwick (or Gunnick) Mill, beneath the area of Papermill Cottage (on the walk just after Point 6) were washed away in a flood in 1852. Traces of the mill leat are still visible. Papermill Cottage stands next to Papermill Coppice, the woodland actively managed for many years.

The only known written mention of paper production at the site is in *The Transactions of the Worcestershire Naturalist Club*. They state that a Welshman, Mr Jones, was producing 'cap paper', a specific writing or coarse wrapping paper. Seasonal hop-pickers from the local area would give their old clothes to the miller who would use the woollen fibres to make paper.

The second mill, also no longer standing, was served by the weir near the orchard, which, until 1973, was one of just a few mills in the country still using direct water power. Just beyond the orchard, the Daffodil Field is so called because of the cultivated daffodils that were once planted there for commercial purposes.

During World War II a Birmingham-based circus was moved to Alfrick for safety. Some of the animals were kept on what is now the reserve. An elephant died and was allegedly buried within the orchard, although the remains have never been found.

The Knapp and Papermill Nature Reserve is within the Suckley Hills, a part of the Malvern Hills Area of Outstanding Natural Beauty. The AONB was designated as such in 1959 and covers 40 square miles (105 km^2), including parts of Herefordshire and Gloucestershire in addition to Worcestershire. Meanwhile, the Leigh Brook Valley was designated a Site of Special Scientific Interest because of the diversity of quality habitats.

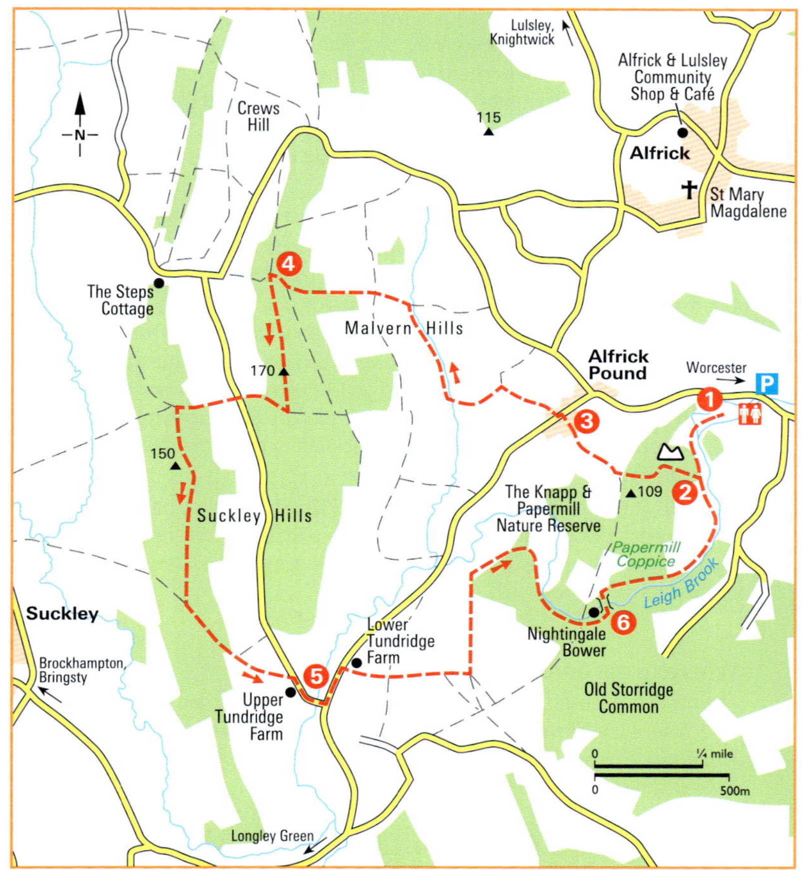

1. From the parking area, take the path through the main entrance of the Nature Reserve with the stream on your left, walking initially downhill then through old orchards (beside a weir) and meadow for 700yds (640m).

2. At a small brick bridge, turn right turn up the field-edge to use the handgate into woodland. Go ahead 50 paces, then turn left (waymark Post 13). In 220yds (201m) fork right (Post 12), soon climbing a long series of wooden steps. Keep ahead to find an information board at a path junction in 400yds (366m). Bend right, following this woodland path to a fork near a forestry hut. Go left, shortly joining a wider track through to Alfrick Pound.

3. Turn left to use a fingerposted gate on the right in 20yds (18m). Beyond the orchard keep to the right edge, through a field gate and, in 75yds (69m), descend the field to a gate-side footbridge at a hedge-gap. Once over turn right at the stile into stream-edge pastures. Beyond the second field cross the gravel track, use the metal kissing gate and turn left to a stile into a sloping orchard. Turn right to the corner oak in 100yds (91m); here keep uphill through the orchard, soon putting the woods on your left. At the higher corner a stile gains a thin, rising woodland path. This hits a wider cross-track; turn right for 80yds (73m).

4. Turn left on the fence-side track, the Worcestershire Way. In 550yds (502m) turn right with the Worcestershire Way, descending to a lane. Cross straight over, rising then beside the orchard to use a handgate into woods. In 75yds (69m) turn left (Worcestershire Way), gently climbing on for 0.5 miles (800m). Fork left on the waymarked crossing bridleway, descending to a split at the woodland foot. Use the gate into pasture and head half-right to the farm and converted oast houses.

5. Turn right and, at a T-junction, go left. In 150yds (137m) turn right up the lane beside the half-timbered barn at Lower Tundridge Farm. Walk the lane to its very end. Turn left through the yard, joining a field-foot track which passes through a neck of woodland. Cross the stile beside double metal gates; then drop half-right to walk beside wood rail fencing (on your left). The track rises through woodland to a pasture-edge gateway. Turn right to use the nearby gate, then go left (waymark arrow painted on tree) on a muddy track within the woods. In 300yds (274m) go left (waymarked), soon passing close to sheds then a garden. At the rough driveway turn back-left to cross the footbridge at Nightingale Bower.

6. Turn left. At the top turn right. In just 40yds (37m) take a gate back down into the woods. A wood-end handgate leads into a meadow; stay beside the stream to the brick bridge (Point 2). Return to the car park by following the track for 700yds (640m).

Where to eat and drink

The nearest refreshments are in Alfrick, at the community run shop and café. A selection of sandwiches, cakes and hot drinks can be enjoyed either inside or out and there is also a takeaway service. Open seven days a week, although limited hours.

What to see

Lower Tundridge Farm is a timber-framed building with mullioned and transomed windows. Built in the early 17th century, it was one of the last of its kind, before brick structures became the norm. Along Leigh Brook the Worcestershire Wildlife Trust has built suitable holts (otter houses). Note the owl and bat boxes throughout Tor Coppice too.

While you're there

You may be able to take part in one of the many events that take place throughout the year at The Knapp and Papermill Nature Reserve, anything from nature photography workshops and guidance on birdwatching to conservation volunteering and family open days.

AROUND DUMBLETON HILL

DISTANCE/TIME	8.75 miles (14.1km) / 3hrs 45min
ASCENT/GRADIENT	610ft (186m) / ▲
PATHS	Mostly good paths, field tracks and village roads, many stiles
LANDSCAPE	Gentle farmland and quiet villages
SUGGESTED MAP	OS Explorer OL45 The Cotswolds
START/FINISH	Grid reference: SP039364
DOG FRIENDLINESS	Mixed farming area, so off lead with discretion
PARKING	On street near church in Wormington
PUBLIC TOILETS	None on route

Wormington sits quietly away from the B4078, perhaps less busy now than in its first recorded mention in 1297. Today, a hexagonal bench, ringing a splendid tree, invites you to sit while donning your walking boots. Tucked behind this tiny green stands St Katharine's Church, a small building of 14th-century origin. It boasts a 9th-century stone crucifix, dug up in nearby Wormington Grange and said to have been salvaged from Winchcombe Abbey, and a 400-year-old brass depicting a mother and child in the lady's bed chamber.

While St Katharine's is spire-less, having just a short bell-turret, the 200ft (61m) Victorian Gothic spire of St Andrew's Church in Toddington is visible from afar. On an ancient site among yew trees, the honey-stone building is largely the work of masons in the 17th, 18th and 19th centuries, funded by the Tracy family, who also built the 17th-century Toddington House, all but demolished in living memory. The 2nd Baron Sudeley gave his name to the side chapel; this is his last resting place, with his wife, in a marble tomb.

What remains of Toddington House is part of the gatehouse, little more than a façade. You can see the remnants over the churchyard wall. Walk a little further round for sight of Toddington Manor. This 19th-century Gothic mansion, owned by artist Damien Hurst, is undergoing extensive restoration.

Dumbleton's history goes back to Saxon times, although the oldest features apparent today are at St Peter's Church, primarily its arched north doorway. The church has undergone several additions and changes; some have suggested that the purpose of the 15th-century south aisle was to provide a place for Masses for the victims of the Black Death. Also of note in the church is the 600-year-old piscina (stone basin). A hall was first built in Dumbleton in the 16th century but that was demolished and the present-day Dumbleton Hall is the 1830 creation of G S Repton. He was commissioned by Edward Holland, the owner of the estate and founder of the Royal Agricultural College in Cirencester. Dumbleton Hall, now a hotel, has a landscaped lake and, from the footpath, a variety of trees worthy of a small arboretum.

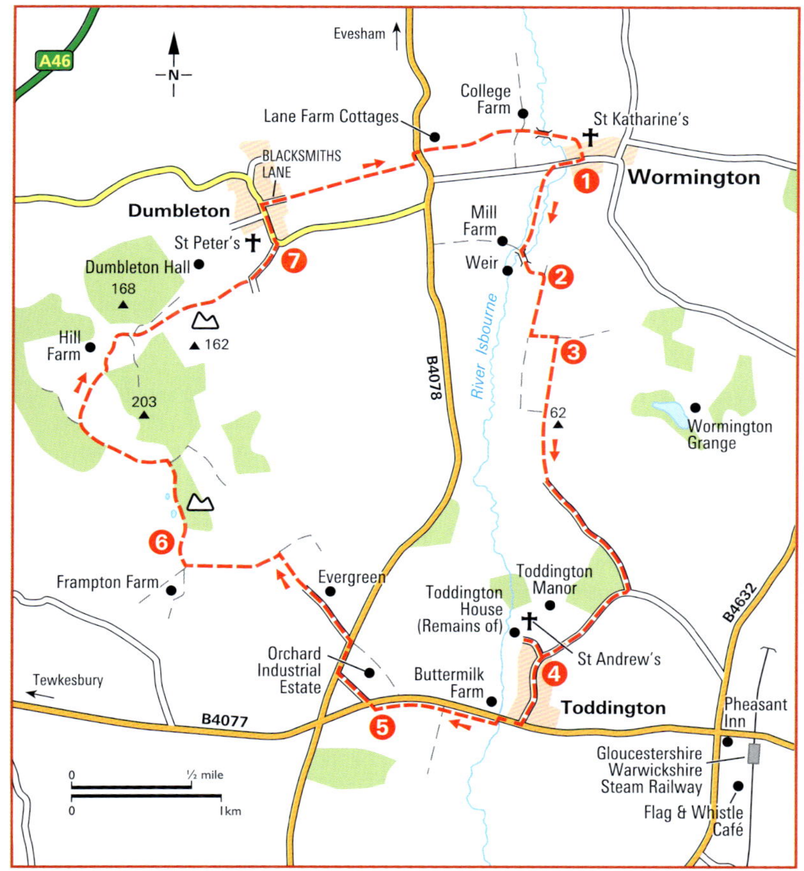

1. Walk west, along the road out of the village, to pass under some power lines. Just after these, take the footpath on the left. Pass through a gate, maintaining this line for a further 600yds (549m).

2. Pass through a gate and turn left away from Mill Farm (view the waterwheel first), to cross the River Isbourne at a bridge. Cross a narrow field, noting the mill's weir to your right, and reach another gate. Go diagonally across another field, under power lines again, bearing right beside a hedge. In about 235yds (215m), turn left to walk along the right-hand field edge. Within 160yds (146m) turn right.

3. Follow this field track – later a green lane and finally tarmac – for nearly 1 mile (1.6km), keeping right at a fork to reach a road junction. Turn right, passing the entrance of Toddington Manor, to reach a junction.

4. Here a sign points to Toddington's church. Visit the church and view the ruin of Toddington House. Retrace your steps, then walk through Toddington village. At the main road turn right. Just after the pavement gives out (before Buttermilk Farm), cross over to a fingerpost and stile. Cross this and turn sharp right to walk behind a screen of trees for 830yds (760m).

5. Re-cross the road to take the minor road through Orchard Industrial Estate. At the T-junction turn right. Go next left, up the driveway, passing the black-and-white painted farmhouse called 'Evergreen'. At the next T-junction turn left along a farm track, contouring the hill. As the track bends left to Frampton Farm, turn right at the footpath sign, avoiding the Winchcombe Way running straight on.

6. Head up the field to a gate near trees. Once through this, the way soon steepens. On the brow join a stony track coming in from the right. On the way up there are good views looking back. Now on the level, continue for about 560yds (512m) to signposts at a junction of tracks. Follow the sign for 'Public Bridleway Dumbleton 1.25 miles', soon coming to a big, open field. A good track now leads all the way down to a minor road, then goes straight on past the driveway to Dumbleton Hall (a hotel).

7. Visit the church, then cross to the crucifix-style war memorial and turn left. About 50yds (46m) beyond Dairy Lane on the left, turn right along Blacksmiths Lane and when you reach a house (Down Callow) keep left for a path ahead that skirts two field edges. Cross the B4078 and, when the drive to Lane Farm Cottages bends left, go forward across one field to a gap in the hedge and then across another field to a stile. Cross the service road to College Farm and continue over farmland to cross over the small River Isbourne on a concrete bridge with corrugated iron sides. Pass under power lines and over a stile into pasture, then walk to the end of a large modern barn. Turn right to a gate, rejoining the road in Wormington. The church is on the left.

Where to eat and drink

There are no refreshments available on the route. You'll find the Pheasant Inn in Toddington, and at the station, the Flag & Whistle café, open April to November, 9am to 4pm.

What to see

Early in the walk at Mill Farm, only a few paces off the route, are the remnants of an overshot watermill, one of many on the River Isbourne. Fragments of the wheel, spokes of wood and rims and paddles of metal are still visible. The mill was in active use, grinding corn, well into the 20th century.

While you're there

At Toddington's Gloucestershire Warwickshire Steam Railway you'll see not just steam trains, but assorted rolling stock and lovingly preserved diesels, too. The station yard seems to be a magnet for old vehicles in general – fire engines, ambulances and buses. Trains run from Broadway to Cheltenham racecourse station. On the same site is the North Gloucestershire Narrow Gauge Railway, which operates a more limited timetable.

AROUND MARTLEY

DISTANCE/TIME	7 miles (11.3km) / 3hrs 45min
ASCENT/GRADIENT	720ft (219m) / ▲ ▲
PATHS	Field paths, lanes, orchard paths, tracks, river meadows, minor roads, several stiles
LANDSCAPE	Arable, orchards, wooded ridges and Teme Valley
SUGGESTED MAP	OS Explorer 204 Worcester & Droitwich Spa
START/FINISH	Grid reference: SO756597
DOG FRIENDLINESS	Off-lead opportunities if under control
PARKING	Just south of St Peter's Church, Martley
PUBLIC TOILETS	None on route

Don't believe everything you read in your dictionary. The entry for 'cyder' could read 'Same as cider'. The entry for 'wine' is scarcely less controversial: 'The fermented juice of grapes; a liquor made from other fruits.' If you can accept that grapes are not an essential ingredient of wine, then our 'cyder' is apple wine; if you can't, then it's fermented apple juice. Authentic, old-fashioned cyder is virtually extinct but some of the smaller manufacturers retain the old word, for example, Healey's Cornish cyders, and from Suffolk, Aspall's range including their 1728 Cyder with a dizzying 11 per cent alcohol by volume.

While being no real authority on drink, Mrs Beeton, writing in the inter-war edition of *Mrs Beeton's Family Cookery*, gives a recipe for cider in which there are just two ingredients, cider apples and water, whereas the adjacent page has a recipe for apple wine, which has three ingredients: sugar, water and… cider. In other words, apple wine is 'cider squared' – a twice fermented-out cider. (By the way, the same publication suggests that one of your servants should clean the silver every Friday.) In the cyder-making process some water was added, because firstly a glutinous pulp was unworkable, and secondly even the hard-working enzymes of farm labourers would not maintain sobriety for (say) scything the corn when drinking copious quantities of a heady ferment.

Cyder was often a safer drink than water as the acids present in it killed off any water-borne diseases. In 1901, when making a critical assessment of the diet of the Dore Workhouse inmates, its medical officer wrote: 'Cold water is a sickly thing to have to drink, especially for agricultural people used to cider.' He may not have been implying that anything was wrong with the water, but his comment shows the ubiquitous nature of cider at that time.

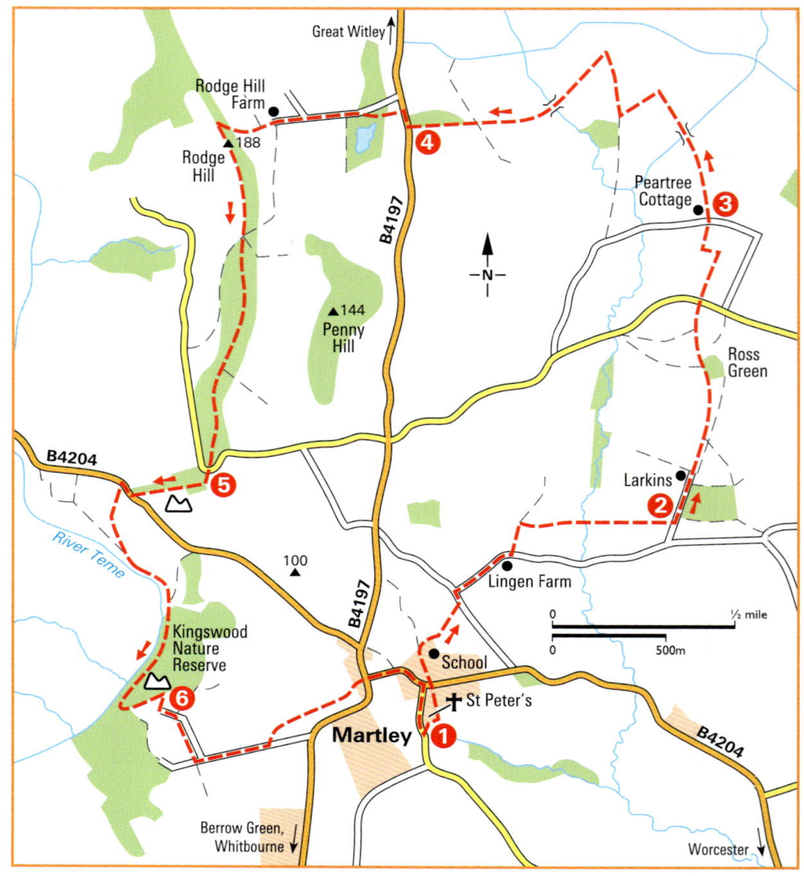

1. Go up through the churchyard to the B4204. Cross to a rough track. In 100yds (91m) walk in trees, parallel to the school. Turn right into a field, then re-enter the grounds. Briefly follow the left edge of the playing fields, then a gate gives on to a field. At the road, turn left. Turn right, signposted 'Highfields'. Beside Lingen Farm go down a track. At the bend take a stile to right, straight across the field. Cross a stream, then ascend, taking the right-hand gates. You will then reach a minor road.

2. Turn left. At Larkins go ahead, taking two stiles and a gate, then a field path, not the inviting parallel gravel track. Go ahead for two fields crossing two stiles and keeping straight ahead. Don't move right, but pass close alongside a breeze-block barn and the driveway of a white bungalow, to walk behind Ross Green's gardens, ignoring the obvious kissing gate to the left. Keep to left of fields to reach another road. Go straight over, to a partially broken, concealed stile, not diagonally to a prominent fingerpost. Walk beside a barn, then in the next field skirt left to another lane. Turn right for a few paces to a finger-post pointing into the apple orchard before the defiantly named Peartree Cottage.

3. Follow waymarkers carefully through this vast young orchard, descending gently. Cross a bridge over a ditch and pass over a stile, before continuing through more orchard. Emerge at a gate beside apple-sorting equipment. Go 200yds (183m) up this track, to a gap in evergreens. Turn left, down an orchard ride. At a T-junction turn right, up to just before a gate beside a small house. Turn left, almost back on yourself. Go very carefully through the orchard, following faded yellow splodges about 1.5ft (45cm) up on the tree trunks, but sometimes obscured by low branches. Leave by a footbridge, keeping to the left field, crossing to the B4197.

4. Turn right for 60yds (55m). Take an excellent track (mostly tarmac) for 0.5 mile (800m) to Rodge Hill's top. Turn sharp left, 'Worcestershire Way'. Follow this for 1 mile (1.6km). Steps lead down to a road's hairpin bend.

5. Turn right. In 20yds (18m) turn left, but in only 15yds (14m) turn right again, into conifers. Emerge to drop down steeply. At the B4204 turn right for 30yds (27m). Use a permissive path across two fields to the River Teme. Follow this beautiful riverside walk, later in Kingswood Nature Reserve, for over 0.5 mile (800m). Leave the river when a wire fence requires it. Ascend a steep path, later a driveway, to a tarmac road.

6. Turn right, uphill; this soon bends left. Near the brow move right (waymarker) just to walk in the field, not on the road. At the tarmac junction turn left but, in 275yds (251m), walk beside a smart wire fence then pass through a gap between hedge and sheds to continue, before emerging between the former Crown pub and the garage. Cross the B4197 straight onto the B4204, then turn right to the church and the start of the walk.

Where to eat and drink

There is currently nothing in Martley, the long closed Crown Inn is being redeveloped. In Berrow Green, 1.25 miles (2km) south, the Rodney has a varied menu that can be enjoyed in the bar or in the converted stables. Further south again, in Knightwick, is The Talbot with its own on site Teme Valley Brewery.

What to see

Martley's red sandstone St Peter's Church claims to have the country's only complete original set of six bells, cast in 1673. It also has some tantalisingly indiscernible medieval wall paintings.

24

GREAT WITLEY CIRCUIT

DISTANCE/TIME	4.75 miles (7.7km) / 2hrs 30min
ASCENT/GRADIENT	1,150ft (350m) / ▲ ▲ ▲
PATHS	Woodland paths, field paths, tracks, several stiles
LANDSCAPE	Wooded hills and farmed valleys
SUGGESTED MAP	OS Explorer 204 Worcester & Droitwich Spa
START/FINISH	Grid reference: SO751662
DOG FRIENDLINESS	Will be driven wild by geese! Running in woods but lead needed over grazing land
PARKING	On-road parking in Great Witley
PUBLIC TOILETS	None on route

What sort of walker are you – 'any weather' or 'fair weather'? Or are you a 'low pollen count walker', suffering from hay fever? Grasses are the most common cause, but just about any pollen can produce allergenic reactions. Between 10 per cent and 35 per cent of people suffer from 'pollinosis' (allergy to pollen), but these reactions may be species-specific. In addition, some species of tree seem to have more potent pollen than others, birch in particular. Pollen is typically released from grasses from May to August, oilseed rape from April to June, and stinging nettles from May to mid-September. These are all good reasons for getting out walking in the winter but, if you are afflicted in January, it could be pollen from alder or hazel, and in March it could be birch. Studies show that the season for birch pollen has shifted to five days earlier every decade over the past 30 years, a clear indication of global warming.

The National Pollen & Aerobiology Research Unit (NPARU), at University College, Worcester, is at the forefront of the science of 'aerobiology'. Supplying pollen forecasts is just one of the NPARU's, diverse activities; others include studying changes in pollen seasons in relation to climate change, and studying asthma in relation to fungi and house-dust mites in homes. Of particular concern is chronic bronchitis – properly, chronic obstructive pulmonary disease (COPD). It is caused primarily by smoking, but there are other, secondary factors at work – this must be the case as in some southern European countries people smoke more but there is less COPD. One possible factor is Britain's higher humidity.

From early spring until mid-December the lane around Walsgrove Farm is awash with geese – about 3,500 of them. (You will see turkeys too.) This is just another of the diverse activities you can come across in the back lanes of Herefordshire and Worcestershire. The geese are allowed to range very freely. Nearly all are destined for the Christmas table, primarily through butchers and retailers, but you can buy one at the farm gate (September–December), too.

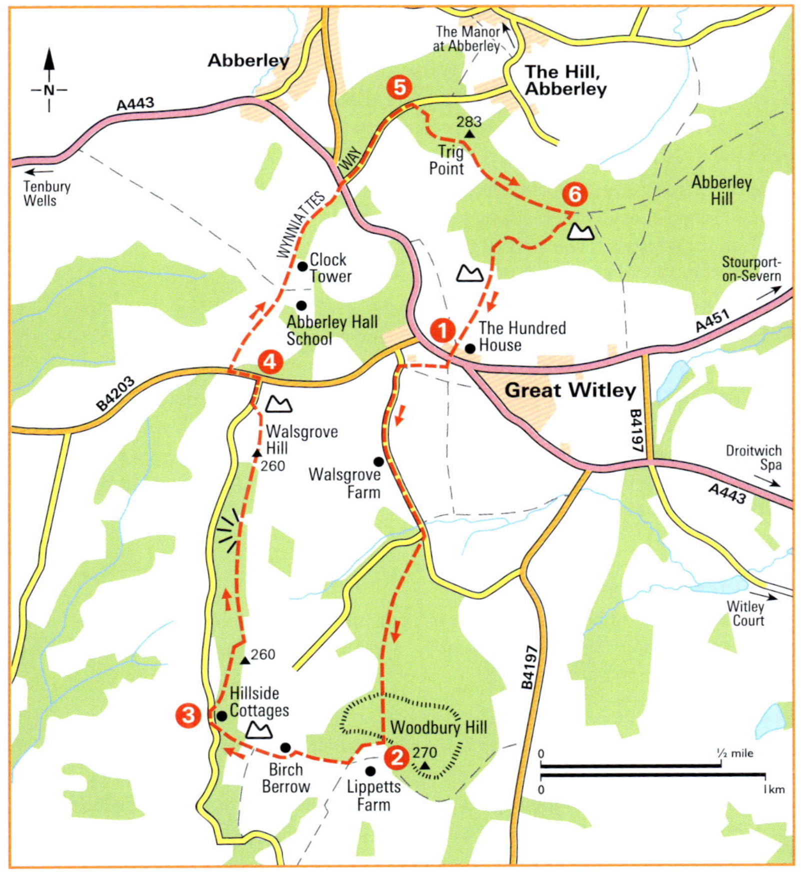

1. Through an opening, nearly opposite The Hundred House, strike sharply right, aiming for the hedge end beside the last house and a marker post. Turn left on this lane. Walk for 0.5 mile (800m) along here, soon passing firstly Walsgrove Farm and secondly (most of the year) thousands of strutting geese. Do not turn right up a lane but go half right, taking the path that becomes a beautiful wooded avenue, to the top of Woodbury Hill. Reach the second information board.

2. Take the path ahead just a few paces to turn right at a partially hidden marker post. In 50yds (46m), turn right. Continue forward to walk along the inside edge of a wood. Skirt to the left of the buildings at Birch Berrow, over two stiles, resuming on a gravel, fenced-in path. Take two stiles. Go steeply down, taking a metal kissing gate into thick pines. In pasture again, descend further, reaching The Woodlands' driveway and a T-junction. Turn right along the tarmac road for 75yds (69m) to a marker post just past 1 Hillside Cottages.

3. Turn right again, back uphill. Continue north for nearly 1 mile (1.6km), with several stiles and gates, walking mostly in trees but later enjoying fine views westwards. Then, on top of Walsgrove Hill, you'll see the elaborate and magnificent clock tower (1883) of Abberley Hall. (Move right to see the geese again!) Now go steeply down this meadow, to take a stile into a lane. Turn right to the B4203.

4. Cross carefully. Turn left, along the verge. Take the driveway to Abberley Hall School. Leave the driveway as it swings right, keeping this direction close to the clock tower and all the way, on a track, to the A443. Take the road opposite, 'Wynniattes Way', up to the brow of the hill.

5. Turn right. In about 400yds (366m), reach an obvious trig point. Walk along the ridge path a further 650yds (594m) to a Worcestershire Way sign at a path junction, just beyond which are four trees growing in a line across the path.

6. Take the path down to the right, initially quite steeply then contouring as it veers right, later descending again. Eventually, at junction with a waymarker, turn left to emerge from the woods over a kissing gate. Walk down two large fields (admire the clock tower, now to your right), meeting the road beside The Hundred House.

Where to eat and drink

The Manor at Abberley serves breakfast, lunch (except Monday and Tuesday) and dinner (except Sunday) and has a very pleasant outdoor area for when the weather is fine. A good range of drinks is also offered.

What to see

Take a good look at Abberley Hall's exceptionally tall clock tower. Built by John Joseph Jones in 1883 in memory of his father – for whom Abberley Hall itself (all Italianate) was built in 1846 – it has an octagonal top section before the spire. You may see some deer in a field just beyond it, too.

While you're there

Visit spectacular Witley Court, 1.25 miles (2km) southeast of Great Witley. The Court's stately architecture, mostly Victorian, is just stunning. Only the skeleton of the house remains since a fire in 1937. English Heritage describes it as its number one ruin.

25

ABBERLEY VILLAGE AND ABBERLEY HILL

DISTANCE/TIME	4.5 miles (7.2km) / 2hrs 15min
ASCENT/GRADIENT	672ft (205m) / ▲ ▲ ▲
PATHS	Quiet lanes, field paths, woodland paths
LANDSCAPE	Wooded hills and farmed valleys
SUGGESTED MAP	OS Explorer 204 Worcester & Droitwich Spa
START/FINISH	Grid reference: SO753678
DOG FRIENDLINESS	Off-lead walks in woodland, but lead required over grazing land
PARKING	Off-road parking on verge 218yds (200m) from village centre. Possible parking in car park of The Manor at Abberley for patrons.
PUBLIC TOILETS	None on route

Abberley is a village of three distinct parts: The Village, Abberley is the oldest and clusters around the minimal remains of the 12th-century parish church of St Michael. Only the Norman chancel remains fully intact. Abberley's 'new' church is dedicated to St Mary.

It lies a couple of minutes' walk from The Village. Although 13th century in style, it was constructed a mere 150 years ago and largely rebuilt following a fire in 1876. Overlooking The Village, Abberley is The Hill, Abberley with a scattering of farms and cottages on the steep slopes of Abberley Hill. The most recent introduction is The Common, Abberley, which includes newer housing, the primary school and village shop, all congregating around the Cleobury Road.

Abberley Hill was at the centre of a protracted standoff between the Welsh and English armies in 1405. The Welsh army of Owain Glyn Dwr took up battle positions on Abberley Hill while King Henry IV's English army occupied the neighbouring Woodbury Hill, an Iron Age hill fort, clearly seen from the trig point on Abberley Hill. Both armies occupied their positions for days without any major action and they never engaged in battle, merely eyeing one another suspiciously. With supply routes blocked, the Welsh army began to starve and headed home.

The distinctive Abberley Clock Tower, seen close to Woodbury Hill, is a Grade II listed building in the grounds of Abberley Hall School. The tower is the setting for the children's book by Gene Kemp, *The Clock Tower Ghost*, renamed Addlesbury Tower. Considered a modern classic, written in 1981, the novel is one of the author's most popular stories.

Along the route, you may notice signs for The Geopark Way. Abberley Hill is within the Abberley and Malvern Hills Geopark, an area that covers 482 square miles and one of ten Geoparks in the UK. Within the Geopark there are rocks that span 700 million years of the earth's history. Abberley Hill, and some of its neighbouring high spots, was formed during the Silurian period around 420 million years ago. At the redundant Shavers End Quarry, seen as you climb Abberley Hill, limestones and shales lie over the top of younger rocks suggesting major mountain building forces when the rocks were uplifted. It is possible that you could find fossils on your walk.

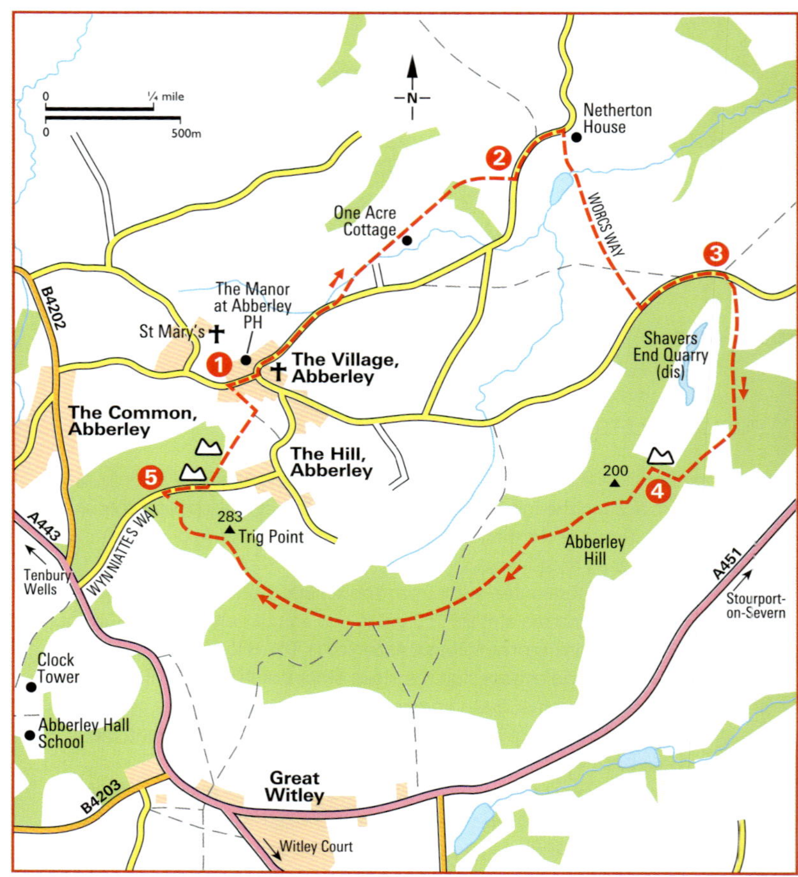

1. With The Manor at Abberley pub in front of you, turn right to walk for 0.25 miles (400m) to a fingerpost on left after the stream at Rodge Cottage's driveway. Leave this meadow by a stile, onto a track heading straight for One Acre Cottage. Just before its garage there is a signposted path to the left, past the cottage's garden. Waymarker posts lead past hop bines on left for some 275yds (251m). Veer right after some woodland through a gate, gently up, then down to the left-hand corner gate.

2. Turn left. Just beyond a private, floodlit tennis court on the left turn right, signposted 'Worc Way & Malvern 24 miles'. Now go straight for 750yds (685m). Turn left at the road. On a bend, where the road is widened for a quarry entrance, do not take the steep flight of wooden steps, but go 80yds (73m) further, downhill, to follow a Worcestershire Way marker.

3. Follow this in woodland for 650yds (594m), then slant across one field before climbing Abberley Hill. You may notice that the trees around you – sweet chestnuts – are classically coppiced. In one place this ascent is particularly steep, with views to the adjacent deep quarry.

4. Having attained the ridge, follow 'Worcestershire Way' to the left, keeping on it for about about 1.5 miles (2.4km), until a lane 400yds (366m) beyond the Trig Point.

5. Walk right on the lane, descending steeply for 180yds (165m). Follow the Abberley Circular Walk fingerpost down many wooden steps. Take a gate out of woods, bear left to another gate and cross meadows continuing down to The Village, Abberley.

Where to eat and drink

The Manor at Abberley in The Village, Abberley. Right in the heart of the village, with a roadside terrace and garden at the back, this is a character pub serving fresh cooked food from seasonal, local produce.

What to see

Take a good look at Abberley Hall School's exceptionally tall clock tower. Built by John Joseph Jones in 1883 in memory of his father – for whom Abberley Hall itself (all Italianate) was built in 1846 – it has an octagonal top section before the spire.

While you're there

Visit spectacular Witley Court, 3 miles (4.8km) southeast of The Village, Abberley. The Court's stately architecture, mostly Victorian, is just stunning. Only the skeleton of the house remains since a fire in 1937. English Heritage describes it as its number one ruin.

A SHORT WALK FROM MAMBLE

DISTANCE/TIME	4.25 miles (6.8km) / 2hrs 30min
ASCENT/GRADIENT	625ft (190m) / ▲
PATHS	Minor roads (one steep hill), field and woodland paths, many stiles
LANDSCAPE	Undulating pastoral landscape
SUGGESTED MAP	OS Explorer 203 Ludlow
START/FINISH	Grid reference: SO685712
DOG FRIENDLINESS	Lead necessary (livestock likely)
PARKING	Lay-by (bend in old road) west of Mamble on A456
PUBLIC TOILETS	None on route

Crude forms of coal mining were probably first carried out on the land around the small village of Mamble in prehistoric times. Much later, the Blount family lived at Sodington Hall, and the Mamble coal pits were part of their estate.

It may have been the case that mining was a part-time activity for what were primarily farmworkers. The inference drawn from the absence of much housing in the Marl Brook area is that mining was never more than a small-scale activity. Mamble's coal was not of premium quality, but it was adequate for domestic use and non-critical industrial processes such as lime burning. Coal mining continued in the locality until 1972. The last pit to close was the Mole Colliery at Hunthouse, about 1 mile (1.6km) southeast of Mamble. The more modern, deep-mining techniques are the ones that cause least disruption at the surface. It is believed that, having won the coal from a pit, the ancient miners put it into wagons, to be hauled by horse along a rudimentary tramway to the (partially constructed) canal.

The rationale for the Leominster Canal, sanctioned by a 1791 Act of Parliament, was simple enough – provide a terminus for the distribution of coal emerging from the pits around Mamble, and reduce the price of conveying other goods between Leominster (pronounced 'Lemsta') and the River Severn. An advertisement displayed in 1797 proclaimed a cost saving, priced per ton, on this route of 25 per cent, and a 'more speedy conveyance'. Indeed, in 1796 the price of coal at Leominster was halved.

Coal was loaded onto barges at Wharf House. For various reasons, the canal company failed to build nearly all of the remaining eastward section and the unfinished Southnett Tunnel later collapsed. Its position is near Broombank Farm, roughly below Ash Coppice. All manner of constructional defects in this, and in the Rea Aqueduct, were reported by a consulting engineer. The Rea Aqueduct was built mostly of brick and was the largest single-span brick acqueduct in the country at that time. It is still standing, but in a crumbling and precarious state. Marked merely as 'FB' on the OS map, it's at Grid Reference: SO 651703 (you need to be committed to find it); the footpath across the aqueduct from the east is closed for safety reasons. Not having the Southnett Tunnel cut off access to essential water from Dumbleton Brook (beyond the tunnel's eastern portal), so a reservoir, the Stocking Pool, was built. The canal was eventually bought by the railway in the late 1850s and wound down.

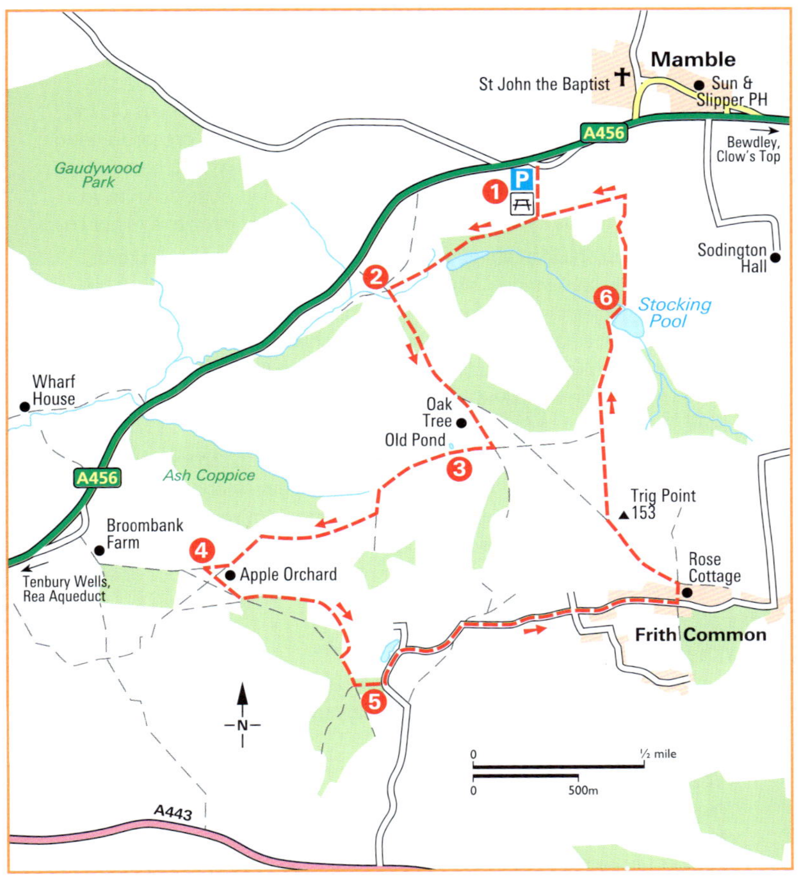

1. Go to the Tenbury Wells end of the lay-by. Take the gate nearest the road to walk down the left-hand field-edge. At the woodland turn right, shortly entering it by a stile. Go forward at a two-plank bridge. In 200yds (183m) cross pastures to join a cinder track by a white house.

2. Turn left for 75yds (69m). At a gate move right on a rising woodland track. At a corner stay in woodland, along a broad green path heading right, ignoring paths to the left. Fork right shortly before a gate. At this, ascend gently by taking the right fork (waymarker), aiming 50yds (46m) left of a skyline oak in a field. At the top turn right, staying within the field and following the hedge to a gateway beside a small, tree-screened dry pond.

3. Keep this line for 250yds (229m) to a stile on the left shortly before a corner; look for a bowl-shaped field and copse to your left. Climb this but don't follow

the waymarker forward and down; instead go through a gate to your right, and continue with this field-edge on your right. In the next field go directly under a large pylon to another stile. Walk initially with the wire fence and an apple orchard on your left, but, within 30yds (27m) of the hedgerow beginning, go through a stile, putting this hedgerow on your right. Reach a seven-bar metal gate, one short field before a cherry orchard.

4. Do not go through; instead turn three-quarters around, to go diagonally down this field, in search of a stile (concealed by a bracken edge) nearly 100yds (91m) left of an old metal gate. Enter an apple orchard, skirting its right-hand perimeter on asphalt and grass for approximately 500yds (457m) and with woodland to your right. Just a few paces around the orchard's bottom corner leave by a stile. Move right a few paces to a wooden post; here fork left (not uphill). In 50yds (46m) go over a stile and see a footbridge down to your left. Across this turn left (waymarker), along a little-used path, to a minor road.

5. Turn left. Keep ahead at a junction, then ascend quite sharply, and drop down past the 'Frith Common' sign. Keep ahead at the next crossroads too. Now ascend again and beside the entrance to Rose Cottage and The Observatory, take a narrow path on the left. Soon in a field, follow the left-hand edge to a stile. Strike half right (waymarked), descending two pastures easily to walk beside woodland on your left. A gate leads you down to the Stocking Pool.

6. Cross the dam to a gate. Turn left and climb for 350yds (320m), skirting woodland on your left. Move right 40yds (37m) to a gate (not another further right). Through this turn immediately left. In 70yds (64m), cross an avenue diagonally. Cross a field, bypassing woods on the left, to a gate. Through this turn right to return to the car park.

Where to eat and drink

If you go into the village you will find Mamble's Sun & Slipper with a beer terrace. Otherwise head east along the A456 to The Colliers Farm Shop and Café at Clow's Top.

What to see

Since trig points (properly, 'trigonometrical stations') were rendered obsolete by technology, some have been adopted and lovingly maintained, whereas others have been neglected. Between Frith Common and the Stocking Pool you are not many paces from an example of the latter: '153' on the OS map can be found, but not easily, for it has suffered the indignation of being directly incorporated into a line of new hedgerow!

TENBURY WELLS TO BERRINGTON COURT

DISTANCE/TIME	5.75 miles (9.2km) / 2hrs 30min
ASCENT/GRADIENT	280ft (85m) / ▲
PATHS	Town streets, field paths, minor lanes, many stiles
LANDSCAPE	Undulating mixed farmland, small market town
SUGGESTED MAP	OS Explorer 203 Ludlow
START/FINISH	Grid reference: SO598682
DOG FRIENDLINESS	Lead preferable most of time
PARKING	Long-stay car park, beside swimming pool, Tenbury Wells
PUBLIC TOILETS	Off Teme Street and on Market Street

The 'Wells' in Tenbury Wells only came about after attempts in the mid- to late 19th century to capitalise on the mineral water in the town's wells. The restored Pump Rooms, dating from 1862, are its other legacy. Built late into the fashion for spas – with Malvern Wells, Droitwich Spa, Buxton Spa and the like already established – it failed to yield prolonged success.

Once upon a time Tenbury was known as 'the town in the orchard'. It has been estimated that between 1970 and 1997, 64 per cent of Britain's orchards were grubbed up. Why? Often it was because the grants system operated by the then Ministry of Agriculture, Fisheries and Food (MAFF) encouraged many farmers to grow cereals, not top fruit. Orchards on urban peripheries were, and still are, ripe for house-building. The cider industry is still thriving – witness the number of young orchards you may see while driving in the two counties – but some varieties of apple are verging on extinction.

One company trying to reverse that trend is the family-run business Frank P Matthews, fruit tree nursery growers for over 100 years, which sells more than 150 varieties of apples for eating, cooking and cider production. The company also has a commercial interest in tree heritage, being the supplier of rare species of fruit trees, not just apples but also plums, pears and cherries – all once a major part of the countryside in the area and throughout the country. Indeed, the company supplies varieties of fruit that were once unique to the different counties of Britain – apples from Cornwall, Surrey, Norfolk and Worcester as well as their 'native' Herefordshire.

Tenbury Wells still celebrates its connections to the apple orchards with an annual apple festival, AppleFest, held every October. However, the town is also noted for its large mistletoe festival, with many events during November and December. (You are likely to see large clumps of mistletoe hanging from the trees during your walk.) An annual wholesale auction is held every December for both mistletoe and holly, and it is deemed that the prices paid here will determine the cost of both commodities in the shops and markets around Christmas.

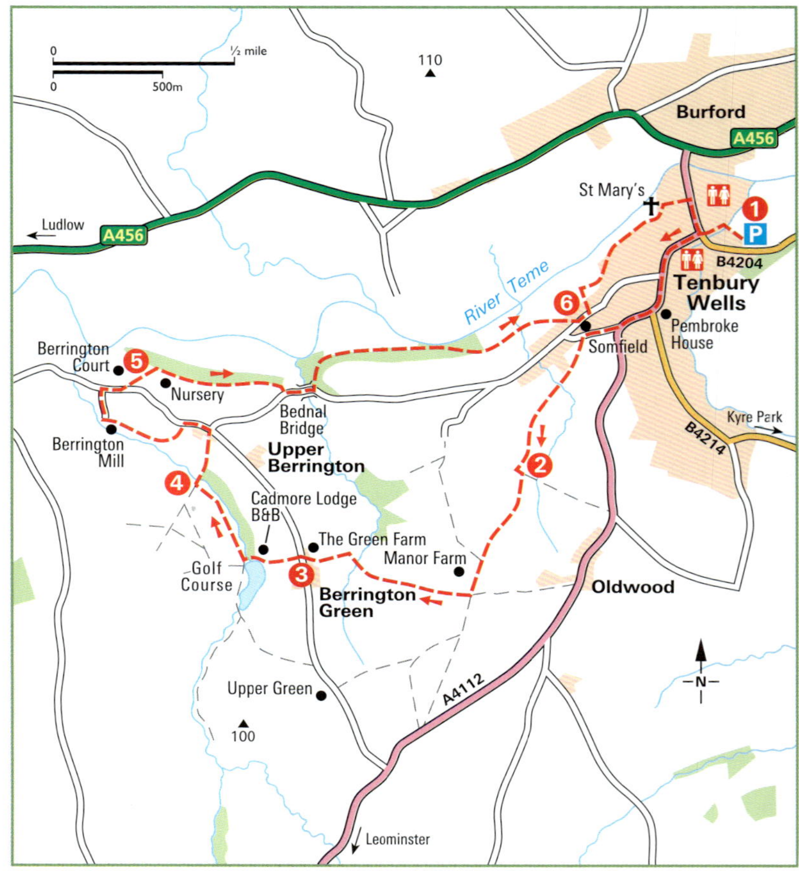

1. Leave the car park by the 'no exit' sign (for cars!). Over the bridge with railings turn left. At The Crow, turn right, then immediately left. Now walk through Tenbury Wells. Cross over beyond the black-and-white pub, Pembroke House, follow Oldwood Road but soon bear right signed 'Berrington'. After 200yds (183m), cross a stile on the left opposite the bungalow, Somfield. Go half right to another, walk on level ground, following power poles. Cross a ditch in a gateway by some willows. Go to the top left corner of a long field.

2. Turn left, then in 30yds (27m) right. Cross fields to join the driveway of Manor Farm. About 40yds (37m) beyond the bridge here turn right at a triple waymarker, and go down steps and across a planked ditch to a stile. Cross fields for 440yds (402m). Veer down and right to the left of a power pole, through a rusty gate, then across the field past two barns, keeping them on your left. Pass The Green's farmhouse to a minor road.

3. Take the footpath directly opposite, down a small, tussocky pasture. At the lakeside turn right, passing the Cadmore Lodge B&B. In the car park's far left corner cross a bridge beside a thatched mill house. Turn right along a gravel track, passing log cabins; within 400yds (366m) reach a junction.

4. Turn right. Around 50yds (46m) before farm buildings fork right, through a gate, to a handrail (overgrown) up to a garden gate. Pass to the right of the house, to a minor road T-junction. Turn left. In 170yds (155m) take the fingerpost left, up some steps. Cross this field diagonally. A path leads through trees to Berrington Mill. Turn right, up the lane, then right to the nursery (Frank P Matthew's Tree Shop) at Berrington Court.

5. Take the track before a house. Enter the nursery. Walk beside mind-boggling numbers of potted trees under glass (or plastic). Leave this gravel track where it cuts down through woodland, taking a stile ahead and right. A meadow leads to Bednal Bridge. Just beyond it take double gates into trees. Keep your line when this ample track runs out. Go up an abrupt bank, crossing a footbridge to do so, keeping out of the trees. It's now straightforward to the outskirts of Tenbury, guided by yellow waymarkers. Round the backs of gardens, emerge through a gate.

6. Turn left, but only for 20yds (18m). Take a hedge-hugging kissing gate, on the left. In the thistle-wrecked meadow, skirt right for 40yds (37m) to a grass track. Turn left, away from houses, for 40yds (37m) more. Turn right (a gate aperture is now behind you) to hit suburbia again. Turn left. Move left at 'No cycling' sign. Keep on the paved footpath, left of No. 14, soon beside tall garden fences. Emerging at the church, turn left. Opposite a church gate turn right, down Church Walk, to Teme Street and thence to the car park.

Where to eat and drink

There are plenty of options in Tenbury Wells, including pubs, tea rooms and takeaway's. At either end of Teme Road are The Crow, which has a beer garden, and The Bridge. On the route out you pass Pembroke House, which serves food and a range of ales.

What to see

No. 18 Teme Street (now an opticians) once housed Tenbury's most famous resident, yet he lived there for less than a year, struck down by tuberculosis when aged 30. Henry Hill Hickman, born in 1800, was a pioneer of anaesthetics, but never a practitioner (and only recognised posthumously), beyond experimenting with animals.

While you're there

About 3 miles (4.8km) southeast of Tenbury Wells is Kyre Park, a large private house, basically medieval with Elizabethan and Jacobean pieces bolted on. It is set in 32 acres (13ha) of landscaped gardens laid out by 'Capability' Brown in 1754, with five lakes, a medieval dovecote (resited in 1756), and a brick tithe barn from 1618. Only the gardens, are open to the public. Dogs, children and picnics in the grounds welcome. (Open daily 10am–5pm all year.)

28

FROME VALLEY: A WALK TO ST MARY'S CHURCH

DISTANCE/TIME	7 miles (11.2km) / 3hrs
ASCENT/GRADIENT	557ft (170m) / ▲
PATHS	Field paths, dirt tracks, lanes and minor roads
LANDSCAPE	Woodlands and rolling green fields
SUGGESTED MAP	OS Explorer 202 Leominster & Bromyard
START/FINISH	Grid reference: SO682515
DOG FRIENDLINESS	On lead near livestock
PARKING	St James' Church, Stanford Bishop
PUBLIC TOILETS	None on route
NOTES	The ruins of St Mary's Church are privately owned, and are currently being restored by the owner and English Heritage. Please observe any warning signs as the structure and surrounding graveyard may be unsafe.

This walk links two churches, both isolated from any significant settlement. St James' Church, at the start of the walk, has a hilltop position with pretty views of the Herefordshire countryside. St Mary's sits in a bend of the River Frome.

The stonework of St James' is Norman and 13th century. Several yew trees dominate the small circular churchyard, the mightiest of which is said to be 1,200 years old; inside, you'll see a certificate to this effect. Also here, nestling in a corner, is the strikingly well preserved wooden chair said to have been used by St Augustine in AD 603 when he met the British bishops of the Celtic church. In spring time the churchyard is carpeted with snowdrops, daffodils and bluebells and is a peaceful place to sit and enjoy the views on the return from your walk.

The village of Avenbury was mentioned in the Domesday Book and St Mary's Church was at its centre. The village has now disappeared, leaving just the odd farm, and the church is now isolated. Built in AD 840 and extended in Norman times, the church was closed in 1931 and now lies in ruins.

Now privately owned, the ruins are currently all but disguised by hoardings and fences displaying 'Danger – Keep Out' signs. Plans are in progress to stabilise this Scheduled Ancient Monument and Grade II listed building for future generations to enjoy. Of the church itself, only parts of the walls and a couple of Norman windows remain.

One of the oldest and most important churches in Herefordshire, St Mary's is believed to also be one of the most haunted. One of the bells, it is said, is to have rung out at the passing of vicars from both St Mary's Church and St Andrews in London. Several stories are connected with the building being haunted, including a phantom organist.

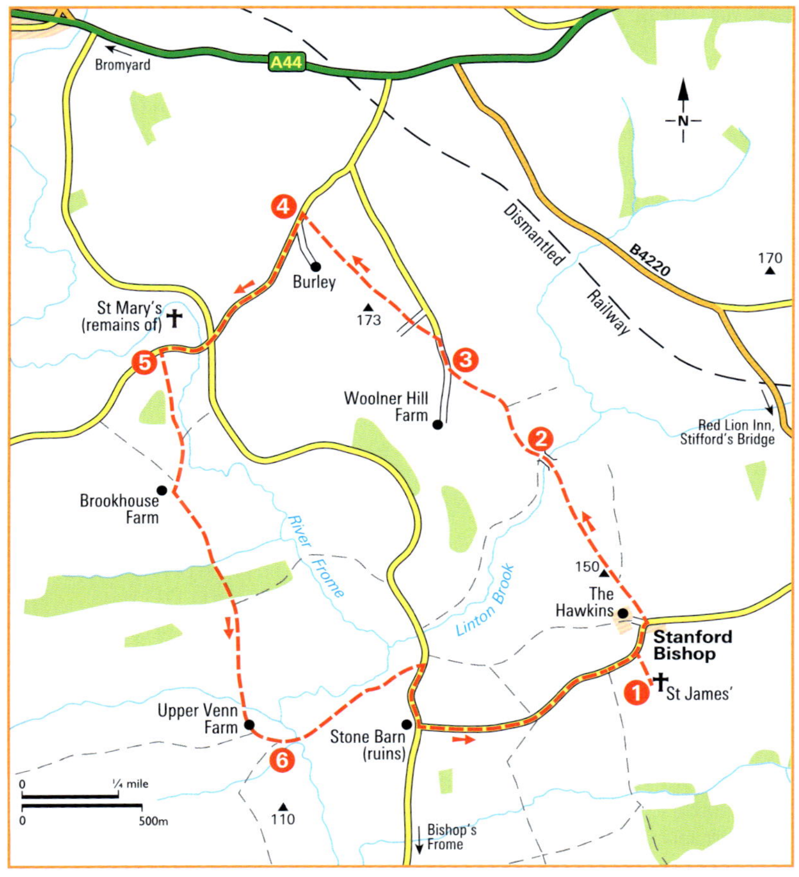

1. From the church, descend to a minor road and turn right. At the entrance to The Hawkins take a kissing gate, then follow waymarkers across a track to skirt this farm. Now head down the pastures to a stile with wooden steps. Keep ahead, descending very gently, for 200yds (183m), to cross a footbridge over the Linton Brook.

2. Cross the concrete breeze block stile, then turn left up the field-edge. Where two stiles span the hedge turn left (waymarked), resuming along the field-edge. At a cluster of gates below a power line go on to the tarmac above left.

3. To your left is a cattle grid and driveway to Woolner Hill Farm. Beside it are two gates – take the right-hand one. Use this grassy track for just 25yds (23m), then take the stile on the right here. Go diagonally, crossing a tarmac drive. Waymarkers are initially clear, following the line of telegraph poles. After several fields, reaching a telegraph pole at the top-left corner, angle right to walk beside and then through a line of trees, guided by a single hidden waymarker on a post. Pass the building, Burley, some 50yds (46m) to your left. Continue to reach a minor road.

4. Turn left. Go steadily down this gated road. About 150yds (137m) beyond the crossroads is the decayed avenue leading to the even more decayed church. Back on the lane, go 80yds (73m) further to a partially hidden stile on the left.

5. Skirt round the plantation of primarily ash trees. Join the driveway to Brookhouse Farm, following bespoke yellow arrows to a tall novelty signpost. Turn left to walk beside an orchard. Look for a wooden handrail and footbridge within 200yds (183m), switching the field boundary to your right. After 400yds (366m), having ascended through trees, keep pretty straight for a good 0.25 miles (400m). Pass in between the tall sheds of Upper Venn Farm.

6. Start down the driveway for 0.5 miles (800m), to a road. Turn right and in 175yds (160m) turn left opposite the remains of a stone barn. Continue along the road for 0.75 miles (1.2km) to reach the turning for St James' church.

Where to eat and drink

Five miles from Stanford Bishop, the Red Lion Inn at Stiffords Bridge, Cradley. Situated on the A4103, the pub is on the banks of the Cradley Brook with a riverside garden, home-cooked food and real ales.

What to see

A half-mile detour will take you to a bridge over the disused Bromyard to Worcester Railway. The track was closed to passengers in 1962 and dismantled in 1965 under the Dr Beeching Plan, although the overgrown route is still clearly in evidence. A one-mile stretch between Bromyard and the Linton Industrial Estate is now the Bromyard and Linton Light Railway.

While you're there

Don't miss a visit to the charming historic market town of Bromyard. The town is at the centre of the hop-growing industry, is a great place to browse local, independent shops and has a large collection of festivals throughout the year – including the Herefordshire Marmalade Festival.

29

EXPLORING THE FROME VALLEY

DISTANCE/TIME	4.75 miles (7.7km) / 2hrs 30min
ASCENT/GRADIENT	475ft (145m) / ▲
PATHS	Field paths, dirt tracks, lanes and minor roads, many stiles
LANDSCAPE	Orchards, woodlands and pasture in gently rolling hills
SUGGESTED MAP	OS Explorer 202 Leominster & Bromyard
START/FINISH	Grid reference: SO680502
DOG FRIENDLINESS	Good early on, but otherwise often among livestock
PARKING	Roadside just before grassy lane to Acton Beauchamp's church – please tuck in tightly
PUBLIC TOILETS	None on route

At first sight the Church of St Giles at Acton Beauchamp is unremarkable, sitting comfortably on a hillside. Parts of it are Norman, but it was largely rebuilt in 1819. However, if you move to the left of the main door you will see a doorway that leads into the tower. The lintel to this doorway is nothing less than a re-used ninth-century stone sculpture, depicting a bird, a lion, and probably a goat – there is nothing like this from the Anglo-Saxon period in Herefordshire.

Through the gate into the churchyard in Acton Beauchamp, a grassy path slants up to the church. Your eye may follow the shiny black line of the handrail that assists people to and from the church door, but right in front of you is an excellent specimen of a wild service tree. It must have been planted there. Wild service trees actually in the wild are relatively rare nowadays, although it is quite fashionable to plant them in urban settings. Their leaves are easily confused with those of a plane tree, but the latter's bark is very distinctive. It is rare for the seeds of the wild service tree to have the opportunity to germinate since they are eaten and, genetically, destroyed by wasps. (This is in contrast to the consumption of hawthorn berries by birds, for example, where the expulsion of the seed, intact, after digestion of its juicy berry coating, is an effective form of dispersal.) Academics are uncertain as to the significance of the name 'service'. Most likely it is a contorted Anglicisation of its Latin name Sorbus torminalis. Before multiple varieties of apples became available, wild service trees were grown in orchards because their fruits are edible. The dictionary says that a 'sorb' is a wild service tree, and that its fruits are called 'sorb-apples'. (In the southern counties of England they were called chequers.) Other less convincing theories are that 'service' derives from the Latin cervisia, meaning beer – not far from the modern Spanish cerveza – since the wild service fruits were fermented to make a beery drink, really as a predecessor to cyder. Alternatively, it could have some association with the

French word cerise (cherry), since, despite being a kiwi-fruit brown in colour, wild service fruits are comparable to cherries in size and shape.

In Stanford Bishop, St James' Church is similarly isolated, but has a hilltop position. Several yew trees dominate the churchyard, the mightiest of which is said to be 1,200 years old; inside, you'll see a certificate to this effect. Also here, nestling in a corner, is the strikingly well preserved, capacious wooden chair said to have been used by St Augustine in the year AD 603.

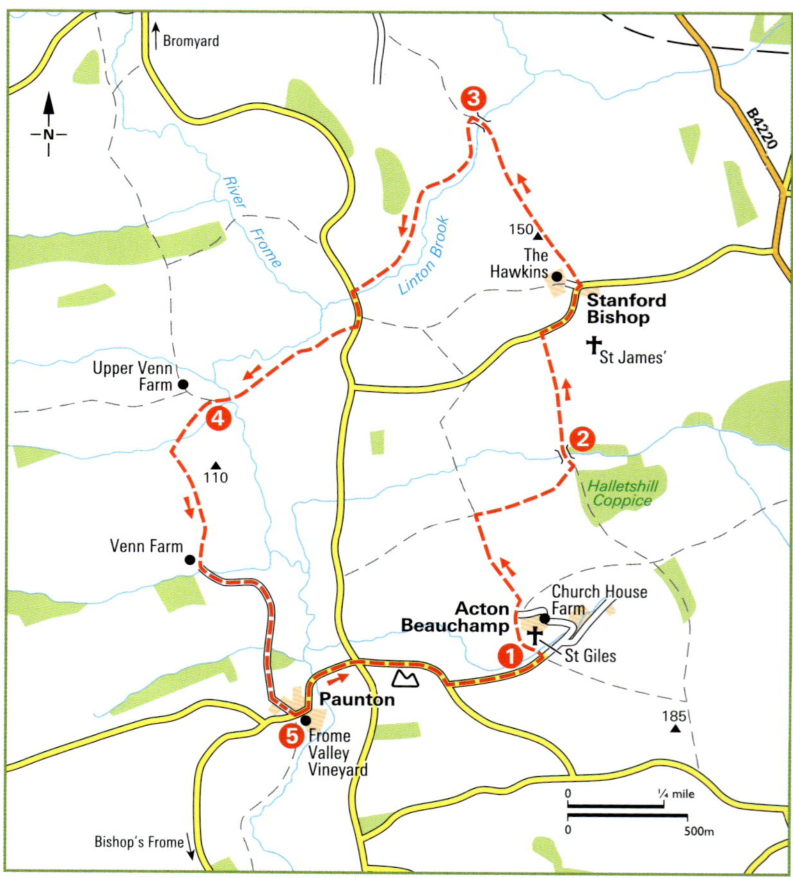

1. Leave the churchyard by an iron gate in the top corner. Ascend to a stile, then follow the line of poplars left along field. Leave by a stile at the first corner. Contour across the next field to a stile, then descend slightly to another, overgrown stile about 100yds (91m) right of a small solitary tree. Turn right, through a gate here, ascending by the field-edge. Keep this line, but, on seeing a dilapidated gate with a faded blue waymarker at a protruding corner of Halletshill Coppice, drop straight down left, finding wooden steps to a footbridge.

2. Now go straight up the bank. After the trees, keep the hedge on your right, through a gate to reach a minor road. Turn right (and to visit the church, right again). Return to the road and turn right. At the entrance to The Hawkins take a kissing gate, then follow way-markers across a track to skirt this farm. Now head down the pastures to a stile with wooden steps. Keep ahead, descending very gently, for 200yds (183m), to cross a footbridge over the Linton Brook.

3. Turn left, walking beside the Linton Brook for 0.6 miles (1km), to a road. Turn left for 160yds (146m). Turn right. Now the driveway to Upper Venn Farm runs for 0.5 miles (800m). Just before the first shed, turn left to a gate 50yds (46m) along the edge of the field.

4. Cross the field diagonally, to a gate in the left hedge. Turn left across a field, aiming slightly uphill, beside residual mature oaks. You'll find a stile beyond an electricity pole. Pick up a rough track to Venn Farm, passing alongside its long black barn. Admire the farm's cream walls and exposed timbers, then turn away, along the drive. Follow this down to the minor road.

5. Turn left, passing Paunton Court (home to the Frome Valley Vineyard) on a sharp bend. At the crossroads go straight over. As you climb this quite steep lane, the Church of St Giles comes into view. Take the first turning on the left to return to your car.

Where to eat and drink

A few miles to the south in Bishop's Frome, the Green Dragon specialises in cask conditioned real ales. Freshly cooked meals are available every day except Monday, as well as local ciders and home-cooked food. A few doors down, The Chase Inn serves reasonably priced, good food and beers.

What to see

As well as orchards, you'll see hop fields and, around Paunton, even vineyards on this walk. They belong to Frome Valley Vineyard. Established in 1992, the product of a modest 4 acres (1.6ha) goes into the making of three dry wines, one medium sweet and a rosé. Tours and tastings can be pre-booked to sample the wines.

While you're there

Nearby Bromyard is a 'black-and-white' market town.

A CIRCUIT FROM ASHPERTON

DISTANCE/TIME	7.75 miles (12.5km) / 3hrs 30min
ASCENT/GRADIENT	260ft (79m) / ▲
PATHS	Field and woodland paths, minor roads, many stiles
LANDSCAPE	Gently undulating, mixed farming, woodland, derelict canal
SUGGESTED MAP	OS Explorer 202 Leominster & Bromyard
START/FINISH	Grid reference: SO642415
DOG FRIENDLINESS	Close control near livestock and on minor roads
PARKING	St Bartholomew's Church, Ashperton
PUBLIC TOILETS	None on route

Unless you know where to look, the only hint of the Hereford and Gloucester Canal in the city of Hereford today is in the street named Canal Road, which led to the canal's western terminus. In the east the canal joined the River Severn at Over, just west of Gloucester. During the 1790s countless canal schemes were promoted, many of which hadn't a hope of making the fortunes promised to their investors. One such was the Hereford and Gloucester Canal. Started in 1793, it took until 1845 to link Hereford to the Severn near Gloucester. Coal, fertiliser, passenger boats and manufactured goods just didn't produce the income needed to keep the canal open. By the 1860s it was a dead duck; in 1881 it was partly reused as a railway south of Newent.

Records show that, typically, a lock keeper would be paid 14s per week but his employers would deduct 2s per week for rent. Lock cottages may have been rudimentary, but what could someone today earning, say, £350 per week rent for £50 per week? This brings to mind the old expression, 'the best place to put your money is in bricks and mortar' – house bricks, that is, not canal bricks.

Since the 1980s the Hereford and Gloucester Canal Trust has striven to restore the canal to its former glory. The Trust's greatest tangible achievements to date have been restoring the skew bridge at Monkhide, a section of canal at Yarkhill, and the Over Basin, across the border in Gloucestershire. Its greatest intangible achievement has been to win over public opinion, perhaps aided by the thriving canal leisure sector in adjacent Worcestershire, where almost as many people overnight on boats (13 per cent) as they do in bed-and-breakfast accommodation (14 per cent). In recent years the planning authorities were successfully lobbied in Hereford city. The service road to a new retail park in the north of the city – connecting Newtown Road and Burcott Road – includes a bridge that spans the course of the old canal, instead of cutting through it or filling it with hardcore or concrete. The Canal Trust is working hand-in-glove with Herefordshire Council to restore a 350yd (320m) stretch of derelict canal through Aylestone Park, just north of Hereford's centre.

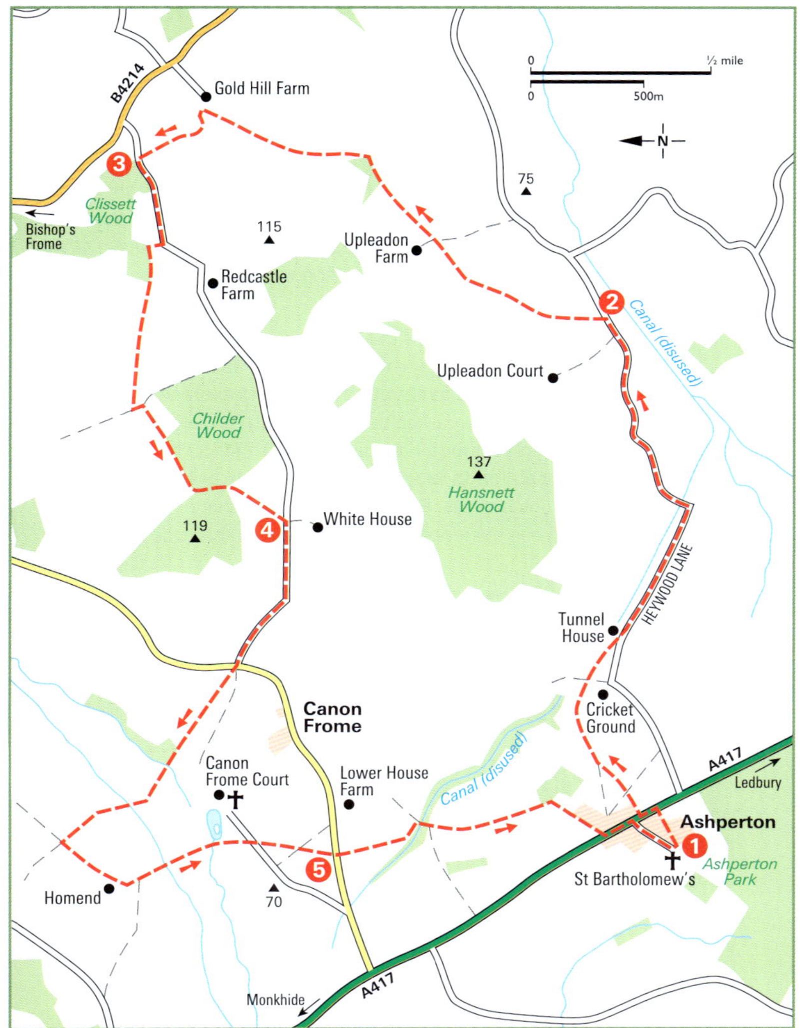

1. From the car park take the wide gate opposite beside the bungalow's hedge, following waymarks through to the A417. Turn left and cross the road. In 80yds (73m) take the enclosed path, right beside the driveway to The Rosary, leading into pasture. Continue past ancient oaks; in the second pasture a gate in the far-right corner leads to a cricket pitch. Cross to use the stile at the white sightscreen opposite. Keep ahead over a drive and past two oaks to a far corner stile into Heywood Lane. Turn left, passing Tunnel House. The lane crosses the old canal; continue for 0.5 miles (0.8km) to a stile on the left 100yds (91m) past Upleadon Court's driveway.

2. Cross the stile, then head diagonally right over several fields, aiming just right of the white farmhouse. Cross the drive and walk to the far-left field corner, near where three wide, waymarked gates lead to a field-side path. Use the stile just past the copse and head for the distant hillside tin barn at Gold Hill Farm. Pass behind this barn over two stiles, look left for the third, then turn up beside the rail-fence. Keep ahead off the corner to a gate 100yds (91m) left of the cottage.

3. Turn left on the lane and continue 440yds (400m) to a sharp left bend. Use the way-marked path here (left gate), initially beside woods. Climb a corner stile; then cross the huge field, in line with the right-end of woods on the ridgetop ahead. Search out and cross a railed footbridge below trees; turn left to the nearby field corner and then right up to the top wooded corner. Go left on the woodland track, crossing a rough road. At the far end head half-right down the field to the farm buildings and a lane.

4. Turn right to the T-junction in 800yds (730m). A waymarked footpath opposite heads for the far-right field corner and through a woodland strip. Beyond, head right of the oak to a footbridge, half-right to another near a pylon, then ahead through a waymarked hedge-gap. Turn left along the field's far edge. At the corner, look left for a handgate; then far-left of the old orchard for a corner stile. Work half-left to wide gates at a concrete bridge. Cross and advance along the line of trees. Beyond a gate, trees shelter a lake; cut half-right to tall elms, cross the fenced driveway, then another track to reach a road by a spinney.

5. Use the gates opposite, walk ahead past the hedge-end poplar to find the old canal. Go left to cross a stone bridge over the water. Walk along a nearby grassy strip up the new orchard; then bear right to the tall corner-oak and a stile. Walk to the offset copse corner ahead; here turn right, and in 250yds (228m) use a handgate to reach the nearby village hall. Turn left; then right for the church.

Where to eat and drink
The Trumpet Inn, 1.5 miles (2.4km) south of Ashperton at the junction of the A438 and A4172, serves good food and real ales, and has a pleasant garden.

What to see
Behind the cricket ground and Tunnel House are the tunnel portals at either end of the Ashperton Tunnel, on the disused Hereford and Gloucester Canal.

While you're there
The Hop Pocket Shopping Village at Bishop's Frome, about 5 miles (8km) north of Ashperton, is a collection of independent shops with a restaurant, café and also a food hall on the site.

31

WOOLHOPE AND SOLLERS HOPE

DISTANCE/TIME	6.5 miles (10.4km) / 3hrs
ASCENT/GRADIENT	525ft (160m) / ▲
PATHS	Country lanes, woodland tracks and fields, many stiles
LANDSCAPE	Hilly, with agriculture and woodland, extensive views
SUGGESTED MAP	OS Explorer 189 Hereford & Ross-on-Wye
START/FINISH	Grid reference: SO630346
DOG FRIENDLINESS	An exciting stretch, but limited off-lead opportunities
PARKING	At top of Glowson Wood Road
PUBLIC TOILETS	None on route

There's an other-worldly atmosphere to this compact area of south Herefordshire. The feeling of remoteness, even isolation, is compounded by the mere handful of lanes that penetrate the woods, fields and orchards here high above the River Wye. Tiny, perfectly formed Woolhope village lies in the heart of a natural amphitheatre. Woolhope Dome is a geological curiosity, a massive upfold of rock uplifted from a tropical seabed some 425 million years ago. Differential erosion has resulted in an almost continual rim of ancient limestone enclosing a hollowed-out saucer of sandstone and shale. Sharp, steep wooded slopes face into the bowl, while longer, gentler scarp slopes face the outside world. There are extraordinary views to the Cotswolds, Shropshire Hills and the Black Mountains from points on this walk; at other points an intimate, closed-in landscape dominates.

Built in the English Gothic style, St Michael's Church at secluded Sollers Hope was altered in 1887, when plaster was removed to reveal the well-preserved timbers of its barrelled roof. Also discovered was a 13th-century stone coffin lid, showing the coat of arms of the de Solers family, who owned the estate and gave the hamlet its name. According to local tradition, in the 14th century the influential Whittington family lived in a house near the churchyard (only the defensive motte now remains). Robert Whittington was instrumental in rebuilding the early church here; his younger brother Richard, possibly born here, became a wealthy merchant and Lord Mayor of London – Dick Whittington.

Near the end of the walk is enigmatic evidence of our distant ancestors. The first hedgerow bank you come to on a short detour off-route is an earthwork delineating Oldbury's northern boundary. Some people believe that while forts such as Oldbury functioned as defensive focal points in times of need, they were built to some extent for 'show', providing a cultural identity. They also provided Iron Age people protection from wild animals such as wolves, lynx and bears, which roamed the countryside 2,000 years ago.

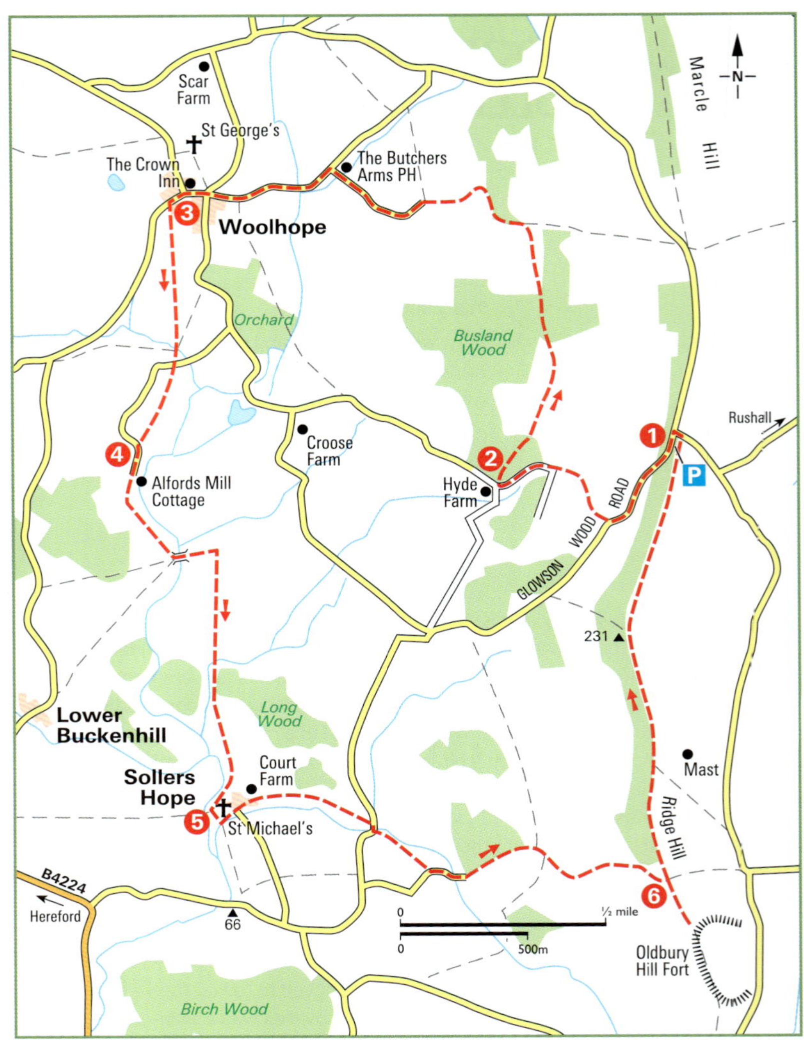

1. Walk down the lane for 500yds (457m). A fingerpost at a set-back pair of gates points right, down-field to a large barn. Turn left at this barn to reach Hyde Farm. Bend right but, within 60yds (55m), find a steep, waymarked track back-right into woods.

2. Follow this and ignore a left fork. As the track bends sharp left, cut to a wood-edge stile. Walk ahead across the huge field; at the distant top-left corner join the track into Busland Wood. Walk for 200yds (183m), again using a wood-edge stile where the track turns left. Go ahead for 250yds (229m) to a marker post above a small, dry valley. A few paces past this turn left on the field track; then join the woodland track beyond a gate. Keep down and left; the track becomes tarred before reaching The Butchers Arms pub. Turn left to Woolhope.

3. Pass The Crown Inn. In 328yds (300m), as the high wall ends, find a fingerpost on the left. Cross two meadows, then, in the third, use a stile in a dip on the right before the corner. Seek out a tree-shaded footbridge ahead; cross and head right past the willow, then left to a stile. Use the stile across the road; then head well right of the field-centre oak to a corner gate onto a lane.

4. Keep ahead, passing Alfords Mill Cottage. Beyond this, take a gate-side stile and cross the field to a stile. Turn left over it, then cross a footbridge. Follow the right-hand field edge for 130yds (119m) to a stile on the right. Walk the waist of the sloping field for 440yds (400m) to a tree-hidden stile in the dip. Keep ahead along the long pasture, looking for stiles and gates taking you well right of Court Farm to St Michael's Church at Sollers Hope.

5. Walk the paved path to the churchyard entrance. Use the handgate 70yds (64m) ahead; then walk right of the modern farm buildings. Past a stile, keep ahead between brook and orchard; then across another meadow aiming right of the stone barn to a lane. Turn left to the bend by the barn. Use the field gate, right, to walk beside a ponded stream; in the next pasture rise to a stile onto a lane. Turn left to the fork; here keep left up a rough woodside track. Keep right at the renovated barn, ascending a tree-lined stony track.

6. Shortly before the brow are wooden steps and a handgate on the left. To view Oldbury Hill Fort, turn right here, then retrace your steps. Climb the wooden steps and simply go straight along the field-side path for nearly 1.25 miles (2km), passing the radio and television mast and using several stiles/gates. At the lane turn left twice to find the car park.

Where to eat and drink

Just outside Woolhope is The Butchers Arms, while in the village centre is The Crown Inn. Both pubs major on local produce and stock locally brewed beers and ciders (The Crown in particular), and are family and dog-friendly.

What to see

The Woolhope Dome is a stronghold of traditional cider apple orchards. Recent years have seen a resurgence of 'farmhouse' cider – and perry, made from pears – with small producers supplying a discerning market. Each May and October the Big Apple festival is held in nearby Putley, but if you can't wait that long then visit Weston's Cider Mill in neighbouring Much Marcle, or seek out Broome Farm, near Ross-on-Wye, for a terrific introduction to real cider and perry.

While you're there

At Brockhampton, just above Fownhope, is the memorable 1902 All Saints Church, built in the Arts and Crafts style. A stunning mix of thatch and pseudo-Norman architecture, with wooden belfry, cedarwood tiles and simple, inspiring furnishings, it contrasts sharply with the area's other churches. There's some wonderful needlecraft here, too.

32

A TOUR OF ROSS-ON-WYE

DISTANCE/TIME	4 miles (6.4km) / 2hrs
ASCENT/GRADIENT	500ft (150m) / ▲
PATHS	Suburban streets, woodland and riverside paths
LANDSCAPE	Classical town built on hill overlooking river
SUGGESTED MAP	OS Explorer 189 Hereford & Ross-on-Wye
START/FINISH	Grid reference: SO582239
DOG FRIENDLINESS	Limited off-lead opportunities
PARKING	Wilton Road car park on B4260 between Wilton Bridge and Ross-on-Wye
PUBLIC TOILETS	Croft Court in town centre and in park alongside river

Although born in 1637 at Dymock in neighbouring Gloucestershire, the name of John Kyrle is as synonymous with Ross-on-Wye as William Shakespeare is with Stratford-upon-Avon. After studying, but failing to qualify as a lawyer, Kyrle settled to live in Ross, in a house overlooking the market place. Kyrle succeeded to a modest inheritance, which included a farm, but rather than indulge in an extravagant lifestyle, he devoted both his time and money to the betterment of his community. He supported many worthy causes, such as child education and improving the environment and amenities by planting trees, setting out a park in which he installed a public fountain supplying clean water to the townspeople. Kyrle employed his legal training in mediating local disputes, in an effort to save the combatants expensive court action, but was as happy to work alongside the labourers on his farm. He lived until the ripe old age of 87 and was buried within St Mary's Church. His achievements inspired the founding of the 19th-century Kyrle Society, formed to 'Bring Beauty Home to the People'.

There is a tradition that St Mary's was a Saxon foundation, although the present building has its origins in the late 13th century. Inside is an impressive collection of funerary monuments to the Rudhalls, curiously crowded together in a small space that was originally a family chantry chapel. The Rudhalls were also benefactors of the town; in 1575, William and his wife Mary rebuilt the picturesque row of almshouses in nearby Church Road, which had been founded some 200 years previously. The cross standing in the churchyard was erected as a memorial to the 315 people of the town who died during an outbreak of plague in 1637.

The market square is dominated by the sandstone-columned market hall, built during the later part of the 16th century. The open space below the arches would have housed trades, while the upper room served the Manor Court. It has since been used for a variety of purposes including a school, library, council chamber and ballroom. It now houses the tourist information centre and a small exhibition area. The impressive building behind it, now a shop, was John Kyrle's house.

Ross has yet another claim to fame: it was the birthplace of English tourism. In 1745, the Rector, Dr John Egerton began organising boat trips to admire the impressive scenery of the River Wye. The area later gained greater popularity when William Gilpin published *Observations of the River Wye and Several Parts of South Wales &c.*, and the troubles in continental Europe encouraged the well-to-do to travel at home rather than abroad.

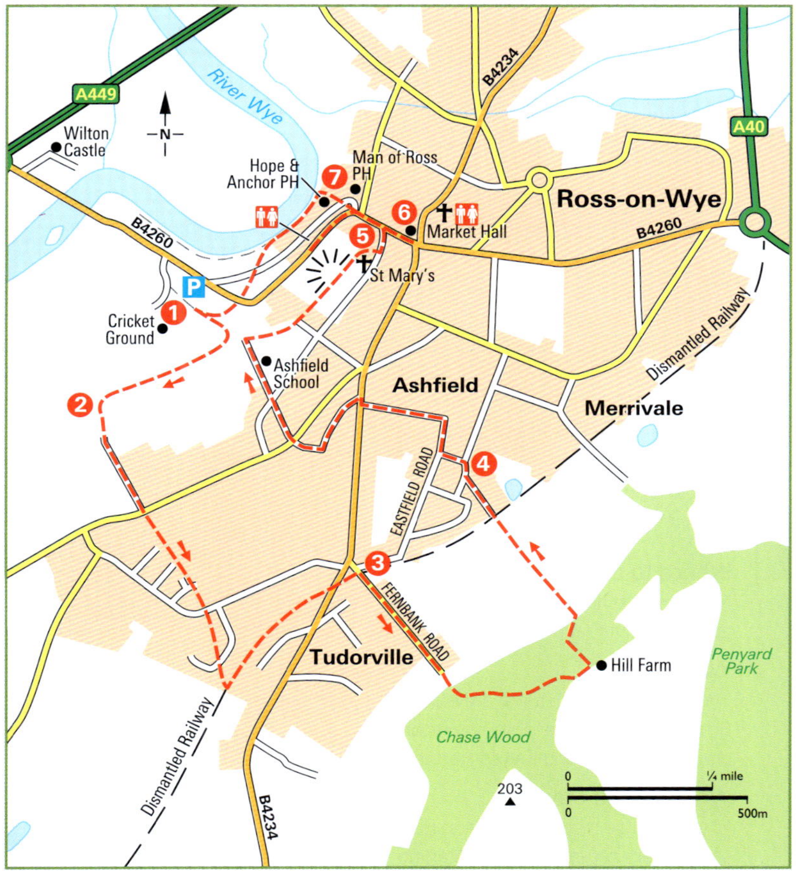

1. At the far corner of the car park, behind a skatepark, look for a path across a footbridge into trees. Bear left up a steep bank to a junction. Follow a hand-railed path right, shortly emerging to walk on at the edge of a couple of fields. Approaching the corner, fork right down to a sunken track.

2. Climb left to continue on a hedged path. Coming out on to a lane, go left to a road. Take the path opposite, which runs between house gardens, later crossing three streets in succession to arrive at a broad track, once the Ross and Monmouth Railway. Go left, shortly meeting a main road. Cross to a path opposite that skirts a playground to reach Fernbank Road.

3. To the right, beyond the houses, the path degrades to a track rising into Chase Wood. At the top by Hill Farm, bear left to a waymarked gate. Through it, fork left but at the next split, stay ahead, the path now dropping steeply. At the bottom, go right on a broader path that soon dips to a junction. Bear left through a kissing gate and follow the field edge. At the far side, re-cross the disused railway and walk out, continuing along a short street to Merrivale Lane.

4. Opposite, diagonally right, a narrow footpath leads to Eastfield Road. Go right and then first left into the Avenue. At the end, turn right and immediately left down Ashfield Crescent. At a crossroads, swing right into Palmerston Road. Keep ahead over the next junction into Redhill Road. Carry on beyond Ashfield School along a wooded track to a barrier and go right beside the playing field. Crossing the end of a lane, the path continues into St Mary's churchyard. Walk forward then wind right and left, passing the walled Prospect (a superb viewpoint) to round the church.

5. Passing a stone cross, leave by the northeast gate, walking past 14th-century almshouses to the bottom of Church Street. To the right is the Market Hall Visitor Centre and, just beyond, John Kyrle's House.

6. Return along High Street past Church Street and go left into St Mary's Street to find the Gazebo, part of mock-Gothic town walls constructed in 1833. Return to continue left along High Street. Cross the main road to the Man of Ross and walk down Wye Street. At the bend, keep ahead down steps, crossing the Hope and Anchor car park to a riverside path.

7. Follow the path left 200yds (183m) to the canoe launch and go left to the road. Cross to the grass opposite and bear right past a bandstand to a twin-arched bridge, through which is the car park.

Where to eat and drink
Ross-on-Wye has plenty of options. On the walk are the Man of Ross Inn, above the river, and The Hope & Anchor, beside the river.

What to see
The architectural historian Pevsner called the Italianate Baptist chapel in Broad Street 'very terrible', yet its architect, G C Haddon, also designed chapels at Dulas and Ewyas Harold.

While you're there
You should go inside the Market Hall, which occupies the prime centre spot. Before returning to your car, go a little further along the riverside to Wilton Bridge. Built in 1597, it was strengthened with concrete ties in 1914. A public footpath circumnavigates the remains of nearby 12th-century Wilton Castle.

AA
★★★
Hotel
The King's Head Hotel
ROSS -ON- WYE
TURKISH RESTAURANT & MEZE BAR
01989 566 637
FULLY LICENCED
Ross
ARTS AND CRAFTS
COURTYARD

OVER COPPET HILL

DISTANCE/TIME	8.5 miles (13.7km) / 4hrs
ASCENT/GRADIENT	900ft (275m) / ▲ ▲
PATHS	Quiet lanes, riverside meadows, woodland paths
LANDSCAPE	River valley and hill top views
SUGGESTED MAP	OS Explorer OL14 Wye Valley & Forest of Dean
START/FINISH	Grid reference: SO575196
DOG FRIENDLINESS	Dogs are welcome in the castle grounds and elsewhere but should be kept on a lead.
PARKING	Goodrich Castle pay-and-display car park open daily; free for English Heritage members
PUBLIC TOILETS	None on route

The name 'Coppet Hill' is a fairly recent introduction to a hill with an Iron Age presence. In the 13th century the hill was named, 'Coppyngwode' and, latterly, 'Coppet Wood Hill', each one referring to its tree-lined status and use as a coppice.

Once belonging to the manor that is now the village of Goodrich, Coppet Hill has also received Roman interest, with two known settlements either side of the main ridge. Both a hoard of Roman coins and a bronze dodecagon gaming piece have been found on the Hill. Born in 1768, Joshua Crystall began work as a china painter in the Staffordshire Potteries but found the work too repetitive and finally gained admission to the Royal Academy School of Art. In 1805 he was a founding member of the Society of Painters in Watercolours and gave the first public exhibition of his works; latterly he became the first President of the Society. He moved to a house in Goodrich at the foot of Coppet Hill in 1822 and spent many happy years there painting local residents in rustic scenes, such as 'A Cottage on the side of Symond's Rock' and 'Coppet Hill Fern Burners'.

The Courtfield Estate owns much of the land through which the walking route follows. Having belonged, in the main, to the Vaughan family since the 17th century, the estate and farm is run on sustainable, organic principles, and has won awards for its outstanding contribution to conserving and enhancing the landscape.

A herd of organic Hereford cattle often graze the large areas of watermeadows through which the walk passes, living outdoors all year round and entirely pasture fed. Originally from Herefordshire, the Hereford is one of Britain's finest native beef breeds and is renowned for the excellent quality of meat it produces. The breed has been exported around the world because of this. Its characteristic red with a white face makes the breed very distinctive. Some of the Herefords at the Courtfield Estate are of the British poll Hereford strain, a hornless variant known for its docile temperament.

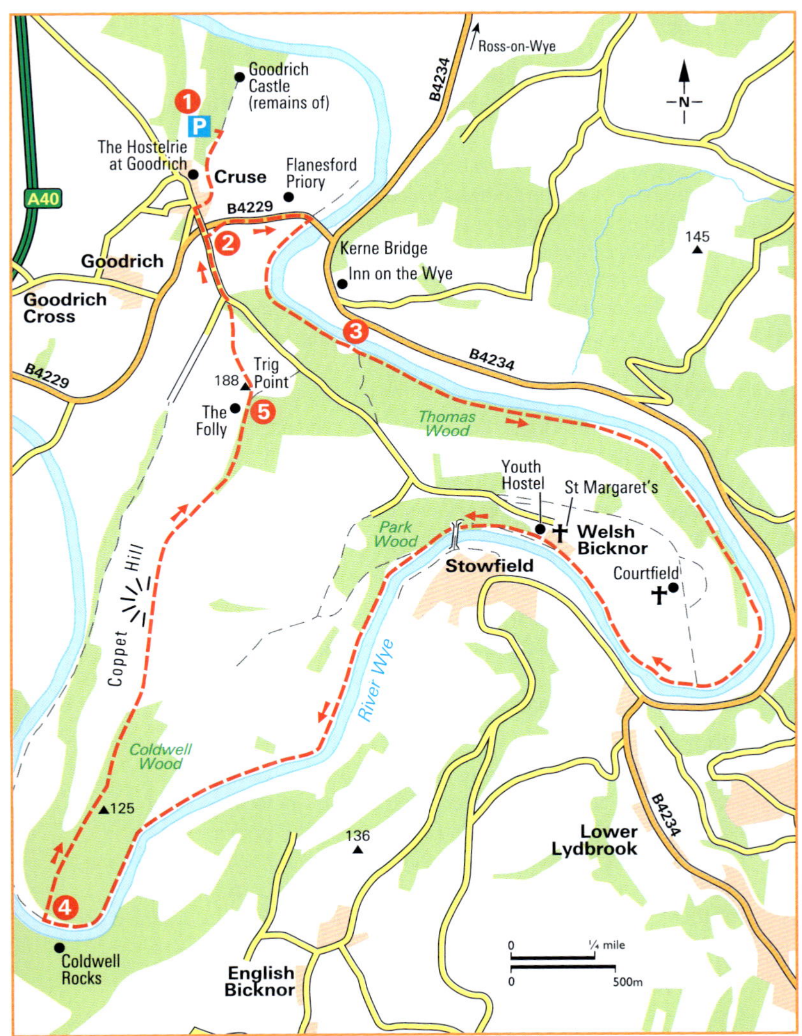

1. Walk down Castle Lane to the village and turn left towards Courtfield and Welsh Bicknor. Follow the lane to a bridge across the B4229.

2. By a fingerpost to Kerne Bridge, cross a stile on the left and descend steps to the main road. Follow it right past Flanesford Priory, founded by Augustinian monks in the 14th century. Today, the restored ruin is run as a self-catering accommodation. Immediately before the bridge, built in 1828, drop down steps on the right and pass through a small metal gate to follow a signposted riverside path at the edge of a field. At the far end, pass into trees and climb a few steps, the way shortly resuming beside the Wye.

3. Ignore a later path signed off right back up to Goodrich and continue along the riverbank. In passing, notice the stone abutments on both banks, all that remains of a demolished bridge that carried the Ross and Monmouth Railway.

The line opened in 1873, crossing the river three times and passing through two tunnels. Carry on beside the river through Thomas Wood emerging at the far side to continue at the edge of long, waterside meadows. Eventually the river sweeps into a tight bend and passing through a gap in a hedge, continue by the river.

4. Keep following the river – the border between Herefordshire and Gloucestershire – through Coldwell Wood by the river. Just beyond a reclining willow. Strike up beside the line of trees to a stile at the edge of the wood and follow a steadily climbing path along the ridge of Coppet Hill. Many of the trees were formerly coppiced to produce a regular crop of poles. These were primarily used for charcoal production to fuel the bloomeries of the Forest of Dean's iron industry. The woodland thins higher up, opening views to the west. Keep right at successive forks and then ignore a crossing, before tackling a final short pull to the folly at the top of the hill.

5. Walk on beyond, bearing left at a fork to descend past the trig column. The narrowing path steepens into more trees. Watch for successive waymarks guiding you left and then right, the path becoming stepped as it winds below a rock outcrop to meet a junction of lanes. Carry on downhill, shortly reversing your outward steps to Goodrich.

Where to eat and drink

Inn on the Wye, on the eastern side of Kerne Bridge. A lovely inn overlooking the River Wye and Goodrich Castle with light lunches, Sunday roasts and evening meals. Accommodation too.

What to see

Stop for a moment by the 'reclining willow' prior to turning into the woodland (at Point 4) and look across the river, where you'll see a collection of craggy rocks peering out of the trees. These are known as Coldwell Rocks and were used as a location in the 1996 film *Shadowlands*, based on the life of author C S Lewis. A little further on along the riverbank is the internationally renowned Symonds Yat Rock. On the other side of the river is Gloucestershire.

While you're there

Hire a kayak or canoe from Wye Pursuits for a gentle paddle on the River Wye. You'll see and pass the landing stage while walking, on the opposite side of the river, just south of Kerne Bridge.

THE RIVER WYE AND AROUND COPPET HILL

DISTANCE/TIME	8 miles (12.9km) / 4hrs
ASCENT/GRADIENT	755ft (230m) / ▲ ▲
PATHS	Quiet lanes, riverside meadows, woodland paths, several stiles
LANDSCAPE	Much-photographed river valley
SUGGESTED MAP	OS Explorer OL14 Wye Valley & Forest of Dean
START/FINISH	Grid reference: SO575196
DOG FRIENDLINESS	Dogs are welcome in the castle grounds and elsewhere but should be kept on a lead
PARKING	Goodrich Castle pay-and-display car park open daily, free for English Heritage members
PUBLIC TOILETS	None on route

The well-preserved remains of Goodrich Castle date from the 12th and 13th centuries, replacing an early 12th-century structure. Some gory traps and ruses kept would-be intruders away, among them a tunnel beneath the gate tower that could be blocked by a portcullis; doomed attackers would then be scalded with hot water from above or burned to death with molten lead.

The castle succumbed to Parliamentarians in 1646 during the Civil War, led by Colonel John Birch, who had successfully attacked the city of Hereford the previous December. The story goes that the colonel's niece, Alice, and Charles Clifford, her lover, fled from the battle, only to meet their deaths trying to cross the River Wye. So watch out for their ghosts on a phantom horse. Goodrich Castle is open daily from spring until autumn, but during winter may be closed midweek.

After the death of his mother, the future Henry V lived for a while at the manor house, which subsequently became known as Courtfield. During the 17th century, the manor was held by the Vaughans, a staunch Catholic family who refused to follow the Anglican faith. In 1651, their recusancy led to the confiscation of their estates, which were given to Phillip Nicholas of Llansoy. The manor became a detached parish of Monmouthshire and thus acquired its title of Welsh Bicknor, although since 1844 it is now back in England.

The rectory, constructed when St Margaret's Church was rebuilt in 1859, is now a YHA hostel, an organisation founded in 1931 to provide simple, affordable accommodation for young people, encouraging them to travel and gain new experiences.

The area around Symonds Yat attracts film buffs wanting to see the locations used for Richard Attenborough's film, *Shadowlands*. It was based on the life of C S Lewis, author of *The Chronicles of Narnia*.

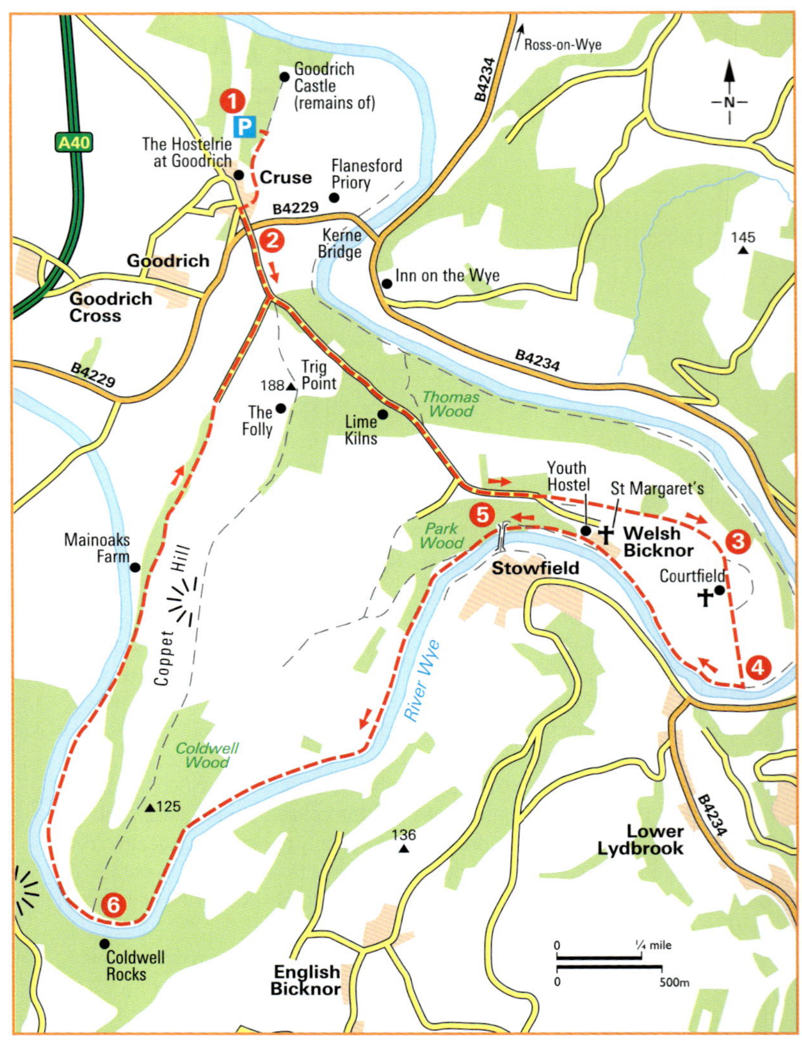

1. Walk back down Castle Lane to the village and turn left towards Courtfield and Welsh Bicknor. Follow the lane to a bridge across the B4229.

2. Keep going along the lane, taking the left branch at a fork. Occasional views open to Goodrich Castle and Kerne Bridge before you break from the trees onto the Courtfield estate. Keep left where the lane later splits, shortly reaching another fork (Youth Hostel signed off right). Continue ahead here on a track towards Home Farm and Glenwye. After 0.5 miles (800m), by the high walls of the estate garden, the track divides again.

3. After 70yds (64m), before a second fork, take a gate on the right. Follow the edge of pasture to the right, passing through an opening to carry on in a second field. Leave through a gate just left of the corner and head downfield beside the hedge to the river. Otherwise follow the original line of the footpath

and keep with the main track ahead past Courtfield's outlying buildings. Through a gate, continue downhill to the Wye.

4. Turn right and follow the river downstream for 0.5 miles (800m) to Welsh Bicknor, where St Margaret's Church and its former rectory, now a youth hostel, overlook the Wye. Keeping to the riverside path, another 0.25 mile (400m) walk brings you to a bridge that once carried the Ross and Monmouth Railway through the valley. Over to the right, past a wartime pill-box, is the southern portal of the Coppet Hill tunnel, in use until the line closed in 1965.

5. Return to the river, and carry on through Park Wood, emerging beyond into meadows. Further on the way, the route enters Coldwell Wood, where on the right a railed enclosure contains a memorial to 16-year-old John Warre, who drowned here in 1804. Beyond the trees, walk on at the edge of another meadow to a redundant stile beside a fallen willow.

6. Continue on beside the river, which sweeps to the right below the dramatic viewpoint of Symonds Yat Rock. Becoming a field track, the way shortly enters woodland again. At the far side, stick with the track towards Mainoaks Farm. Just before the entrance, climb a stile on the right into the Coppet Hill Common Local Nature Reserve. A path slants up across the wooded hillside, breaking from the trees above Rockland Cottage. A stony track leads past more cottages to meet the lane by which you first climbed out of Goodrich.

Where to eat and drink
A visitor centre beside the castle car park serves hot food and drinks. The Hostelrie at Goodrich serves coffee, tea and lunchtime bar food.

What to see
Around 100yds (91m) to the right from the first junction on the Courtfield estate are some partly covered lime kilns, marked by a clump of trees growing on top.

While you're there
For a 35-minute river cruise, try Kingfisher Cruises at Symonds Yat East, where you'll also find the Saracen's Head (a former cider mill) and the hand ferry. The aMazing Hedge Puzzle and Wye Valley Butterfly Zoo are at Symonds Yat West.

ON THE WYE AT HEREFORD

DISTANCE/TIME	4 miles (6.4km) / 1hr 45mins
ASCENT/GRADIENT	180ft (55m) / ▲
PATHS	Farmland and woodland paths, old railway bed, several stiles
LANDSCAPE	Orchards, arable fields and riverside pastures
SUGGESTED MAP	OS Explorer 189 Hereford & Ross-on-Wye
START	Grid reference: SO470414
FINISH	Grid reference: SO503400
DOG FRIENDLINESS	Some arable fields, but many cattle beside Wye
PARKING	Several pay-and-display car parks in city centre, including West Street and Friars Street
PUBLIC TOILETS	None on route but several in city
NOTES	Bus routes 71, 71B and 446 leave Hereford along Eign Street (A438); ask for Hereford Garden Centre

Percy and Fred Bulmer, the founders of H P Bulmer, were brought up in Credenhill, where their father was rector. His education interrupted by asthma, Percy lacked qualifications and decided to set up in business on his own. In 1887, inspired by his father – a contributor to the Herefordshire Pomona, a beautifully illustrated catalogue listing the varieties of apples and pears – and taking his mother's advice to select a business in 'eating or drinking – activities that do not go out of fashion', Percy tried his hand at cider-making. It must have been a promising start, for his brother Fred, having completed a degree in history at Cambridge, turned down an opportunity to tutor the children of the King of Siam (present-day Thailand) and joined his business.

With a loan from their father, the brothers purchased land beside the city for a new cider mill and began fermenting the cider in 100-gallon casks. Cider production was still not mechanised and the brothers often worked 16-hour days, sleeping overnight in the mill. The outcome of their labours was often uncertain, too, for the natural yeasts could unpredictably turn the brew sour. Their business also depended upon the annual harvest, which in 1890 was disastrous, forcing them to buy Somerset apples at inflated prices. Their fortunes began to turn, however, when a university friend of Fred's, Dr Herbert Durham, isolated the wild yeast necessary to produce a pure cider. The brothers started to expand, mechanising the process and installing tanks to store excess stock as insurance against a poor harvest. The also began planting their own orchards, developing suitable varieties that they could supply to the local growers. Marketing their product was a challenge, since much of Britain had little or no tradition of drinking cider. Fred began travelling the country, taking their product to agricultural shows, but soon realised that to succeed, they had to create a new demand. Publicity was expensive, but the brothers began trawling directories for appropriate contacts, targeting them with specially produced informative pamphlets. They accumulated a list of some 20,000 names and the business generated finally enabled them to become a 'wholesale only' company. Their famous Woodpecker brand was first sold in 1896.

During his schoolless childhood, Percy taught himself French and as the business blossomed took himself to France, where he learned from the cider-makers of Épernay, found out about new bottling techniques and discovered the methode champagnoise. This he subsequently employed to make a champagne cider, which the brothers marketed as Pomagne. Bulmers continued to grow and was granted a Royal Warrant in 1911. It finally became a public company in 1970. Now part of Heineken, it remains a top brand and is still based in Hereford. Fred's book *Early Days of Cider Making*, published in 1937, is available from the Cider Museum. Written in the language of its day, it is a delightful read, a story of sweat, endeavour, opportunism and good fortune.

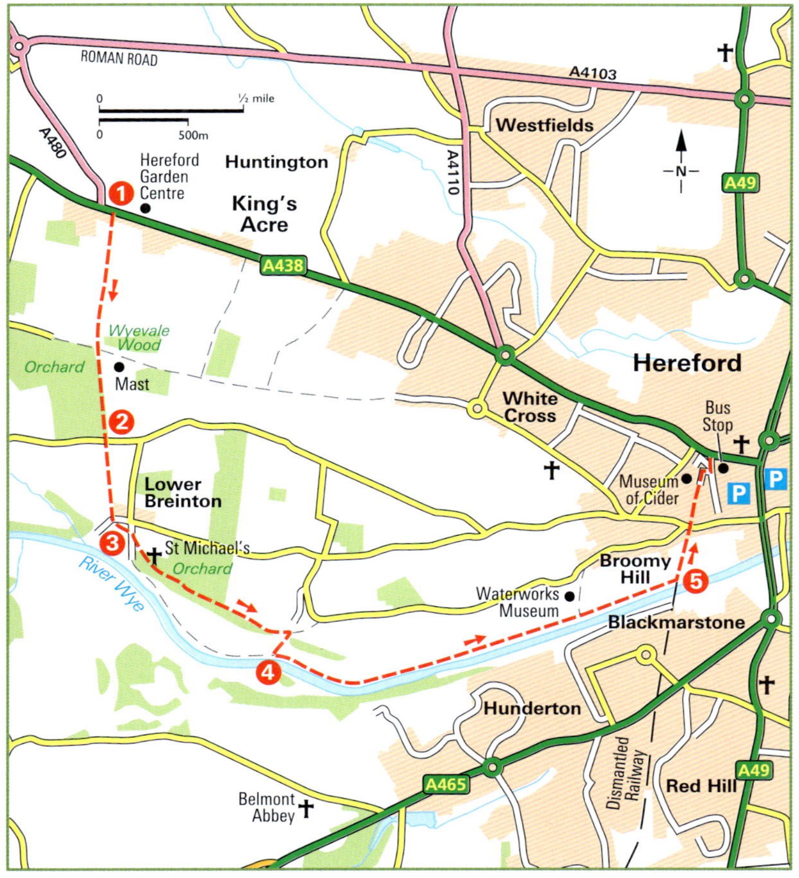

1. From Hereford Centre (Eign Street) take the bus to Hereford Garden Centre, King's Acre. From the bus stop a hedged bridleway leaves the main road. Follow it to its end at the corner of Wyevale Wood. Cross another bridleway to a small gate opposite and continue along the right-hand edge of successive fields beside orchards, eventually coming out onto a lane.

2. Cross and go over a stile into the field opposite. Carry on with the boundary now on your left down two fields to exit by a kissing gate in the corner. Swing right beside a house to emerge onto another lane.

3. Cross to a small metal gate opposite and strike half-left in an old orchard. Beyond a second gate, skirt a tennis court to a lane. Through a kissing gate opposite, continue the same line across another orchard to a stile. Keep going to join a green path that passes to the right of St Michael's Church and graveyard. After another kissing gate, walk on above a wooded bank past the foot of the extensive vicarage garden and then orchards beyond. Keep going at the edge of a field, passing through a gate partway along to continue within a narrow pasture. At a fork beside a large tree, branch right downhill to a kissing gate and walk beside the hedge down to the River Wye.

4. Go left over a gated bridge and follow the river downstream towards Hereford. After 1 mile (1.6km), a track on the left leads to the Waterworks Museum. Otherwise, carry on along the riverbank to Hunderton Bridge.

5. Climb steps beside the bridge onto the course of the old railway and go left. After passing beneath a road bridge, keep left at a fork and wind past buildings to emerge on a supermarket car park. Follow the path ahead, which joins a street past the Museum of Cider. To return to Eign Street where you caught the bus out of town, carry on a little further to a mini-roundabout and go left.

Where to eat and drink

Although famous for cider, Herefordshire is also proud of its (small) breweries. In the city, at No. 88 St Owen's Street is The Victory pub and Hereford Brewery. Bill's Kitchen is a café in All Saints church that's moved with the times.

What to see

From the riverbank you'll see an Italianate water tower, part of the Waterworks Museum. Beside it is a little railway line, run by the Hereford Society of Model Engineers (open some Sundays).

While you're there

Visit the Cider Museum or the child-friendly Waterworks Museum, which combines the history of drinking water with the engineering of Victorian steam pumping engines (check for opening times).

THE HISTORIC CITY OF HEREFORD

DISTANCE/TIME	3 miles (4.8km) / 1hr 30min
ASCENT/GRADIENT	Negligible
PATHS	City streets, riverside path and tracks
LANDSCAPE	Riverside and city
SUGGESTED MAP	OS Explorer 189 Hereford & Ross-on-Wye
START/FINISH	Grid reference: SO510403
DOG FRIENDLINESS	Busy city streets are not great for dogs, which should be kept on a lead
PARKING	Garrick House long-stay, pay-and-display multi-storey car park, Widemarsh Street
PUBLIC TOILETS	Blackfriars Street, Castle Green, East Street and Union Street
NOTES	Care needed crossing busy junctions

The old city of Hereford overlooked the Wye from its northern bank and, as its name suggests, was an important river crossing. A Celtic see from the sixth century, it has seen much conflict both as a Marches town (established by the Normans to subdue the Welsh) and during the English Civil War (1642–1651). Founded around 1050 by the Anglo-Saxons to repel the Welsh, its castle was rebuilt by the Normans and remained in use until the 17th century. All that survives of the fortifications are fragmentary city walls and part of the moat by Castle Green.

The city's prosperity grew out of the surrounding land, where apple orchards and cattle production thrived. The famous Hereford breed, developed at the end of the 18th century for beef production, is celebrated in a life-size bronze statue of a bull beside the Old House in High Town. Apples grown in orchards scattered across the county's sheltered vales are largely used for cider production, and both Bulmers and Westons are based in the city. Herefordshire has even adopted an apple for its logo.

Largely unscathed during World War II, Hereford's older buildings make an attractive tour. At the city's heart, the cathedral occupies the site of the first stone church, built over the tomb of St Ethelbert around 825. Destroyed when the city was sacked by the Welsh in 1056, it was later rebuilt by the Normans, a process that took some 70 years to complete. It has seen many changes during the last 1,000 years, including the disastrous collapse of the western tower in 1786. Inside are the famous 14th-century Mappa Mundi, with Jerusalem placed at the centre of the world, and the Chained Library. Other buildings to seek out are St Xavier's Church, its entrance flanked by imposing Greek Doric columns, and the Museum and Art Gallery, both in Broad Street.

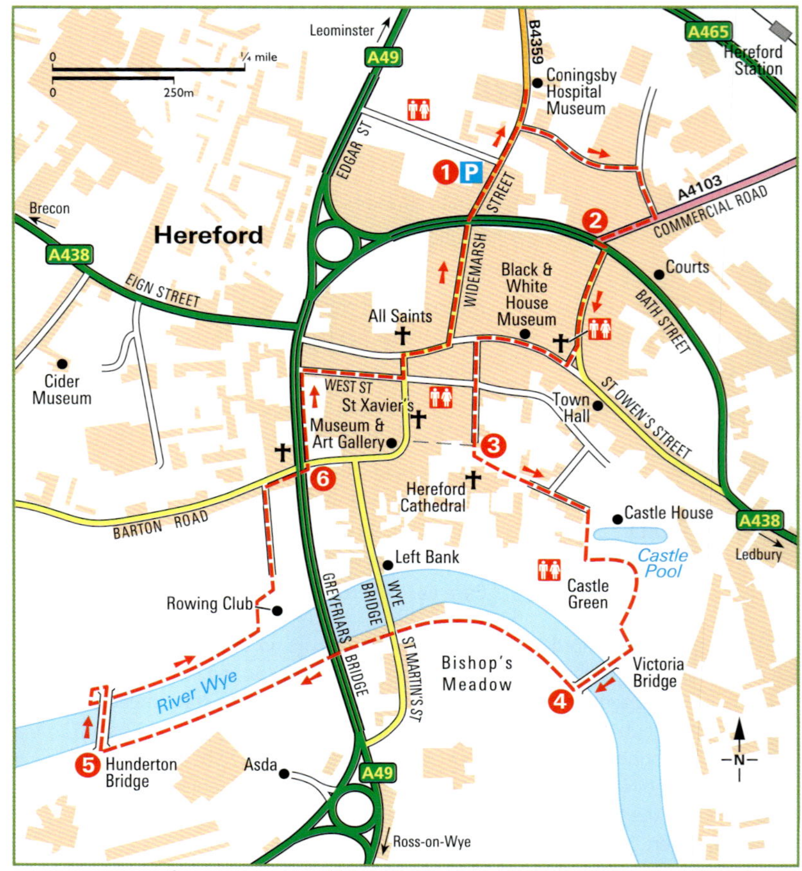

1. Turn left out of the car park and walk up Widemarsh Street to the Coningsby Hospital Museum, housed in a hospital built in 1614 for ex-servicemen beside a Black Friars' monastery. Its remains and a preaching cross can be seen in the secluded rose garden behind. Briefly retrace your steps and go left into Coningsby Street. At its end, Canal Road to the left led to the triple canal basin terminus of the Hereford and Gloucester Canal. The route, however, continues to the right along Monkmoor Street and then right again along Commercial Road to a busy junction opposite the Kerry. Cross at the lights.

2. Briefly detour left along Bath Street to see a remnant of the old city wall opposite the Magistrates' Court, then return to go down Union Street beside the Kerry pub. Union Street leads to St Peter's Square. Just to the left along St Owen's Street is the Town Hall, which was opened in 1904. Turn around and walk back past St Peter's Church into High Town. A short distance past the Black & White House Museum swing left through an archway down a narrow passage, Capuchin Lane. It leads into Church Street and on to the cathedral, where the famous Mappa Mundi can be seen.

3. Go left past the cathedral into Castle Street. Approaching Castle House at the end, walk right along a narrow passage which leads past Castle Pool (the last remnant of the city's defensive moat) to Castle Green. Turn left on a rising path that skirts two sides of the park to a viewpoint overlooking the Wye. Steps left of the belvedere lead down to Victoria Bridge.

4. On the far bank turn right beside Bishop's Meadow, continuing beyond to cross St Martin's Street at the foot of the 15th-century Wye Bridge. It carried all the city's traffic until Greyfriars Bridge was built in 1966. Carry on beside the river to Hunderton Bridge, constructed in 1854 to carry the railway from Newport and Abergavenny.

5. Cross here, descending to the riverbank to double back downstream past the Rugby Club. Approaching Hereford Rowing Club, the path leaves the river to skirt the clubhouse. Continue up Greyfriars Avenue. Immediately before the main road, go right along a footpath above the car park. Emerging from a pedestrian subway, glance right through a gateway to see the base of one of the city wall's towers before turning up steps to cross St Nicholas's Street.

6. Continue along Victoria Street beside the old city walls and then turn right into West Street. At the crossroads, go left into Broad Street, heading towards All Saints Church at the top. A popular meeting place, it houses a café and exhibitions while maintaining its original spiritual function. Go right to High Town, taking the first left into Widemarsh Street. Follow it up across a junction with a main road back to the car park.

Where to eat and drink

Continental-style 'alfresco piazza lounging' has arrived in Hereford's High Town. The Moka Bar at No. 8 Church Street can be quite a crush – always a good sign. At No. 10 is a coffee shop, and at No. 17 is La Madeleine, a French inspired café. Also within the city centre numerous pubs and other cafés.

What to see

Visit the Black and White House Museum (open every day except Monday, April to September) in High Town. Nearby, on the High Street, is the relocated Marchants' House. Near the cathedral, the sign 'Tower open today' means you can climb the cathedral's stairs, all 218 of them.

While you're there

Only devout heathens avoid Hereford Cathedral; this, and the Mappa Mundi and Chained Library (entrance fee) are the city's biggest draws. Within the Museum and Art Gallery, a timeline on the walls describes the main chapters in Hereford's history, while mounted on the stair wall is a stunning Roman mosaic floor from nearby Kenchester. Upstairs in the museum you can see bees working in a hive behind only a sheet of glass. On Bishop's Meadow you'll find an endangered species, municipal grass tennis courts – use them or lose them.

Sunday Carvery £14.95
THE KOFFIE POT

QUEENSWOOD COUNTRY PARK AND THE RIVER

DISTANCE/TIME	7.5 miles (12.2km) / 3hrs
ASCENT/GRADIENT	492ft (150m) / ▲▲
PATHS	Woodland paths, bridleway tracks and field footpaths
LANDSCAPE	Woodland park and riverside meadows
SUGGESTED MAP	OS Explorer 202 Leominster and Bromyard
START/FINISH	Grid reference: SO506515
DOG FRIENDLINESS	Lots of off-lead opportunities in country park (on lead in the car park and picnic area) and through the woods. On-lead near livestock.
PARKING	Large car park at Queenswood Country Park
PUBLIC TOILETS	In car park
NOTES	This route requires crossing the A49 and is therefore not suitable for very young children

The only designated country park in Herefordshire, Queenswood Country Park includes 123-acres (50ha) of semi-natural ancient woodland covering much of Dinmore Hill. Queenswood is just a fragment of what was a vast ancient oak wood that once stretched to the Welsh borders and beyond. It was held by the crown and changed its name from Kings Wood to Queenswood in the reign of Queen Elizabeth I. During the 17th-century Queenswood became part of the Hampton Court House Estate, which still borders the country park on the opposite side of the main A49 Leominster to Hereford road.

The wood was clear-felled during World War I to provide timber for the war effort and in 1935, with concern that the land could be sold off for development, it was handed to Herefordshire County Council to be managed 'as an open space for the enjoyment of the public for all time'.

The coppice and hillside woodlands in Queenswood Country Park are designated as a Site of Special Scientific Interest (SSSI) and the whole site is designated as a Local Nature Reserve. Much of the woodland, aside from a central 47-acre (19ha) arboretum, has regenerated naturally since the clear-felling 100 years ago. Oak, wild service and small-leaved lime trees are prominent but the woodland is also abundant with wildlife, particularly woodpeckers. The park is also involved in a national monitoring scheme to help protect the rare dormice that are found in the woods.

In 2009 Dr Owen Johnston, on behalf of the Tree Register, surveyed the trees at Queenswood. He discovered that the Queenswood Arboretum was home to a number of champion trees. Some of the trees are Herefordshire champions, the finest in the county, and others are UK champions, the finest or biggest in the country. These number 148 and small plaques by the trees identify which are champions.

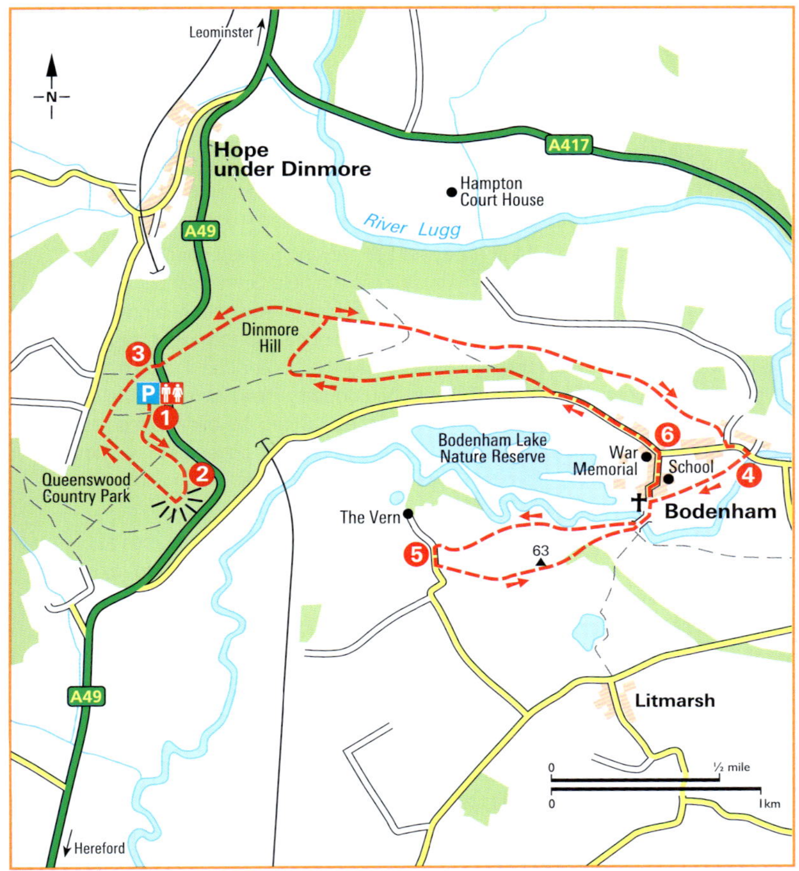

1. From the car park, pass under the Border Oak building. In 27yds (25m) turn left on a track just before 'Lime Avenue'. At a fork, take left path and keep six very tall, straight Redwood trees on left before turning half-left to find a track beyond the Redwood Grove. Cross a ditch to fork left. Turn left onto a wider path and in 11yds (10m) left again. Continue for 328yds (300m) and at a 4-way junction, turn left. Walk for 0.25 miles (400m), ignoring a crossing path after 328yds (300m), to turn left and follow the well-trodden path round until it meets with another to rise uphill. At a 5-way junction (with a bench), take the 3rd right uphill. In 328yds (300m) turn to a clump of pines and within 33yds (30m) right to a viewpoint. Here, on a clear day, you can see towards the Malvern Hills, Ledbury, Orcop Hill and the Black Mountains.

2. From the viewpoint, take the widest path uphill and at a junction with a stone to mark Queen Elizabeth II's coronation, take 2nd left to a clearing and a sign, 'Oak Avenue'. Leaving the sign behind, walk up between the avenue of trees for 50yds (45m) and take the path on left. Continue round, ignoring a turning to the left, and at a junction with a rusty gate, turn right. In 219yds (200m) turn left to pass through the 'Autumn Garden'. Beyond the garden turn onto a tarmac drive and follow this to the right for approximately 328yds

(300m), keeping forestry buildings on right. Cross the main road (with extreme care) to a bridleway opposite.

3. In 656yds (600m) turn right onto a woodland track. Continue on this for 0.25 miles (400m) passing through a metal gate with cattle grid. Keep a second cattle grid on left and follow the line of a copse, then keep the line across the field to a gate. Keep to the right-hand field edge to pass through two further gates. Beyond, go half-right to the top right-hand field corner. Follow the sunken lane to a gravel track and turn right to the road. Turn left.

4. In 82yds (75m) turn right at a waymarker. Beyond a small paddock, take a gap in the hedge by tall poplars to cut across the field behind school playing fields, towards the church. Into the churchyard follow the path behind the church to a gate in the far corner. Cross a footbridge and turn right, signposted 'The Vern ½ mile'. Follow the riverbank to a further footbridge and turn half-right (beyond you can see Queenswood Country Park). Cross the field to a 3rd footbridge 16yds (15m) from the riverbank. Climb the bank to a double stile and turn left into a field. Cross the field on a well-trodden path, keeping a house and poplars on your left. Take a path between hedges to a lane by 'The Vern'.

5. Turn left following the lane for 219yds (200m) then left again across a way-marked stile. Follow the right-hand field edge for 0.5 mile (800m) to come out against stock fencing for 109yds (100m). Cross a stile on left to follow right-hand field edge. Take a stile/footbridge on right just before field corner and cross the field back to the blue footbridge over the Lugg, returning to the church. Walk back through the churchyard and under the Lych Gate. Walk forward to go right then left along the lane past the school for a road junction by the war memorial.

6. Turn left and keep on the road for 547yds (500m), climbing past orchards and with views of Bodenham Lake Nature Reserve. At a driveway on the right take the waymarked footpath uphill through trees. In 656yds (600m) take the right fork just past a hide chair and ladder. At a junction with a cherry tree (marked with a white arrow directing straight on) turn right, then right again after 109yds (100m). At a wide gravel turning area, turn left and retrace your steps along the bridleway back to Queenswood Country Park.

Where to eat and drink
Queenswood Café at the start and end of the walk, within the country park, serves hot and cold drinks, home-made cakes and light lunches, including hot food.

What to see
Some of the half-timbered buildings at Queenswood Country Park are 'rescued' buildings from elsewhere in the county. The Queenswood Café was, once, The Essex Arms, a 17th-century coaching inn from Widemarsh Street in Hereford. The National Trust shop on site was once a tannery from Leominster.

AYMESTREY TO YATTON

DISTANCE/TIME	4.75 miles (7.7km) / 2hrs 15min
ASCENT/GRADIENT	525ft (160m) / ▲
PATHS	Excellent tracks, field paths, minor roads, steep woodland sections, many stiles
LANDSCAPE	Wooded hills and undulating pastures
SUGGESTED MAP	OS Explorer 203 Ludlow
START/FINISH	Grid reference: SO426658
DOG FRIENDLINESS	Several opportunities for controlled, off-lead walking; lead needed on two stretches of lane
PARKING	At old quarry entrance, on east side of A4110, 0.25 miles (400m) north of Aymestrey Bridge
PUBLIC TOILETS	None on route

On your way here, you may have seen signs to the village of Shobdon and the adjacent Shobdon Airfield. It was one of the many airfields built in 1940, as part of what was collectively perhaps the biggest civil engineering project undertaken in Britain. At that time a modest, privately owned quarry was operating at Aymestrey. The wartime government used its compulsory purchase powers, ensuring a local supply of stone for the airfield. In its latter years, the quarry was run by Hanson Aggregates.

I don't suppose that anyone at Hanson Aggregates expects, in the fullness of time, to be remembered for their landscape architecture in the same way as Lancelot 'Capability' Brown or Richard Payne Knight, but they should at least be commended for trying. Unfortunately, you will not be best placed to judge the quality of their 'seamless' landscape restoration, since you've now been primed to look out for it. Nevertheless, towards the end of the walk, as you descend to the former quarry area, there is little to indicate that the immediate landscape has been recently manufactured, although your curiosity may be alerted by the absence of any really substantial trees. Unlike many quarries, the plan here was not to provide any sort of lake-based recreation, but to return the land to a mixture of agricultural use (sheep grazing, it seems) and woodland.

West of Aymestrey, the River Lugg runs in a small but spectacular gorge. This is a glacial overflow channel that exploited a fault in the rock, associated with the glacial Wigmore Lake. The paucity of contours on the suggested map a few grid squares to the north shows the position of the former lake.

At Mortimer's Cross, Richard of York's son Edward defeated the Lancastrian army in 1461 in one of the battles that changed the course of the Wars of the Roses (Edward was crowned King later that year). The battle site is 0.5 miles (800m) south of the road junction named Mortimer's Cross. The cross itself dates from 1799.

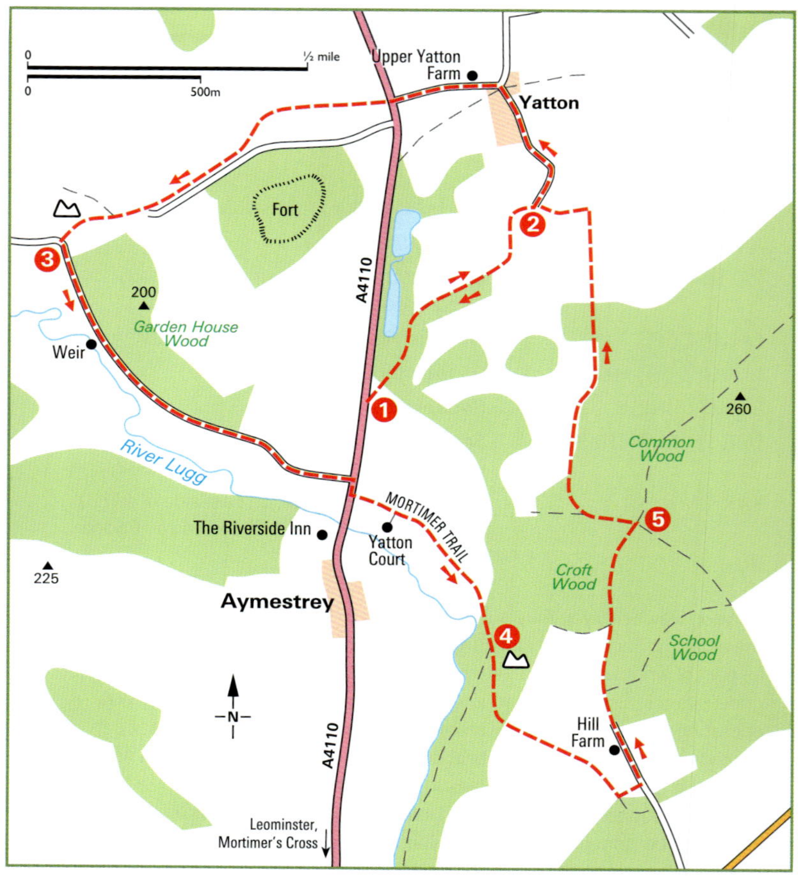

1. Walk up the access road for 750yds (686m), until just before a junction of tracks. Note a stile on the right – your route returns over this.

2. Turn left then, in 25yds (23m), curve right, passing a seemingly nameless house with a stone wall relic in its garden. Shortly curve left to walk through Yatton, to a T-junction. Turn left to the A4110. Cross directly to a stile, striking across this field to a gap. In the next field veer left to skirt round the right edge of (not over) an oak and ash embankment, to find a corner stile. Walk up the left edge of this field but, at the brow, where it bends for some 70yds (64m) to a corner, take a stile in the hedge to walk along its other side. Within 60yds (55m) you will be in a clear path, steeply down through woodland, a ravine on your left. Join a rough driveway to a minor road. (The glacial overflow channel is directly ahead.)

3. Turn left here, joining the Mortimer Trail. Enjoy this wooded, riverside lane for nearly 0.75 miles (1.2km), to reach the A4110 again. Cross, then walk for just 25yds (23m) to the right. (The Riverside Inn is about 175yds/160m further.) Take a raised green track, heading for the hills. Then go diagonally across two fields, to a kissing gate and wooden steps.

4. Within a few paces fork left to ascend steeply through the trees. Leave by a stile, to cross two meadows diagonally. Over a double stile, walk along the left-hand edge of a field, still heading downhill. At the trees turn left. Soon reach a tarmac road. Turn left along the road, now going back uphill. Beyond Hill Farm, enter the Croft Estate. Walk along this hard gravel track. After 110yds (100m), ignore a right fork but, 550yds (503m) further on, you must leave the track. This spot is identified where deciduous trees give way to conifers on the left and you see a Mortimer Trail marker post on the wide ride between larches and evergreens on the right, approximately 250yds (229m) on from a large, green Croft Wood sign.

5. Turn left (there is no signpost). Within 110yds (100m) go half right and more steeply down on an aged stone path. Within 250yds (229m) look out for a metal gate, way-marked, leading out of the woods. Walk along its right-hand edge, admiring the former quarry's new landscape. Walk briefly in trees then out and, at the far corner, within the field, turn left to Point 2. Retrace your steps to the start of the walk.

Where to eat and drink

The Riverside Inn at Aymestry serves locally made alcoholic and soft drinks, and has a fine bar and dinner menu. The Grange at Mortimer's Cross Café, at the junction of that name, serves good food and has a large garden.

What to see

There are stunning brick-arched barns at Upper Yatton Farm. These tall stone structures have brick apertures; one is filled in with attractive gridded brickwork. Later, look back from the other side of the A4110 to see more arches.

39 LEINTWARDINE TO DOWNTON ON THE ROCK

DISTANCE/TIME	10 miles (16.1km) / 5hrs
ASCENT/GRADIENT	1,200ft (366m) / ▲ ▲ ▲
PATHS	Pastures, leafy paths, grass tracks, dirt tracks, tarmac lanes, three steep banks (care needed on one), 15 stiles
LANDSCAPE	Rolling country, wooded and farmed, above River Teme
SUGGESTED MAP	OS Explorer 203 Ludlow
START/FINISH	Grid reference: SO403741
DOG FRIENDLINESS	Mostly on lead, lots of game birds
PARKING	Village hall and community centre car park, Leintwardine
PUBLIC TOILETS	None on route

By the end of the 18th century, formal neatness in landscape architecture had fallen from favour; the new word on the lips of those who counted was 'picturesque'. This craving for a laissez-faire type of landscape had been of great benefit to Ross-on-Wye, where the Wye Tour had become the must-do trip. Downton on the Rock was to benefit from Richard Payne Knight, under whose direction Downton Castle was built between 1772 and 1778. If you like regimented rows of trees, twee fountains, manicured lawns and symmetrical paths, then it's not the castle for you.

Richard Payne Knight knew exactly the sort of landscape he wanted for Downton Castle, having travelled extensively, particularly in Italy. He sought a rugged, wild view, like those seen in the landscape paintings of Nicolas Poussin, Claude Lorrain and Salvator Rosa, who had produced their best works in the mid-17th century.

As for the privately owned Downton Castle's interior, it is wholly classical in style. Some alterations and additions were made in the 1860s.

The Romans built a fort beside the River Teme here, and stayed at Leintwardine until the late fourth century AD. Where an early church is found within a Roman earthwork, the inference is that usage of the site continued when the Romans left, as is the case with Leintwardine. The High Street lies on the line of the Roman Watling Street. Today Leintwardine's population is well below half its late 19th-century figure of nearly 2,000.

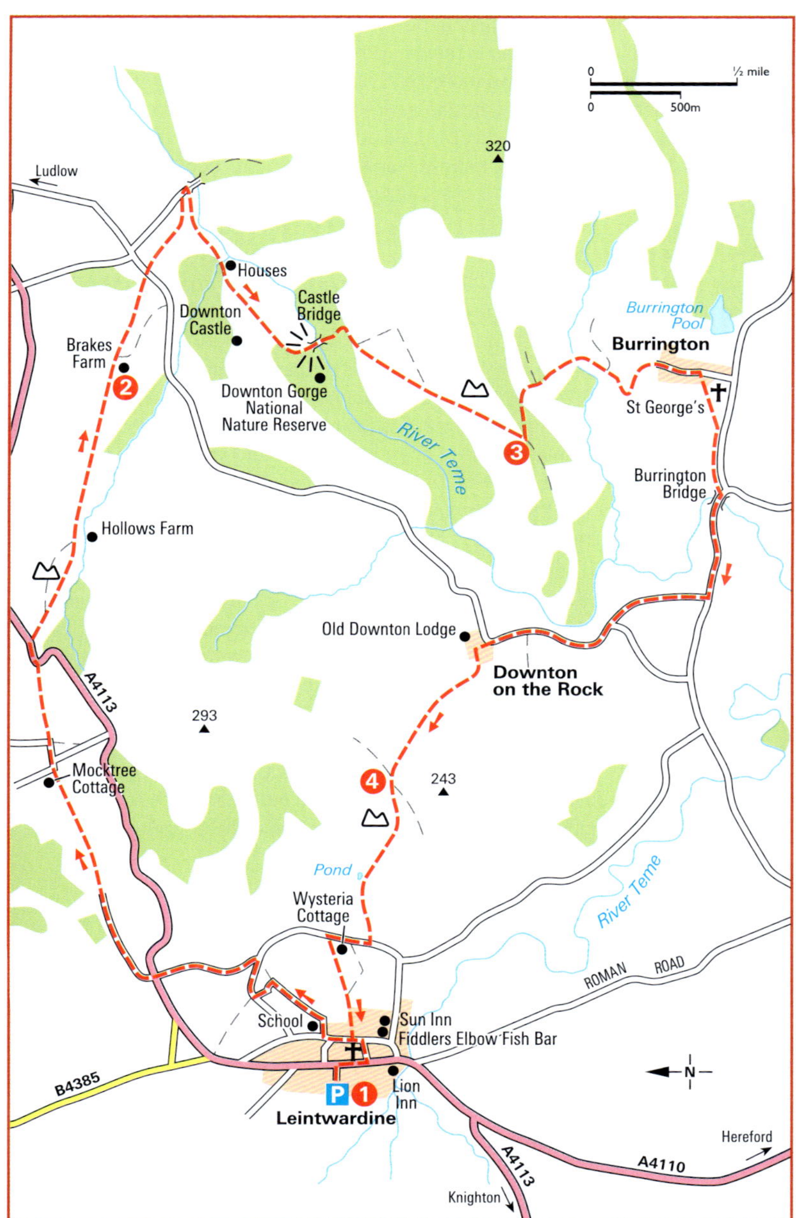

1. Begin downhill, very soon taking the first left, Church Street. Turn left. As you reach the primary school, turn right. Aim for a brick, brown-and-white house but, after a two-plank footbridge, go left to a tarmac road. Turn right. In 300yds (274m) turn left, to the A4113. Cross, turning immediately right up a lane. Ascend for a short mile (1.6km). Soon after a skew junction go forward beyond a corrugated shelter, taking the left of two gates. Just beyond a second corrugated shelter, take a gap in the hedge by a defunct stile on the right. Go three-quarters left, across two more fields, to replanted woodland. At the A4113 turn left but soon right, beside a wire fence. At the end follow the field-edge round to the left for 40yds (37m). Go down a very steep, earthy bank (care needed) in trees to pass Hollows Farm on your right, then along a good road, soon dead straight for 0.5 miles (800m) to Brakes Farm.

2. Go straight ahead (waymarker), across a field to find a stile/gate beside a pond in the far left corner. Cross a minor road diagonally, then cross fields to a minor lane beside houses Nos 20 and 19. The parallel minor road could be used if the field is ploughed. Turn left. Soon turn right, downhill. Turn right, along the river, just before a bridge over the River Teme. Skirt two unnamed houses. Up a bank, join a dirt road. Follow this to Castle Bridge. Ascend but within 110yds (100m) of leaving woodland go half right, across a field, rejoining the dirt road into forest for perhaps 60yds (55m). (If the footpath is not established, it would make sense to go round the road, not trample the crop.) Scramble up a bank (waymarker). Traverse the steep meadow to a gate in the top, among oaks. Keep this line to go across a wide meadow, locating a stile on the left into harvested trees.

3. Turn left and descend. When you reach open meadow, curve round a dry valley. At a left bend go through a gate on the right. Go left of a specimen oak to a hidden gate in the bottom corner (marked by a bright red disc). Cross over a footbridge and turn right. Cross meadow to a gate, and soon reach a minor road. Turn right. Descend easily through Burrington, to St George's Church. Behind the church, cross meadows to Burrington Bridge. Cross the River Teme. After 650yds (594m) take the right turn. When you reach Downton, head towards Old Downton Lodge, and skirt around the Lodge buildings. Beyond a wall take the rightmost gate (waymarker), along an old lane. Shortly move right to ascend a right-hand field-edge, soon following a beech-lined avenue to reach a junction with a dirt track.

4. Over a stile into an expansive field, swing left to descend, initially steeply. Past a small (possibly dry) pond veer left along a right-hand field-edge to a hidden stile in the corner and a road. Turn right. Within 275yds (251m), at Wysteria Cottage, take a kissing gate. Cross three fields to soon emerge on Watling Street. Turn right to Church Street and back to the start.

Where to eat and drink

In Leintwardine fish and chips are available Tuesdays to Saturdays from the Fiddlers Elbow Fish Bar. Weekend walking groups can phone in advance and have their fish-and-chips lunch served to them at the Sun Inn, next door, washed down with a beer. Leintwardine's Lion Hotel has a riverside beer garden.

What to see

At St George's Church, Burrington (now closed as a place of worship), are several iron slab tombstones, among which is that of 'Richard Knight, MDCCXLV' (1745). He was the grandfather of Richard Payne Knight, who had purchased the Downton Estate with money earned from his life as one of the Shropshire ironmasters.

HARLEY'S MOUNTAIN

DISTANCE/TIME	7.5 miles (12.1km) / 3hrs 30min
ASCENT/GRADIENT	1080ft (329m) / ▲ ▲ ▲
PATHS	Meadows, field paths, woodland tracks with roots, many stiles
LANDSCAPE	Wooded hillsides and farmland, views to higher Welsh hills
SUGGESTED MAP	OS Explorer 201 Knighton & Presteigne
START/FINISH	Grid reference: SO364672
DOG FRIENDLINESS	Horses near Lingen but few sheep, 88 exciting woods
PARKING	At St Michael's & All Angels Church, Lingen (tuck in well)
PUBLIC TOILETS	None on route

After World War II, the nascent European Economic Community devised the well-intentioned Common Agricultural Policy (CAP) to address food shortages. In its later years the CAP fell into disrepute because surpluses resulted, and maintaining these perishable stores was costly. It was also contentious because many of the larger players in the global food market, in particular the United States, complained (correctly, it seems) that exportation of such surpluses was illegal because they arose from subsidised production.

To reduce the European output, 'set-aside' was introduced in 1992. Under the scheme, farmers essentially left some fields 'unfarmed' and received financial compensation for loss of income. In 2001, for example, farmers were obliged to leave 10 per cent of their food acreage out of food production. The payment received was partly dependent upon which side of the Welsh border the land lay. In England the rate was £88 per acre (£218 per hectare) but in Wales it was £77 per acre (£190 per hectare). Set-aside land could be used for growing 'industrial' as opposed to food crops and land could be either part of a crop rotation or left for successive years. In environmental terms, favoured fields would be those adjacent to existing hedgerows, copses, commons and the like.

The government replaced Set-aside with the Single Payment Scheme in 2005, which was then superseded by the Basic Payment Scheme ten years later. In 2024 'delinked payments' will be introduced as the latest plan for farmers to follow. Clearly the solutions to the agricultural economy will continue to tax policymakers for many years to come.

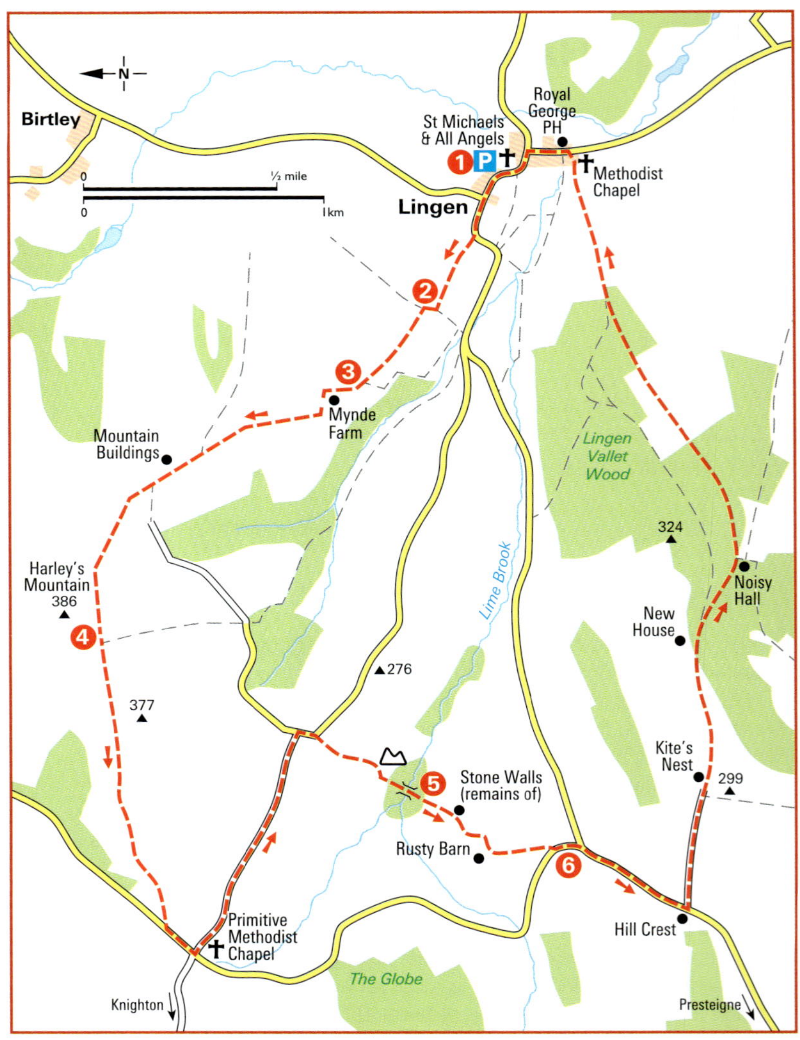

1. With the church tower behind you, walk forward and cross over to take the minor road signposted 'Willey'. When you reach the first bend, follow the fingerpost directly ahead. Walk up the left-hand edge of one paddock, followed by the right-hand edge of next and move right to find a stile, with a barn on your left and a muddy track in trees on your right.

2. Five paces to the right climb another stile and follow the left-hand field-edge marked by square fencing. With trees and power lines half-left, follow a waymarker up and slightly right. In the corner, go through a narrow metal gate (waymarked) to the side of a track. On reaching a brick-built cottage skirt right of this, and around the buildings of Mynde Farm (loose dogs may be present). Find a gate on the right behind a low building.

3. Turn right to go down and up a wide meadow to a stile seen from afar beside a prominent tree in the hedge. Go diagonally across (right) to a top field corner towards power lines and trees on the horizon, passing beside Mountain Buildings on a stony track. Where the track divides, take the left fork to two pine trees some 160yds (146m) further. Enter a large field. Go diagonally to a protruding hedge corner; then follow the hedge left for two field-edges. Within 200yds (183m) take a gate on the left. One field further along this breezy ridge reach another gate with a small pool to the right (possibly dry in high summer). Above and behind you is the trig point in the hedge.

4. Go straight ahead, not left, for over 0.75 miles (1.2km). Crossing arable fields and pastures using a farm track and following 'Herefordshire Trail' markers, descend to reach a minor road. Turn left for 120yds (110m), then left, signposted 'Lingen', soon passing the diminutive Primitive Methodist chapel. More than 0.5 miles (800m) further, turn right at a T-junction. Now in just 70yds (64m) take a fingerpost right, across a field to a stile, and down into the valley. Veer a fraction right, but don't be misled by sheep tracks – pick your way down this, at times inordinately steep, pasture, to find a gate then a double-stiled footbridge in a boggy patch below three large ash trees.

5. Scramble up a short, wooded bank to walk with a field boundary on your left for about 250yds (229m), taking a deeply rutted farm track into a miniature valley with tall trees. Here ignore an option to fork right on a track, instead swinging left, ascending, alongside an old, square-wire fence. However, in just 80yds (73m), at a fence corner, keep ahead, to pass through a gap beside a defunct stile, to the left of a rusty barn. Walk 80yds (73m) diagonally left to a working stile. Walk up the left side of the field to a minor road.

6. Turn left, along the road, for 650yds (594m). Turn left at Hill Crest. Just past a large metal barn at Kite's Nest take a track between hedges, not into a field 50yds (47m) beyond a new metal gate. When the outbuildings of New House are near your left take the lower, wider track, into pleasant woodland. On seeing a garden shed before Noisy Hall, fork left. Beside the house, initially keep just within the trees, on a narrow path close to pasture on your right. This goes deeper into woodland but after 600yds (549m) a kissing gate gives on to meadows. Two fields later, go into trees again (at a stile and gate, a large oak has grown around a gate bar), for a gently descending track. This becomes a deeply sunken, barrel-like lane between meadows once more. This ends at a dirt track to the public road, beside the Methodist chapel. Turn left through the village, then the lychgate to St Michael's and All Angels Church.

Where to eat and drink

Lingen's pub, the Royal George, has fine ales from Wye Valley Brewery, and a beer garden. It is open lunchtimes Friday to Sunday. Lingen's pub, the Royal George, opens everyday late afternoon to 11pm, closed on Monday and Tuesday. It has fine ales, a beer garden and serves classic pub dishes. If visiting Presteigne, you'll find several options, from traditional pubs to cafés and little restaurants.

What to see

In Lingen, St Michael's & All Angels Church has attractive 19th-century wooden shingles on its bell-turret. On the slopes of Harley's Mountain, notice how the eroded farm track has a bed of rock, illustrating the shallowness of the soil.

HERGEST RIDGE

DISTANCE/TIME	7.5 miles (12.1km) / 3hrs 50min
ASCENT/GRADIENT	1,115ft (340m) / ▲ ▲ ▲
PATHS	Meadows, field paths, excellent tracks, many stiles
LANDSCAPE	Panoramas on Hergest Ridge
SUGGESTED MAP	OS Explorer 201 Knighton & Presteigne
START/FINISH	Grid reference: SO295565
DOG FRIENDLINESS	Sheep country and some horses
PARKING	Mill Street car park (east and west sides of Crabtree Road)
PUBLIC TOILETS	On Mill Street

The first thing you need to know about this walk is that 'Hergest' rhymes with 'hardest' – but don't let that put you off. Kington was essentially a wool-trading market town, on an important drovers' route. St Mary's Church was certainly visible from afar, a tall spire on a hilltop position. The Norman tower had to be rebuilt in 1794. The remainder was built mostly in the 13th century, but with Victorian additions. The suggested map shows 'Race Course (disused)' along Hergest Ridge. It was a focus of entertainment from 1825 to 1846. It had replaced the one on Bradnor Hill (north of the town), first used in the 1770s. Racing stopped circa 1880, but being up on the hill must have given considerable relief from the nauseating stench of the town's surface sewage.

The Hergest Ridge section is one of several highlights for walkers undertaking the Offa's Dyke Path. The path and the ancient earthwork itself often do not coincide, but that doesn't seem to matter – they still represent a mighty piece of history and a fine long-distance route. Adjacent to Bradnor Hill is Rushock Hill, and a particularly well-preserved section of the Offa's Dyke that the National Trail route follows – you will have to make a separate excursion on foot to see it. The industrial estate that straddles the road southwest of Hergest Bridge stands on the site of a 'camp', a wartime military hospital, dilapidated parts of which remain. Closer to the town, on the opposite side of the road to the toll house, the (almost) level field once served as a landing strip – all 300yds (274m) of it!

During the 1970s, the musician and composer Mike Oldfield lived on Bradnor Hill just north of Kington, and seen from Hergest Ridge. Following the success *Tubular Bells*, which catapulted him onto the world stage, he released a second album, *Hergest Ridge*, inspired by the countryside around his home. It is an instrumental composition that reached number one in the album charts in 1974. His house, The Beacon, was turned into a recording studio where he recorded his third album, *Ommadawn* in 1975.

Hergest Court was once one of the many properties owned by the Vaughan family. Vaughan's wife's brother had been murdered, for which she effected revenge in dramatic fashion. Dressed as a man, she attended an archery contest where her brother's killer was, and despatched him with a fatal arrow. She then fled. Sir Thomas Vaughan was killed in the Wars of the Roses. Their alabaster effigies lie in Kington's St Mary's Church. Hergest Court is also rumoured to be haunted by a black dog, the story – and the house – allegedly the inspiration behind Arthur Conan Doyle's story, *The Hound of the Baskervilles*.

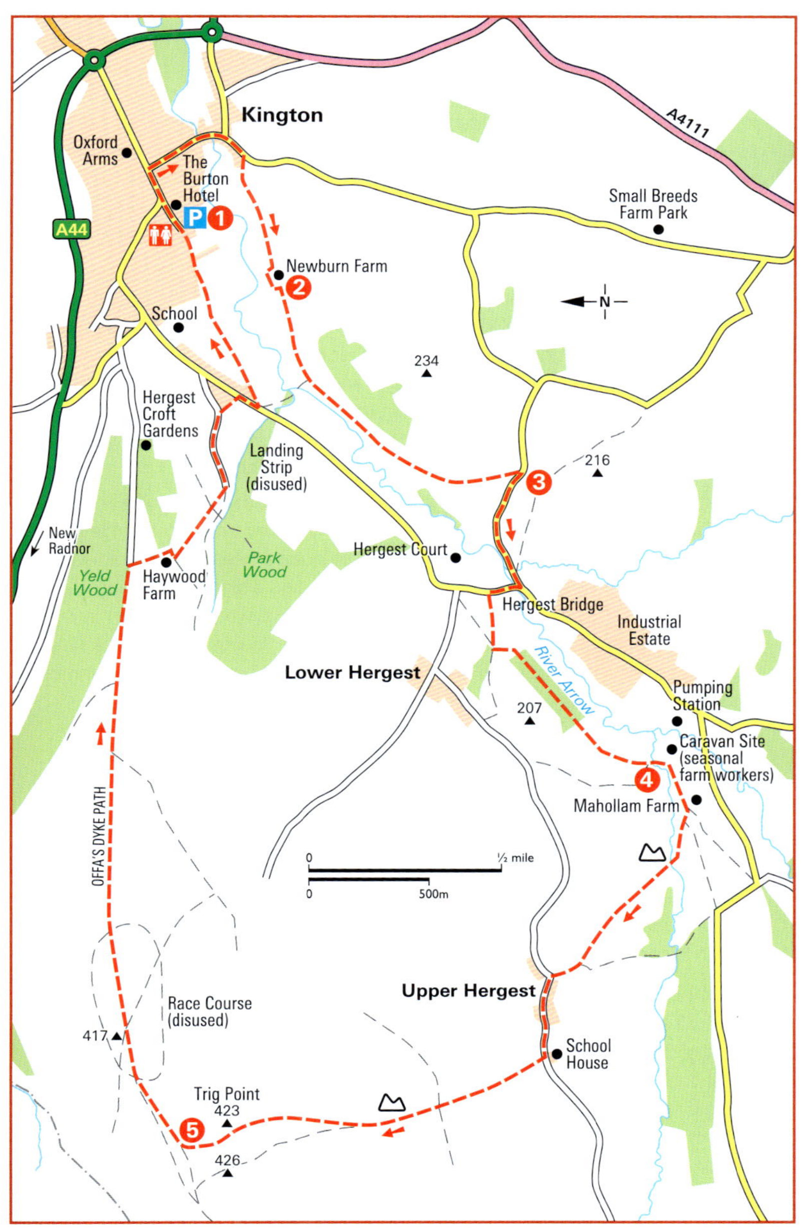

1. Walk down the High Street and turn right into Bridge Street. Cross the River Arrow and turn right into Kingswood Road. Take the driveway to Newburn Farm.

2. Go round three sides, then take a gate beyond a corrugated shed and stables into a field. After an area planted with trees (including cherry and ash), when you see a footbridge, move up and left to take a stile to a right-hand field-edge, under huge oak limbs. Walk for over 0.5 miles (800m) through meadows, curving left to a stile and steps, between two houses, down to a road.

3. Turn right, then right again to cross Hergest Bridge, but after 125yds (114m) take a left fingerpost. Within 100yds (91m) veer right to cross a stile into trees. Out of trees, at a three-pronged waymarker, see a stile on your right, but go beyond it and veer left, to cross the bottom corner of a meadow towards a line of sweet chestnuts. Over a difficult stile, turn right, along an awkward path across a steep, wooded bank. After 325yds (297m), a stile puts you into another meadow. Pass by a bracken bank to cross a footbridge hidden in undergrowth (care needed). Contour to a gate then cross waymarked meadows using a two-plank bridge, a double-stiled footbridge and steps down to a metal footbridge.

4. At a road on a caravan site for seasonal farm workers turn right. After 40yds (37m) find a stile, right. Almost immediately, take a second stile beside a huge oak stump. At a track beside Mahollam Farm bear right, downhill. Do not stay on this green lane, but go right, finding another metal footbridge. Ascend steeply, soon in farmland. Cross fields to a lane, first following a left-hand field-edge, then cutting a left-hand field corner, then on to a red metal gate. Turn right. At a junction, go left for 325yds (297m), to a gate way-marked 'Bridleway'. Now go straight up to the '423m' trig point on Hergest Ridge.

5. Keep ahead for 80yds (73m) and, on seeing a wide path cut through bracken, go through and then around a pool. Turn right. Now stride out for 1.5 miles (2.4km), initially heading for a clump of monkey puzzle trees, ignoring an early left fork. On the road again, when 30yds (27m) beyond a sign proclaiming 'Kington – the centre for walking', turn right. Round Haywood Farm, continue down to a cattle grid; cross this. Down this road after 350yds (320m), look for a fingerpost beside the white 'No. 31'. Go down this field. Turn away from Kington for 120yds (110m), then turn sharply left, following 'Tatty Moor'. Cross a meadow and school playing fields to the recreation ground. Join Park Avenue, which becomes Mill Street.

Where to eat and drink

Kington has many pubs to choose from; you'll find fish and chips, Indian cuisine and a Chinese take-away here too. The Burton Hotel has lengthy menus that include Indian, Thai and classic British options. Just down the High Street is the Oxford Arms, which is now community owned and run.

While you're there

The 70 acres (28ha) of Hergest Croft Gardens are open daily April to the end of October, so that you can enjoy the dazzling autumn colours of the National Collection of maples and birches here. You can meet European eagle owls eyeball to eyeball just south of Kington, at the Small Breeds Farm Park. It is very child friendly and has tearooms, but you can take your own picnic too. Dogs are only allowed in the picnic area.

A WALK FROM WEOBLEY

DISTANCE/TIME	5 miles (8km) / 2hrs 15min
ASCENT/GRADIENT	230ft (70m)
PATHS	Minor lanes, meadow paths, village streets, several stiles
LANDSCAPE	Gentle farmland and orchards, village
SUGGESTED MAP	OS Explorer 202 Leominster & Bromyard
START/FINISH	Grid reference: SO401517
DOG FRIENDLINESS	Lead needed on lanes and preferred in fields
PARKING	Village car park off B4230
PUBLIC TOILETS	None on route

Pronounced 'Webbley', the village is one of those included in the famous Hereford Black and White Village Trail, a 40-mile (64.5km) route around the county's prettiest villages, which contain a wealth of beautiful timber-framed buildings. After a heavy snowfall Weobley is at its blackest-and-whitest, taking on an almost surreal, monochrome guise, but at any time of the year the village is a delight: in spring it's inspiring, in summer it's beautiful and in autumn it's simply exquisite.

The village was originally a Saxon settlement and its name describes a 'ley' or woodland clearing held by a local headman called Wibba. In Saxon times, in addition to farming, glove-making and brewing developed as local industries. Weobley remained a prosperous settlement and before the Reform Bill of 1832 returned two Members of Parliament. Weobley is also associated with the development of the famous Hereford cattle. Prior to the 18th century, cattle were bred primarily as beasts of burden, with the production of milk and beef being secondary, and it was only towards the end of the century that the Hereford cattle we know today emerged. The Tomkins family became noted cattle breeders, with Benjamin Tomkins beginning selective breeding in 1742. The marketplace where they would have traded their cattle has long since gone, the market hall demolished in the mid-19th century and the adjoining row of late medieval houses destroyed in a bakery fire in 1943. The site is preserved in the triangular rose garden at the top of the village.

A place of such importance required protection and Weobley's castle was founded shortly after the Norman Conquest by the de Lacys, one of the important Norman families upon whom William had relied. The impressive earthworks are still visible to the south of the village, although the later extensive stone castle has entirely disappeared. The church, however, is a prominent landmark and boasts the second tallest spire in the county. Dedicated to St Peter and St Paul, it has a Norman south doorway, parts of the chancel are 13th century, and the soaring tower dates from the 14th century. Inside is a statue of Colonel John Birch. Originally a Royalist supporter during the English Civil War, he changed allegiances, becoming one of Cromwell's right-hand men and a signatory to Charles I's death warrant. Foreseeing the winds of change, however, he later donned his Royalist hat again to welcome Charles II to the throne.

Despite its industrious and sometimes turbulent past, the village was remote from the canals, and later railways, that began criss-crossing the country from the 18th century and thus was largely bypassed by the Industrial Revolution. It is to this, at least in part, that its wonderful heritage of old buildings remains.

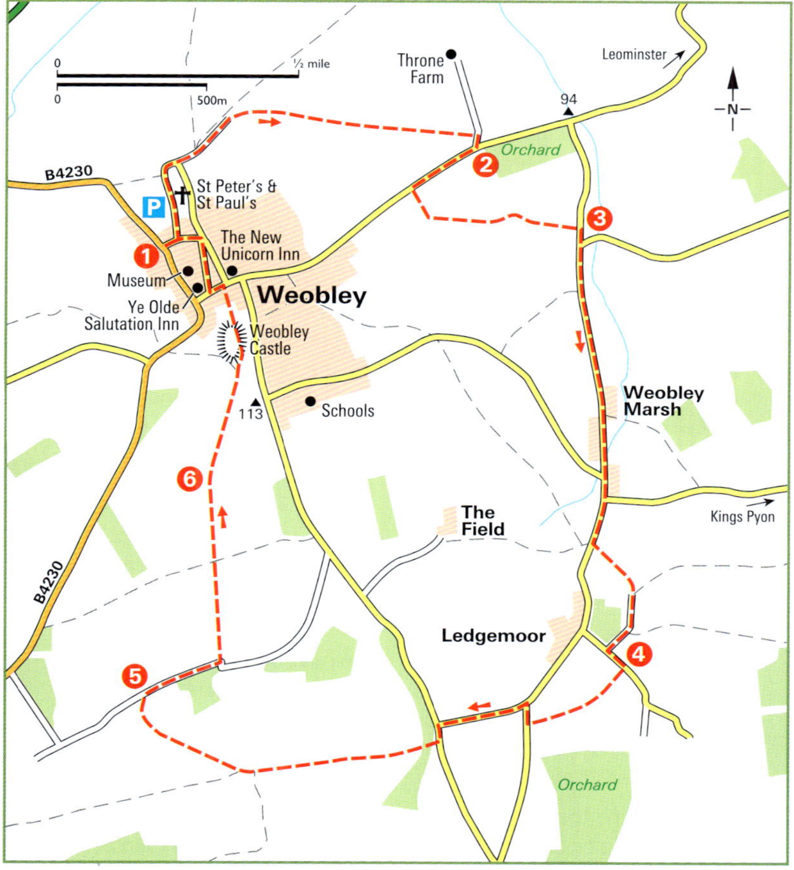

1. Leaving the car park, go left and left again past the church. Continue beside the burial ground and swing right. At the next bend go forward on a track. Stay with it as it later curves right, but where it subsequently bends left, keep ahead through a gap into a field. Follow a power line across the field, leaving through a kissing gate onto a lane.

2. Go right. After 300yds (274m) look for a stile beside a gate on the left into an orchard. Follow waymarks along an avenue between the trees, passing an ancient oak. After a further 20yds (18m), watch for a waymark directing the path half-left across the rows of trees. Through a gate, keep the same line across two fields, leaving onto a lane.

3. Follow it right for nearly 0.75 miles (1.2km) through Weobley Marsh. Beyond the turn to Kings Pyon and 50yds (46m) after a brick cottage, go over a stile in the left hedge. Strike across to a stile just left of the far-right field corner. Turn right by the hedge for 10yds (9m) to a footbridge. Over that, follow a narrow passage to come out onto the end of a lane. Walk left to a junction and go left again.

4. After 100yds (91m), go through a break in the hedge opposite Arrow Cottage. Head away by the left edge to another lane. Go right to a T-junction and then left. At the next T-junction turn left again. Walk 30yds (27m) then take a track off right through a wooded strip to the field behind, a kissing gate on the left bypassing a locked gate. The track runs away, later climbing a low rise and passing through a couple of gates. Immediately beyond the second, bear half-right across the field, making for the left end of a tall brick wall. Exit over a planked ditch onto a track.

5. Go right, passing through a gate to continue at the edge of pasture. Swing left at the end to a kissing gate and head along a green track towards Weobley's church. Ignore a crossing track and carry on to a gate.

6. Bear slightly right to pick up a trod across a pasture. Through a kissing gate, continue along a grass track, cutting across the moat and earthwork defences of Weobley's castle. Beyond, leave through a gate and walk out to a street at the top of Weobley. The Throne and the old grammar school can be found to the right, past the New Unicorn Inn and round a left bend. The way back to the car park, however, lies ahead down the main street and then left down Bell Square.

Where to eat and drink

In Weobley are the Salutation Inn and the New Unicorn Inn. The long established Jules restaurant in the heart of the village serves lunch, dinner and coffee, teas and cakes from 9am.

What to see

In the village, find the grandly named Throne, a 400-year-old house where Charles I spent the night of 5 September 1645, after the Battle of Naseby. Diagonally opposite, and dating from roughly the same era, is the former grammar school, constructed before schools were built to look like schools; it had 25 pupils in 1717.

While you're there

Weobley's small museum is only open Monday's (10-1pm) and Thursday's (2-5pm) displays include documents, photographs and items relating to the history of the village and its residents from the last 200 years.

A CIRCUIT FROM CLIFFORD

DISTANCE/TIME	6.25 miles (10.1km) / 3hrs
ASCENT/GRADIENT	675ft (205m) / ▲▲
PATHS	Field paths and lanes, awkward embankment, many stiles
LANDSCAPE	Rolling hills and Wye Valley views
SUGGESTED MAP	OS Explorer 201 Knighton & Presteigne
START/FINISH	Grid reference: SO251450
DOG FRIENDLINESS	Numerous stiles and farm livestock should be considered
PARKING	Roadside parking at St Mary's Church, near Clifford
PUBLIC TOILETS	None on route

Clifford was a planned Norman town of perhaps 200 dwellings, surrounding a castle built around 1070 by William Fitz Osborn (later the 1st Earl of Hereford) overlooking a ford across the river. It appeared in the 1086 Domesday survey, and maps from the 1360s show it to be one of only three significant settlements in the county; Wigmore and Hereford itself being the others. It prospered in the relative stability of the 12th century, but by the 15th century was no longer of importance.

Supplementing the natural defences afforded by the knoll on which the fortification stands, an earth dam impounded a shallow lake across the flood plain to the south of the castle. Earthworks remain from the original motte, with much of the surviving stonework being from the mid-13th century.

Although contemporary with the castle, St Mary's Church on the hill above has escaped the ravages of war and withstood the test of time. It was probably associated with the now vanished Clifford Priory, which overlooked Hardwicke Brook, just to the south. The monastery was founded under the Cluniac order around 1130 and contained extensive fish ponds to ensure a ready source of food. Although some original stonework remains in the church nave, the present edifice is largely the product of Victorian rebuilding. Among its features are four family shields on the belfry roof and a rare 13th-century wooden effigy of a priest in vestments, which bears a striking resemblance to one in Hereford Cathedral of Bishop Aquablanca. Local legend decrees it to be of Simon FitzRichard, who founded the priory, and it was processed around the church on Founder's Day.

On the route you'll cross and re-cross the dismantled railway that connected Dorstone, in the heart of the Golden Valley, with Hay-on-Wye. Running for 19 miles (31km), it joined the line that served Hereford and Hay (and continued on to Brecon) about 1 mile (1.6km) southwest of Clifford, the line from Hereford having been built some 25 years earlier, in 1864. It survived only 10 years before becoming bankrupt, but was re-opened as part of the Great Western Railway in 1901. It was finally closed in 1953.

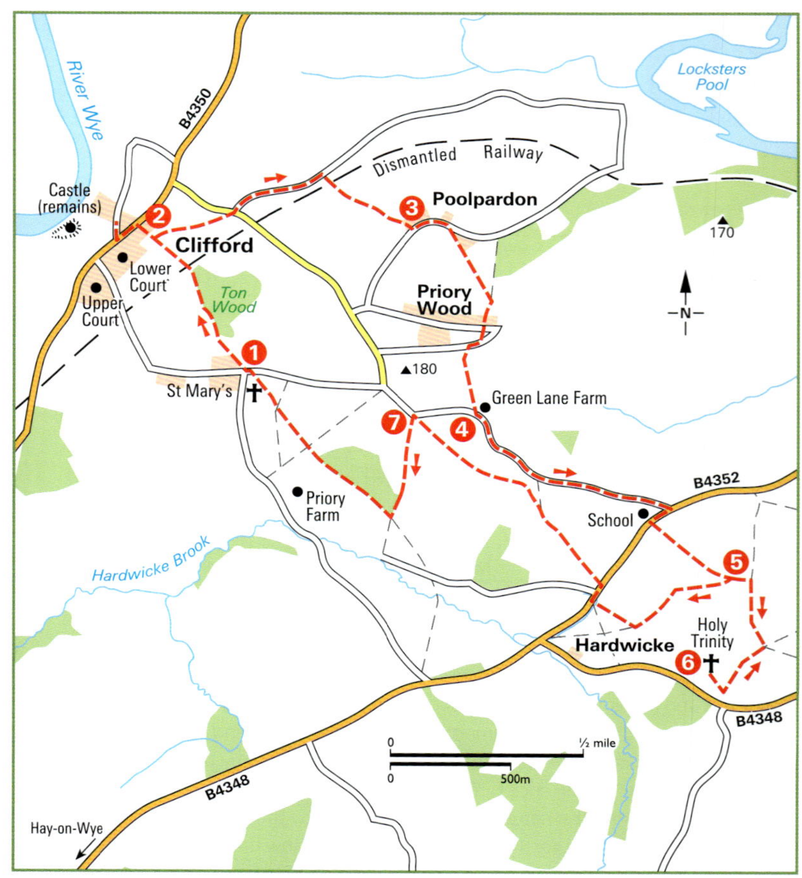

1. Walk downhill from the church past a junction to a fingerpost indicating a path off right. Entering a field, strike diagonally left to the bottom corner. Over stiles go right and soon right again into Ton Wood. Follow a winding path left through the trees. Beyond, bear right downfield, cross the embankment of a former railway and continue down towards Clifford.

2. For a distance glimpse of the castle, follow the holly-tunnelled path in front into the village and go left, then first right. Otherwise, strike sharp right, following a sparse line of trees to exit at a junction. Take the narrow lane opposite for 0.25 miles (400m). Through a kissing gate on the right, cross a narrow field, then the old railway to climb away at the field edge. After 150yds (137m), slip through a gap to continue up on the opposite side of the boundary and finally follow a contained path to a lane at Poolpardon.

3. Go left. Some 100yds (91m) beyond a right-hand bend, leave right over a stile. Follow the left wall then make for the top-left field corner. Over a stile, keep with the right hedge to emerge onto a lane. Take the track opposite and go right past a cottage. Bear left beside a green, crossing a track to continue forward through trees to a kissing gate. Head downfield to reach another lane.

4. Walk downhill for 0.5 miles (800m). Turn right at a junction by a school then leave left over a stile. Strike up half-left to a hedge corner, curving past it to a stile by a white cottage.

5. Leaving the yard, take a gate on the right. Follow the field-edge right into trees and walk on along an old way. Leaving the wood, continue another 100yds (91m) to a stile on the right. Cross the field to more stiles and then keep with the left hedge to a track. Turn right to Holy Trinity Church.

6. Return to Point (5). Entering the field, follow the left boundary to a stile tucked behind a corner. With the hedge now on your right, go around two sides to a stile. Swing right and follow the hedge out to the B4352. Go right past a track to a stile on the left. Head across a couple of fields. Initially by a hedge, keep the same line in the next field to a gate near the far corner. Diverging from the right hedge, make for a stile in an indented corner. Strike past a solitary oak, crossing into another field to a gate at the top.

7. Turn sharp left back across the field, passing through a gap to continue down a second field. Through a gate, keep going by the right hedge. Halfway down, turn right over a stile and walk on below a wood above two fields to emerge beside a cottage. Cross a track and keep ahead towards St Mary's Church. Over a stile in the top hedge, walk to a kissing gate in the left boundary. Pass through the churchyard to the lane.

Where to eat and drink
Clifford lost its pub decades ago, but northeast of Hardwicke, along the B4352, you'll find The Castlefields pub and restaurant. The interior of this family-run establishment includes a well, discovered during the pub's renovation. Alternatively head west for the pubs and cafés of Hay-on-Wye.

What to see
Besides its lush, cattle-grazed meadows and orchards, Herefordshire is important for potatoes. Consequently ridge-and-furrow patterns have been mostly lost to the deep workings of the modern plough. However, a fine example is in the pasture from Poolpardon up to Priory Wood. Hardwicke's Holy Trinity Church is a picture in sunlight. This 14th-century style structure was only built in 1851.

While you're there
Any visit to the Golden Valley should include Hay-on-Wye, famous for its secondhand and specialist bookshops and many attractive corners among the back streets. For something serene and different, try paddling a very stable canoe down the Wye – Celtic Canoes and Paddles and Pedals are both in Hay.

MERBACH HILL:
A CLIMB TO THE TOP

DISTANCE/TIME	4.75 miles (7.7km) / 2hrs 30min
ASCENT/GRADIENT	1,330ft (405m) / ▲ ▲ ▲
PATHS	Minor lanes, good tracks, meadows
LANDSCAPE	Hills and livestock meadows with very attractive hill views
SUGGESTED MAP	OS Explorer 201 Knighton & Presteigne or OS Explorer OL13 Brecon Beacons National Park
START/FINISH	Grid reference: SO332445
DOG FRIENDLINESS	On lead across farmland (many fields potentially with sheep), but some freedom on the Common
PARKING	Roadside parking in Bredwardine
PUBLIC TOILETS	None on route

A truly idyllic and peaceful setting at the foot of Merbach Hill and in the valley of the River Wye, Bredwardine offers a get-away-from-it-all destination.

On the banks of the River Wye, across the water from the village of Bredwardine, sit the Victorian terraced gardens of Brobury House. Originally laid out in the 1880s, when the house was built, the formal gardens offer panoramic views of the beautiful surrounding countryside.

Most of the trees within the garden were a part of the original design although subsequent owners have enhanced these plantings with striking features such as the stand of Paper Birches.

It is the present owners Keith and Pru Cartwright, however, who have embarked on an ambitious programme of restoration since 2001 in conjunction with garden designer Peter Antonius. Water is a recurring theme, complementing the riverside setting. Three formal water features have been introduced within the original terraces including a Lutyens inspired pool. A bog garden is well established with a feeder stream in woodland leading to the watermeadow. Elsewhere borders are alive with colour all year round with magnolia trees, wisteria, rhododendrons and dahlias.

From the grounds you can look across the valley to the Regency-style Bredwardine Vicarage, where the Reverend Francis Kilvert, the Victorian diarist, lived and is buried. Brobury House is built on the old vegetable garden of the vicarage and Kilvert is said to have planted the Mulberry tree that graces the top lawn. The eight-acre gardens are open to the public all year.

One mile south of Bredwardine is Moccas Park, a National Nature Reserve managed by Natural England. It is one of the largest and most diverse examples of wood pasture remaining in Britain. The ancient area of wood pasture was enclosed in Norman times and was subsequently transformed into a designed landscape park in the 17th century. There continues to be a managed herd of fallow deer in the park today.

It's not just deer that inhabit the Park, which is unfortunately not open to the public, but over 200 species of lichen have been recorded and some are very rare. The reserve also has considerable importance for invertebrate groups with 1000 species of fly recorded there. Thirteen bat species are present as is the polecat, once thought to be extinct in England.

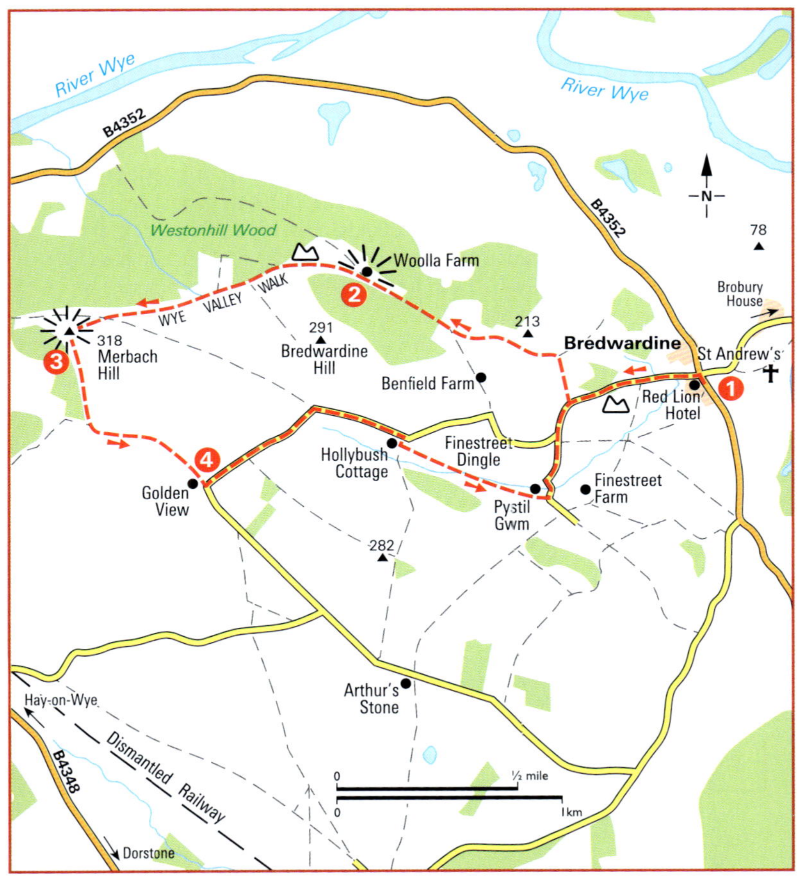

1. Take the steep lane right from the pub. Continue 500yds (458m), turning right along a bridleway track past a cottage. At a sharp right bend, go forward through a field gate. Climb beside the left hedge to find a small gate. In the adjoining field, climb across the slope of the hill, passing through a broad gap in the end hedge. Keep the same line, shortly intersecting a gravel track from Benfield Farm by a telegraph post. Follow it to the right.

2. Approaching Woolla Farm, watch for a path branching off left. Rising into the woodland fringe, skirt the farm to rejoin the track. Carry on uphill to a gate. Ignore the crossing track beyond and climb to a small gate beside corrugated barns. Keep going by the right boundary, then along a short track to continue with the hedge now on your left. Later crossing a stile onto bracken common, walk forwards a few paces before turning right to another crosspath. By a

plaque explaining Merbach Hill Common to the left, a bridlepath cuts through the bracken and scrub. Ignore a later path off right and then, at a three-way split, take the middle branch. A final pull leads to the hilltop trig column. The view is superb. To the north beyond the Wye Valley is distant Hergest Ridge, and to the southwest Hay Bluff and the Black Mountains. Below your feet lies the Golden Valley.

3. Walk forward past the trig column and swing left above the edge. Carry on towards a wicket gate that soon appears at the far side of the common. Keep ahead across open grazing above a fringe of scrub, the trod later curving left above a boundary. Eventually, join a track rising from Golden View to leave on to the bend of a lane.

4. Turn left and follow the lane for 0.6 miles (1km). At Hollybush Cottage turn right signposted a bridleway and then left in a few paces through a gate on a footpath. Follow the stream across three fields, crossing a small spring at the third and pass through a small wooden gate by a large hazel bush to pass by the garden and house of Pystil Gwm. Turn left and follow the lane down, up and round, back to Bredwardine.

Where to eat and drink

The attractive Red Lion Hotel serves home-cooked food using fresh, seasonal produce. Log fires in winter, a charming garden in summer, there's accommodation too.

What to see

St Andrew's Church in Bredwardine, a short detour from the start of the walk, is very much Kilvert's church, being where the Victorian diarist was rector when he died of peritonitis in 1879. It has a huge 12th-century font.

While you're there

The Red Lion Hotel owns and allows access to four miles of riverbank on the Wye for keen anglers, with both coarse fishing and salmon fishing options available. Day tickets are available from the hotel – they'll even provide a riverbank breakfast or packed lunch.

EXPLORING THE GOLDEN VALLEY

DISTANCE/TIME	6.5 miles (10.4km) / 3hrs 30min
ASCENT/GRADIENT	1,245ft (380m) / ▲ ▲ ▲
PATHS	Minor lanes, good tracks, meadows, couple of short but severe descents over grass, many stiles
LANDSCAPE	A route with many picnic opportunities!
SUGGESTED MAP	OS Explorer 201 Knighton & Presteigne
START/FINISH	Grid reference: SO313416
DOG FRIENDLINESS	On lead across farmland, but some freedom in woodland
PARKING	Car park opposite The Pandy Inn
PUBLIC TOILETS	Beside village hall, near green

Bees are fascinating. One could write a book just on the biology and sociology of bees, and still have much to write. We shall have to content ourselves with a little bit about how Herefordshire has benefited from them. Beekeeping is a combination of science, art and skilled labour, an all-consuming hobby, or occasionally, a way of earning a living.

At one time Golden Valley Apiaries in Peterchurch managed over 540 colonies of bees, although today the number is greatly reduced. A typical year would yield 8.5–10 tonnes of honey – about 20,000 1lb jars – but one exceptionally good year produced over 13 tonnes. Their honey, which has won prizes at the Three Counties Show and the Royal Welsh Show, is largely sold through local shops, with some being sold in bulk to packing companies.

Fruit growing is financially a high-risk venture – apples and pears, but more so the soft fruits such as blackcurrants, raspberries and strawberries – so rather than leave pollination to chance, growers hire colonies of bees. Although almost impossible to measure scientifically, it is generally reckoned that hiring bees during the flowering period can improve the fruit yield by 30–40 per cent compared with merely relying on the local, wild bee population.

Most of Golden Valley Apiaries work is within a 40-mile (64km) radius. Bees are early risers – to deliver bees to a site means getting the hives into a vehicle before first light – otherwise, particularly on warmer mornings, the bees may have taken flight. Typically, the hives are kept on a site for four to six weeks. Bees don't like the rain but yields of honey are only seriously affected if there is very protracted wet weather. The greatest danger to the flowers they are pollinating is a late frost, but the fruits themselves are also vulnerable to adverse weather such as heavy downpours and freakish hailstorms at picking time.

Any species is susceptible to diseases and viruses, and more than 100 colonies were lost in the Golden Valley when varroasis struck in 1994–95. Across the UK, between winter 2007 and winter 2008, the varroa mite destroyed 30 per cent of our wild bee colonies. Shockingly, perhaps only remote regions of northern Scotland and some UK islands now remain free from the varroa mite. The control of the mites is not an easy process for beekeepers – chemical treatments and biomechanical methods are mostly used. In addition to the varroa mite, there are now three other reportable diseases and pests for beekeepers to be concerned about. Not only that, but the loss of habitat, climate change and the wide use of pesticides, it's a never-ending struggle for our bees.

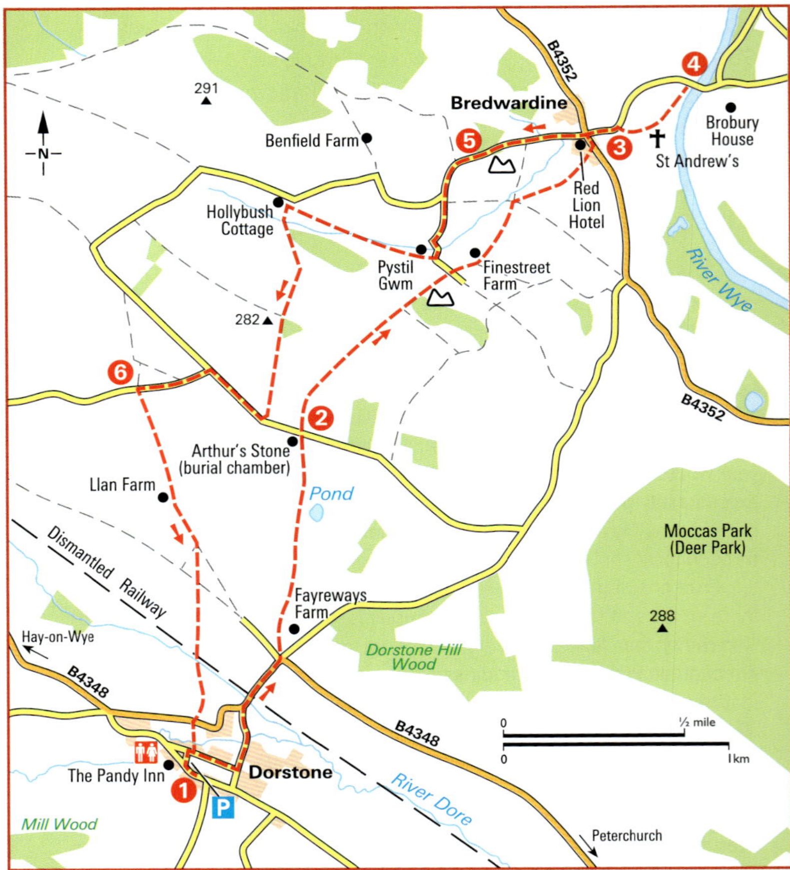

1. Walk from the car park to the Pandy Inn and go right beside the green. Turn right again along Chapel Lane, then swing left to the B4348. Mindful of traffic, follow the main road forward to a sharp right bend and junction. Branch left on a rising track to Fayreways Farm. Continue past barns, but as the track curves right through a gate, go on to a stile. Continue uphill on the opposite flank of the hedge and then head straight across the top field to reach Arthur's Stone.

2. Cross the lane to a gate and follow the right-hand field-edge. Strike ahead across the middle of a second field, maintaining the same line down more fields to an awkward stile beside a wood. Continue downhill, eventually emerging beside a cottage. Walk forward on a track towards Finestreet Farm, leaving just before the farm through a gate on the right. Follow the fence past the buildings to a hand gate in the corner. Bear left to a stile and head down by the right boundary. As it curves right, bear left past two oaks, one fallen, to a gate in the bottom corner. Strike a right diagonal across a final field, joining a track past a timber-frame house into Bredwardine.

3. Take the lane opposite, branching right to Bredwardine's church. Keep left past the church then cross a stile from which a path leads to the old bridge.

4. Return to Point (3) and take the steep lane right of the pub. Continue 500yds (458m) to a track off to the right.

5. Continue uphill past a junction to a cottage, Pystil Gwm. Just beyond, go right beside the garden along a rough bridleway up through Finestreet Dingle. Emerging at the far end by a house, go left over a plank and stile. Keep by the left perimeter, skirting a plantation before swinging up beside an old hawthorn to a stile. Accompany the hedge uphill, then, past scrawny pines, angle slightly left. In a final field, follow the left boundary to the lane. Go right, then next left. After 325yds (297m), look for a stile on the left.

6. Drop to a track and go left to Llan Farm. Leave along its access, but after 200yds (183m), as the right hedge finishes, bear half-right across an open field to a gate partway along the bottom boundary. Cross an old sunken lane and maintain the diagonal line to reach a track, the course of a former railway. Cross again to a playing field, leaving at its far-left corner onto a lane. Opposite right, take a path skirting the churchyard and follow Church Lane back into Dorstone.

Where to eat and drink
In Dorstone, The Pandy Inn, a 12th-century free house, overlooks the village green. It has a delightful beer garden and serves award-winning food. Roughly halfway round, in Bredwardine, the handsome Red Lion Hotel is an irresistibly convenient place to stop, particularly as you'll pass it twice.

What to see
On the village green in Dorstone is a simple sundial. The stone post on which it stands is reputedly the remains of a cross, the top of which was detached during Oliver Cromwell's time. Arthur's Stone is a chambered tomb dated 3700–2700 BC.

While you're there
St Andrew's Church at Bredwardine is very much Kilvert's church, being where the Victorian diarist was rector when he died of peritonitis in 1879. It has a huge 12th-century font. Brobury House Gardens – seen from Point 4 – extend to 8 acres (3ha) in formal Victorian style.

ON THE BLACK HILL

46

DISTANCE/TIME	8.25 miles (13.3km) / 4hrs
ASCENT/GRADIENT	1,575ft (480m) / ▲ ▲ ▲
PATHS	Muddy patches, stony descent, lanes, minor roads, several stiles
LANDSCAPE	Narrow mountain ridge and moorland plateau incised by green valleys
SUGGESTED MAP	OS Explorer OL13 Brecon Beacons National Park
START/FINISH	Grid reference: SO288328
DOG FRIENDLINESS	A good yomp, but may be sheep grazing on tops
PARKING	Black Hill car park (signposted)
PUBLIC TOILETS	None on route
NOTES	Being in remote hill country with no easy escape routes, this walk is not recommended for inexperienced hill walkers

On the western edge of Herefordshire are three valleys: the River Dore in the Golden Valley, the Escley Brook in the Escley Valley and lastly the Olchon Brook in the Olchon Valley. The Black Hill lies, sometimes literally, in the shadow of the Black Mountains that here delineate the Welsh border.

Even at the car park – almost 1,300ft (396m) – you are higher than most tops attained elsewhere in this book. Known locally as 'the Cat's Back', Black Hill distinguishes itself by being the highest peak in Herefordshire (and in Worcestershire) that the Ordnance Survey names on its maps. The Ordnance Survey gives no such attention to the actual highest point in Herefordshire, a knuckle on one of the Black Mountains' splayed-out fingers, lying as it does along the boundary with Wales'. In fine, summertime weather you cannot fail to enjoy this airy walk, but should you do it in cold and wet conditions, you will need a heart of stone not to empathise with those upland farmers who have no choice but to be working outdoors in such conditions.

Bruce Chatwin's 1983 book *On the Black Hill* was largely biographical, tracing the history of the Jones family through some 70 years of farming on the Black Hill. He had spent much time in the Herefordshire borders and had befriended several people. At first it may seem odd that a book about outdoor, farming people should be claustrophobic, but it is a short distance from solitude to isolation, and even in the 21st century people who work on the land are often in solitude for protracted periods of time. In the case of the novel's Jones brothers, Benjamin and Lewis, they are emotionally intense, largely because they have so few relationships and because of their blood ties. (In the film of the same name, directed by Andrew Grieve and released in 1988, the actors playing the brothers were real brothers too.)

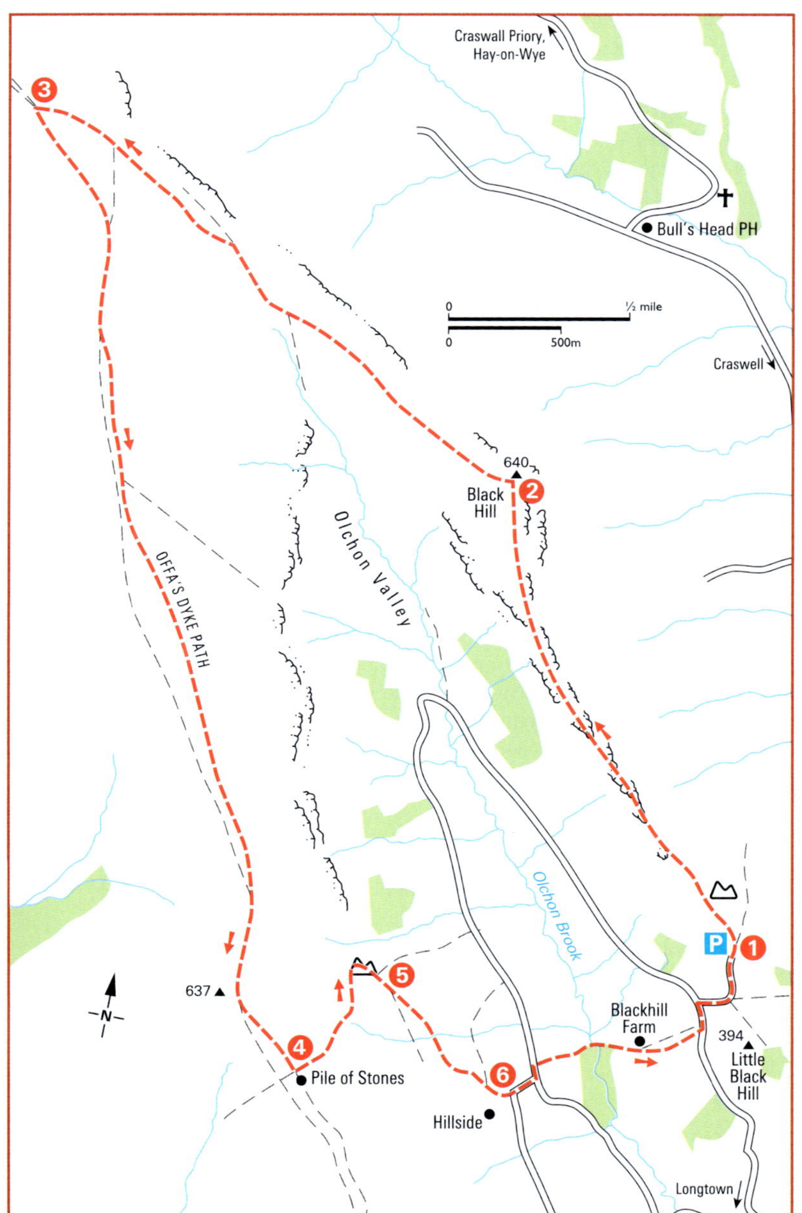

1. Over a stile behind the car park, follow a steep path up the spine of the hill. The ridge shortly narrows and in strong wind or poor weather, may be intimidating. But, the way soon broadens to continue as a fine, airy walk, which offers superlative views on either hand.

2. Fork left at the trig column, passing a shallow tarn on your right. The clear path gently rises across the moor for 1.5 miles (2.4km), eventually meeting a crossing of paths by an Offa's Dyke stone marker.

3. To the left, the way initially climbs over an un-named top, but which, at over 2,300ft (700m), is the highest point of the walk. The trail runs on, intermittently slabbed along the broad ridge, which here marks the boundary between England and Wales. After nearly 3 miles (4.8km), and almost level with the car park across the valley, look out for a cairn and another Offa's Dyke waystone marking a crossing of routes.

4. Take the grass path off left, which soon curves left down the steepening slope. Lower down, after 700yds (640m), the way swings sharply right.

5. Soon, a waymark indicates a junction from which a path drops to the lane. However, carry on ahead through bracken, ignoring a later intersecting path. Eventually cross a brook and enter a grove of alder to reach a fence. Turn right in front of it, crossing a stream to reach a kissing gate. Through that walk on within the fringe of trees, passing an opening and a stile before reaching another kissing gate. Negotiate a fallen tree just beyond and follow the line of an old hollow way. Disregard a later stile on the left, but then shortly cross a stile. Stay with the groove, passing through a kissing gate at the end to meet a lane.

6. Walk downhill to a junction and go left. Approaching a small bridge, leave over a stile on the right and head downfield beside the stream. Cross the stream lower down and bear right to a footbridge spanning Olchon Brook. Climb away to Blackhill Farm. Over a stile, walk up beside the buildings to find a waymarked handgate in the top-right corner. Head up a wooded gully to a stile and bear left, soon emerging onto a lane. Turn left along the lane and first right to return to the car park.

Where to eat and drink

The menu at the Bull's Head, in Craswall, is very tempting and includes locally produced meat and cheeses. In Michaelchurch Escley The Bridge Inn, offers home-cooked food also using local produce. It has a brookside beer garden. Dogs and children are welcome.

What to see

Look out for energetic Offa's Dyke Path walkers. They started in Chepstow and so are only a couple of days into the walk. Those who started in the north are probably tiring, so won't overtake you!

While you're there

A few miles along the road to Hay-on-Wye, not signposted and tucked out of sight in a valley, are the forlorn remains of Craswall Priory. Craswall is the third and final Grandmontine priory in England, the others being in Grosmont, North Yorkshire, and Alderbury, Wiltshire. The priory was probably built in the 1220s, and abandoned in 1441. It is a listed Grade II, Scheduled Ancient Monument.

47

THE LOWER OLCHON VALLEY

DISTANCE/TIME	5.25 miles (8.4km) / 2hrs 45min
ASCENT/GRADIENT	820ft (250m) / ▲ ▲
PATHS	Lanes, tracks and field paths in mixed farmland, many stiles
LANDSCAPE	Rolling farmland and the Black Mountains ridge
SUGGESTED MAP	OS Explorer OL13 Brecon Beacons National Park
START/FINISH	Grid reference: SO324287
DOG FRIENDLINESS	Under close control; small dogs may need help on stiles
PARKING	About 300yds (274m) north of The Crown, Longtown, on Castle Road, in long bay fronting houses
PUBLIC TOILETS	None on route

Longtown is a typical linear village, strung out for almost 0.5 miles (800m) along the narrow road through the Olchon Valley between Hay-on-Wye and Abergavenny. It is suggested that the site, lying in the shadow of the Black Mountains on a spur of high ground between the Olchon and Monnow valleys, may have originally been fortified during the Iron Age or Roman period.

Whether or not this was the case, it was ideally suited to the Norman Marcher lords, charged to keep the border with Wales under control. Like the castle at Weobley, Longtown was commissioned by Walter de Lacy, but here, the later stone fortifications as well as the earthworks have survived and it remains an impressive site. At its heart is a soaring earth and rubble mound, the motte, the original wooden tower at its top replaced by a stone keep in the 13th century. Although an English castle, the keep is circular, a design more usually seen in neighbouring Wales, and was carefully built to avoid collapse. Its foundations slope outwards and the structure is supported by three round buttresses. A spiral staircase gave access to an upper storey containing the lord's private apartments, with a garderobe added for his convenience. For a while, the castle must have been an important link in the Norman strategic line of defence, for there is another, probably earlier motte and bailey just 1 mile (1.6km) to the south at Pont Hendre. As peace settled upon the area, however, the castle became redundant and, apart from being re-garrisoned in the early 15th century in response to Owain Glyndwr's uprising to reinstate Welsh sovereignty, fell out of use.

Clodock takes its name from a sixth-century Celtic saint, supposedly buried here, with an early church founded over his tomb. A ninth-century tombstone found in the nave is evidence of a Saxon church, with the Norman building evolving out of that. Inside, the pews are laid out in an unusual manner with box pews in the centre, overlooked by a splendid three-decker pulpit; the priest's preaching platform overlooking the clerk's stall and a reading desk. There are three ancient parish chests, one dating to the 12th century. The parish money-box has three separate locks, a key being held by the priest and each of the churchwardens to avoid embezzlement. Look, too, for the elegant Norman font and, on the wall tucked beneath the minstrels' balcony, a stone tablet setting out the 1805 judgement of the Hereford Assizes that established monetary payments to be made in lieu of tithe payments. The dove (a symbol of peace) carved in one corner is thought to mean that both sides were happy with the judgement. Just downstream is Clodock Mill, a restored watermill dating to the 13th century. Although privately owned, it is opened on National Mills Weekend (second weekend in May).

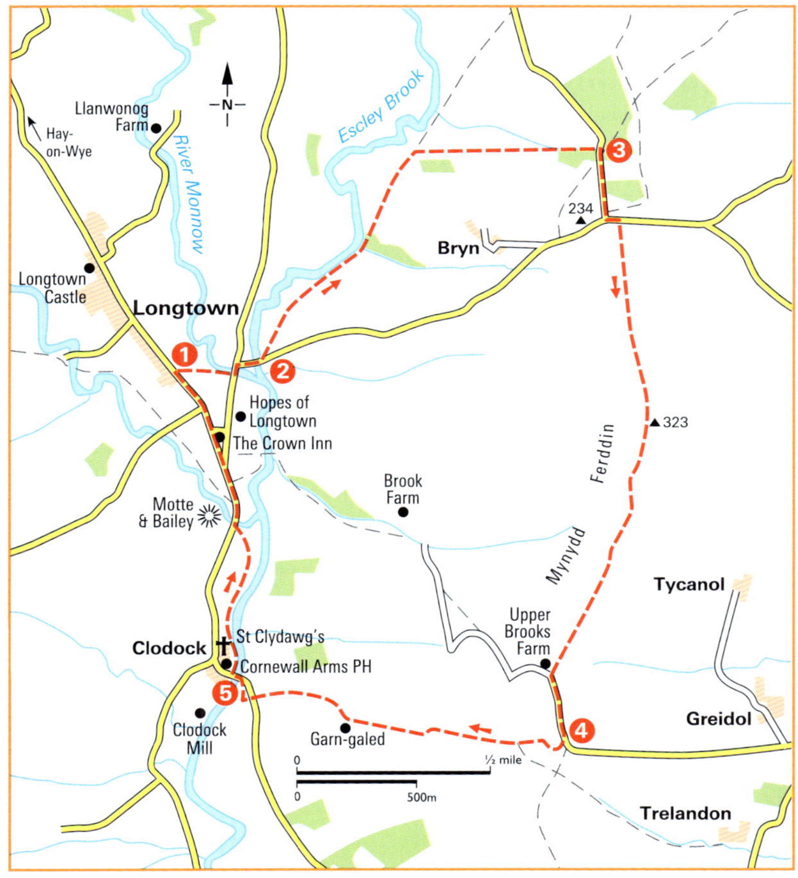

1. A path opposite Greyhound Close at the foot of the lay-by leaves between houses to a field. Cross to a stile part-way along the right boundary and continue in the next field, rounding an indented corner to exit over a stile at the bottom on to a road. Go left over the River Monnow and then right.

2. Just beyond a second bridge, cross a stile in the left hedge. Bear right to overgrown steps part-way along the bank, and then go left on a rough track past a scrapyard to a field gate. Walk forward with a hedge on your left,

continuing over a stile in the next field above Esclay Brook. Fording a stream, pass into a wood and climb right. Emerging from the trees, bear right across rough pasture to a gate. Carry on by the left boundary, then, over a stile, angle right down to a gate. Follow a permissive path within the boundary of a wood. Emerging at the top, continue ahead across successive meadows. Eventually over a footbridge, pass through more woodland and then a meadow corner to reach a lane.

3. Go right to a T-junction and turn left, leaving almost immediately beside a gate on the right. Climb with the hedge from field to field up Mynydd Ferddin. Strike across the top field to adjacent gates in the far corner. Go through the left one and maintain the diagonal line, passing through more gates in the corner onto a track. Over a stile at the end, go right alongside the hedge, passing through a tree windbreak to continue in the next long pasture. Exit over a stile, passing Upper Brooks Farm to walk away left along a narrow lane.

4. At a sharp bend, leave right through a gate into a field. Disregard the signpost pointing confidently ahead and instead swing half-right across the field to find a gate tucked in the hedge corner. Ignore the gate and instead bear right through a gap. Follow the left hedge for 40yds (37m) to a gate and carry on downfield, the hedge now on your right. Keep going through the next two fields, then, near a ruined barn, Garn-galed, descend a bank to a metal gate. Walk down two more fields and on past a high-hedged house to join a rough track. Emerging at the edge of Clodock, go right into the village.

5. Over the bridge, turn right behind cottages and through the churchyard on a riverside path. Parting from the Monnow in the second field, cross two more fields. Now follow the left hedge, crossing stiles to a lane. Turn right to Longtown, keeping left at a fork to return to the start.

Where to eat and drink

Hopes of Longtown is the proudly independent village stores and post office; here, in season, you will find locally sourced produce. The Crown has an open fireplace and serves home-cooked food. In Clodock is the Cornewall Arms.

While you're there

Longtown Castle has just enough to fire the imagination, and stunning views. St Margaret's Church (between Longtown and Vowchurch on a minor road) has a beautiful rood screen.

AROUND ABBEY DORE AND EWYAS HAROLD

DISTANCE/TIME	8.5 miles (13.7km) / 4hrs
ASCENT/GRADIENT	1,020ft (310m) / ▲ ▲
PATHS	Meadows, tracks and woodland paths (one stony, awkward descent), many stiles
LANDSCAPE	Quintessential Herefordshire
SUGGESTED MAP	OS Explorer OL13 Brecon Beacons National Park
START/FINISH	Grid reference: SO386302
DOG FRIENDLINESS	Mostly on leads
PARKING	On east side of B4347, by the Abbey, south of the lychgate
PUBLIC TOILETS	None on route

Abbey Dore Court occupies the site of the Red Lion where, in 1837, the inaugural meeting of the Board of Dore Union Guardians took place. Under the Poor Law Act of 1834, responsibility for administering relief was transferred from individual parishes to Unions, in this case a group of 29 parishes. It enabled the construction of large workhouses and required compulsory schooling for workhouse children. Hereford had five workhouses, one of which subsequently served as part of the County Hospital. Right up until its partial demolition in 2002, the building still bore the poorhouse stigma among elderly people, who were reluctant to be admitted.

Riverdale, the Dore workhouse, is a remote place, well away from the village of Abbey Dore itself. The most disliked rule, and perhaps the least necessary, was the one that forbade inmates to leave the premises. The rules of the workhouse were strict but not Draconian; criminal acts were rare, with breaches often punished by reducing diet (but such punishment could not be given to children). The key elements of the workhouse diet were bread, gruel (an inferior porridge of oatmeal and water) and potatoes. Each person was allowed 5oz (140g) of meat two days per week and 1.5oz (42g) of cheese on four days per week. Riverdale accommodated between 80 and 100 men, women and children. Most of the adult residents were aged or infirm; many had additionally suffered some other misfortune: there were blind people, abandoned wives, unmarried mothers, and so on. Nevertheless, physical conditions may have been little worse than those experienced by agricultural workers, who often endured the discomfort of damp and cramped cottages without a solid floor.

In 1929 legislation transferred responsibility for poorhouse residents to county councils. During World War II the Dore workhouse was used for tractor assembly and the buildings were subsequently converted into private dwellings.

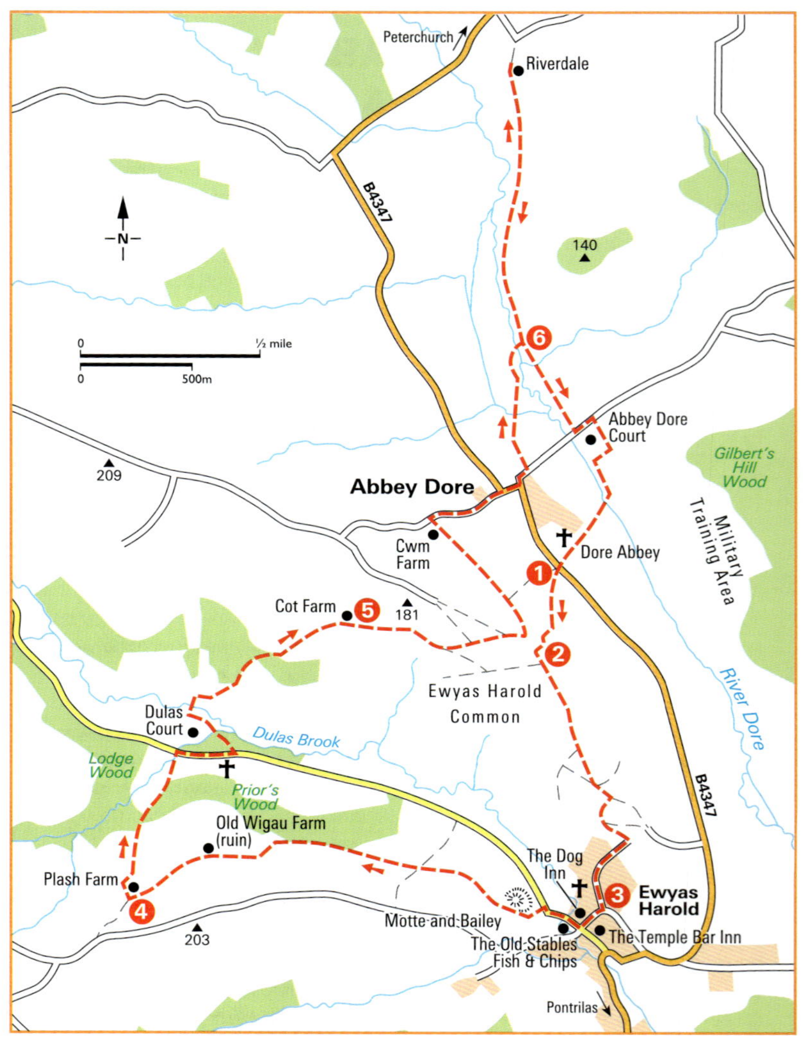

1. From a stile opposite the lychgate, head for the top-left field corner. Continue towards a white cottage. Ignore the stile and turn up beside the boundary, leaving the top of the next field along a hedged path onto Ewyas Harold Common.

2. Over a track, bear left to a junction of grass paths. Go left and arc right in front of a shingled cottage. Where paths fragment after 350yds (320m), take the right branch, but as that splits, bear left. At another fork bear right and, ignoring crossings, descend through bracken and trees to emerge onto a gravel track (grid reference: SO 388292) in around 0.25 miles (400m). Turn left, then fork right to merge with another gravel track. Continue down with the lane ahead into the village.

3. At the end go right past Priory School and right again past The Dog Inn. As the road bends, branch left up fingerposted steps. Bear left across a field below the castle tump, the raised mound upon which the keep stood, and walk through a yard left of buildings to another gate. Carry on by the left hedge to a shallow corner. Passing through the left of two gates, the boundary is now on your right. Slipping over a stile in the third field, continue on the other flank. Through a small gate, walk on beside a wood. Over stiles, pass briefly through trees and then bear left towards the crest of the hill. Round an indented corner and remain beside the right hedge through fields to Plash Farm.

4. In the yard, bear right and then left beside a barn. Climbing stiles, turn right and right again into a paddock behind the house. Cross to a gate and continue down a large pasture to the bottom-right corner. Follow a descending rough track through trees, beside a plantation and then an old hedge to come out onto a lane. Go right past redundant St Michael's Church, then sharp left along a drive towards Dulas Court. Following 'Visitors' Car Park' signs, wind right past bungalows and over a bridge. Just beyond, take a track right into a field and bear left to the top corner. Follow a green path up to the right through trees. Walk right at a crossing and again at a fork, but reaching the next split, keep left. Emerging from the wood, continue climbing right across rough pasture to Cot Farm.

5. Walk forward between house and barns, progressing along the top edge of the field beyond. Cross the next field to a stile in the far lower corner. Back on Ewyas Harold Common, walk forward to a track and bear left. At a bend, keep ahead to join another gravel track, following it down past Hill Place to more cottages. Immediately before the first house, turn left through a wide gate and walk away beside the top edge of a sloping field. Over a high ladder stile, keep ahead across a deer park. Exit over another ladder stile to drop past Cwm Farm to a lane. Walk down, keeping ahead and then left towards Abbey Dore Court. Around a bend and over a small bridge, cross a stile on the left. Pass farm buildings and go through consecutive gates to another gate in the far corner. Continue across the next field, leaving through a field gate, some way along the right boundary.

6. Over the river, go left, passing through a gate to follow a waymarked route across the fields to Riverdale. Retrace your steps to Point 6 and continue ahead to emerge by Dore Bridge. Go left, leaving after 50yds (46m) along a track on the right. Approaching high gates to an army training range, bear right on a grass path around the perimeter fence to a bridge. Strike across pasture to Dore Abbey and walk out to the lane.

Where to eat and drink

Ewyas Harold has the Temple Bar Inn, the Dog Inn and Old Stables Fish & Chips. A few miles away is The Kilpeck Inn, which uses local and seasonal produce in a tasty menu and local ales, ciders and gins behind the bar.

What to see

The lychgate was erected in memory of a soldier, killed in the last weeks of World War I.

While you're there

Part of Cistercian abbey built between 117 and 1220, Dore Abbey, is a scheduled monument.

49

A CIRCUIT FROM KILPECK

DISTANCE/TIME	5 miles (8km) / 2hrs 30min
ASCENT/GRADIENT	640ft (195m) / ▲ ▲
PATHS	Field paths, tracks and minor lanes, many stiles
LANDSCAPE	Wooded, grazed and cultivated hills
SUGGESTED MAP	OS Explorer 189 Hereford & Ross-on-Wye
START/FINISH	Grid reference: SO445304
DOG FRIENDLINESS	Best kept on leads and not allowed in Kilpeck churchyard
PARKING	Spaces beside St Mary's and St David's Church, Kilpeck
PUBLIC TOILETS	None on route

While Kilpeck may be a quiet and sleepy little village today, it was once an important, bustling market town that has been in both Wales and England.

Kilpeck's first recorded name, from Anglo-Saxon records, is 'Ecclesia Cilpedic', suggesting that it was once a religious community – the cell of St Pedic. After the Norman Conquest, William the Conqueror gave the manor of Kilpeck to William Fitz Norman, the first Lord of Kilpeck, who began building a timber motte and bailey castle around 1090.

His son and heir, Hugh Fitz Norman, was also the King's forester for the Royal Forests of Dean. As a result, the village grew rapidly and the castle became more important, with a stone rebuild in the first half of the 12th century. At the same time, a stone walled bailey was added along with two further baileys and a modern, planned and defended medieval town and a Romanesque church. Much of the land north of the village today formed part of the ancient forest of Treville, which was used as hunting grounds for the Lords of Kilpeck. In 1259 King John made a visit to Kilpeck and he granted a charter for a Friday market and an annual fair. The town flourished well into the 14th century, but with the then lord, the Earl of Ormond, absent, the town began to lose its prosperity. Poor harvests, disease resulting in the Black Death of 1349 hit the town hard.

Kilpeck Castle was virtually in ruins by the time of the English Civil War but it was, however, utilised. It was garrisoned for the King but in 1645 Parliamentary forces stormed the building and demolished it to prevent re-use.

Stone carvings and sculptures heavily adorn Kilpeck's Church of St Mary and St David. The Herefordshire School of Romanesque Sculpture is largely responsible for the work. A hypothetical group of master masons from the 12th century, the stone carvers have created a very distinctive set of Romanesque sandstone and limestone carvings, which are to be found in parish churches across Herefordshire. However, Kilpeck Church is one of the finest examples of their work, which includes animals, Celtic patterns, bestiaries and graphically bawdy figures.

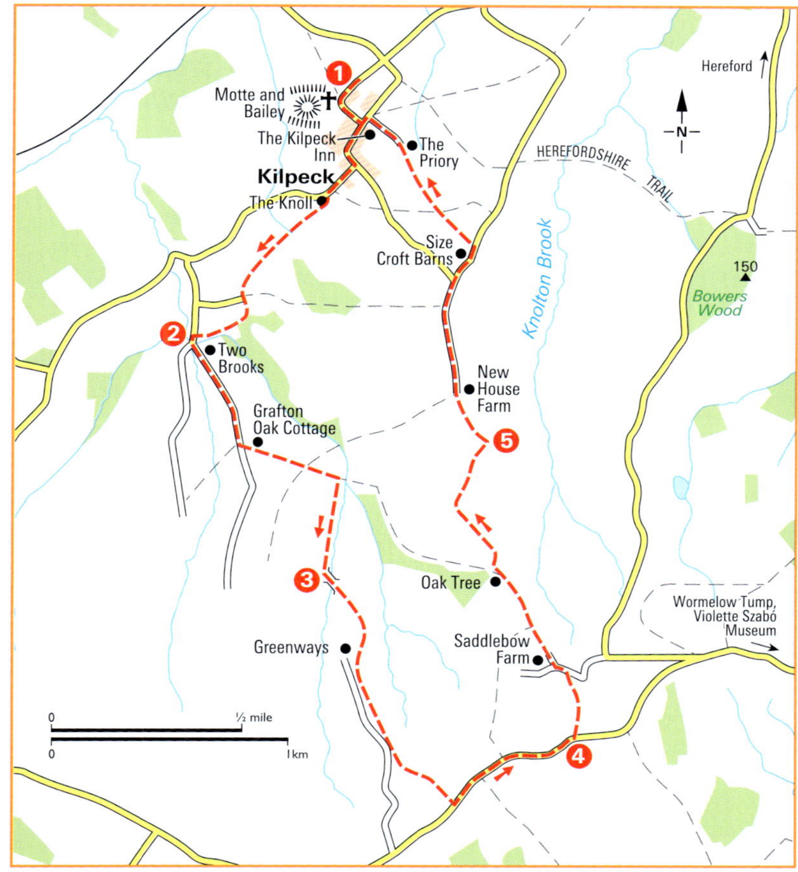

1. Walk into the village and go right at the Kilpeck Inn. Keep right again toward Garway Hill. After 200yds (183m), approaching a cottage, cross a stile on the left. Walk right to a gate opening and turn right down the adjacent field-edge. Curve left within the corner and continue at the bottom of more fields towards a white house. Leave over a stile to its left and follow a track left towards trees. Over a stile, a waymarked path winds through the wood. Carry on down a field to emerge at a junction.

2. Go left over a bridge and up a hill. At the crest, turn left through a field gate beside Grafton Oak cottage. Follow the top fence to a stile. Don't cross, but bear left, slanting down past a solitary oak. Approaching the corner, go over a stile on the right into the adjacent field and continue above the left hedge. Partway along the third field, cross a footbridge on the left.

3. Leaving the bridge, climb diagonally right to a stile and then by the right fence up a long field. Reaching the top corner, go through a gate and forward over a stile. Walk on uphill, passing through a gap beside a hollow oak. Keep going at the left edge of more fields to emerge onto lane. Follow it left for 0.5 miles (800m). At the crest, look for a discrete fingerpost on the left.

4. A path drops through bracken, becoming a track between trees. At the end, swing right and then left to Saddlebow Farm. Fork right past the buildings and continue forward along a hedged path. Keep by the right field-edge in the field beyond. Through a gate follow a field track right then left, slipping through a gap into the adjacent field. Wind round to three gates.

5. Through the waymarked middle one, walk beside the left hedge to New House Farm. Leave along its access to a junction and follow the lane ahead. At a fingerpost just beyond Size Croft Barns, go left into a field. Head across to a stile, left of an indented corner. Pass through coppice and carry on across two more fields, leaving over a fence stile by the Priory. Beyond the buildings, an avenue leads into the village.

Where to eat and drink

At Wormelow Tump, on the A466, is The Tump Inn. It has a beer garden, a children's play area, bar meals, snacks and a restaurant. Booking is advisable for Sunday lunch. The Kilpeck Inn at Kilpeck stands just two minutes from the end of the route.

What to see

The exterior of Kilpeck church is adorned with a large number of decorated corbels. As Norman churches go, it is one of the best preserved in England. Beside the church is a substantial motte and bailey (12th century like the church).

While you're there

In Wormelow Tump, just down from the pub, is the Violette Szabó Museum, which commemorates the life of the WWII resistance fighter. Her story was later turned into film, *Carve Her Name with Pride* (1958) staring Virginia McKenna in the lead role (see walk 50)

50

FROM KILPECK TO ORCOP HILL

DISTANCE/TIME	6.75 miles (10.8km) / 3hrs
ASCENT/GRADIENT	640ft (195m) / ▲ ▲
PATHS	Field paths, tracks and minor lanes
LANDSCAPE	Wooded, grazed and cultivated hills
SUGGESTED MAP	OS Explorer 189 Hereford & Ross-on-Wye
START/FINISH	Grid reference: SO445304
DOG FRIENDLINESS	Best kept on leads and not allowed in Kilpeck churchyard
PARKING	Spaces beside St Mary's and St David's Church, Kilpeck
PUBLIC TOILETS	None on route

The bottom of a garden seems an odd place for a museum, but the Violette Szabó, GC Museum is a very personal one. It stands in the grounds of Cartref, the modest house to which Violette Szabó would come to visit her cousins. Rosemary Rigby, who lives there now, is both the museum's creator and curator. Among the many attending the museum's opening in 2000 was Violette's daughter, Tania.

Violette Bushell had a French mother and an English father. When Violette was 11, they moved to London. Violette met Etienne Szabó, a Hungarian-born French national who was 12 years older, at London's Bastille Day Parade in 1940. After a whirlwind romance – not uncommon in wartime – they married 41 days later. In February 1942, Violette gave birth to Tania, whom Etienne was never to see, for he succumbed to chest wounds inflicted in the Battle of El Alamein that October. Seeking revenge, Violette joined the Auxiliary Territorial Service (ATS), from where she was head-hunted by the French section of the Special Operations Executive (SOE). Her second mission on the ground in France was to be her last. Among the museum's exhibits is a door of the car believed to have been the one in which Violette Szabó, Jacques Dufour (the local Maquis leader) and a friend of his had been travelling to visit another Maquis member when they encountered a Nazi road block. In the ensuing gun battle her two companions escaped, uninjured, but Violette had to surrender when she ran out of ammunition. She was – posthumously – awarded the George Cross, the first woman to be honoured in this way. Although unaware of major Nazi troop movements, it isn't clear why Dufour, who was driving, decided to take on the soldiers at the road block, rather than turning the car round and hoping they wouldn't be pursued, or at least hoping to find a better escape route, for example, but this was the beginning of the end.

From her capture on 10 June, 1944 until her execution on 28 January, 1945, Violette was moved eight times, enduring rape, brutal assaults and inhumane living conditions, particularly at Ravensbrück concentration camp and three months at Königsberg on the Russian Front. The outcome could have been so different. Alerted to where Violette was being held, two SOE colleagues intended to rescue her from Limoges Prison, which wasn't heavily guarded. Tragically, just hours before they planned to do it, she was moved to Fresnes Prison in Paris.

Of the SOE's 55 women members, 11 were killed in service, either in France or in concentration camps. R J Minney's biography of Violette Szabó was published in 1956. In the 1958 film, *Carve Her Name with Pride*, Virginia McKenna – who attended the museum's opening – portrayed Violette. Although Steve Tomlinson's summary account of Violette Szabó's life, available at the museum, doesn't dwell on Ravensbrück's horrors (where 92,000 women died), it still leaves a grim memory of a fanatically and remorselessly cruel regime.

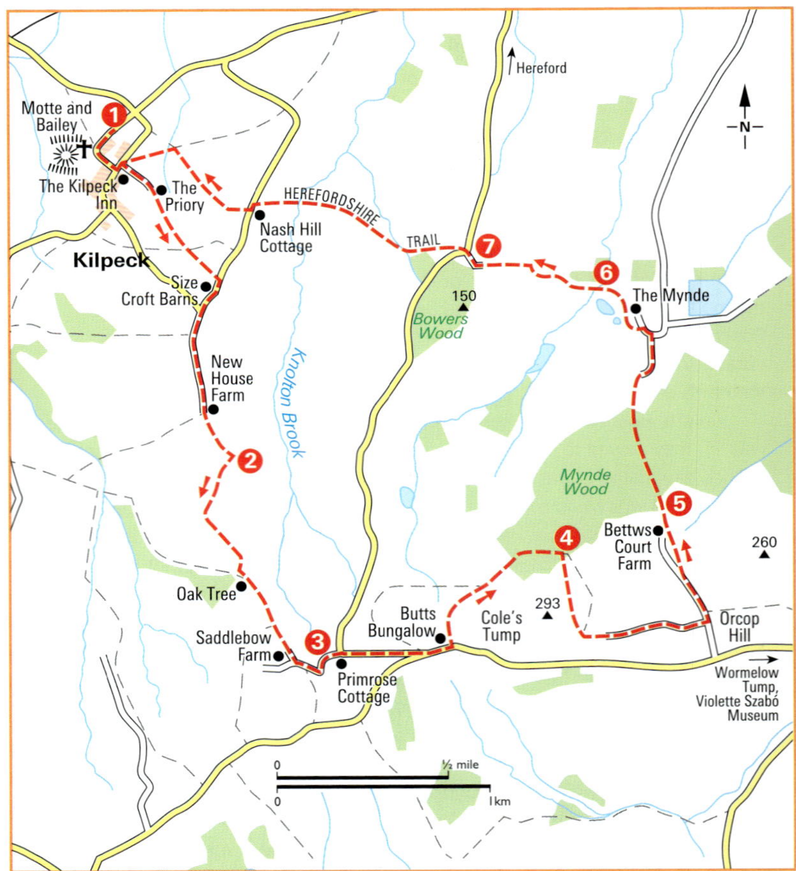

1. Walk into the village and follow the driveway between The Kilpeck Inn and a stile into pasture to the left. Pass brick stables to cross two stiles. Keep the line crossing a further two stiles leading into a spinney. A narrow path leads up to a waymarker. Head up the field to a stile by houses on a lane. Turn right at Size Croft Barns and keep straight on at a junction marked 'No Through Road'. Passing through yard of New House Farm to a stile, keep the right-hand hedge beside stock fencing.